THE
Kings &
Queens
OF
ENGLAND
& SCOTLAND

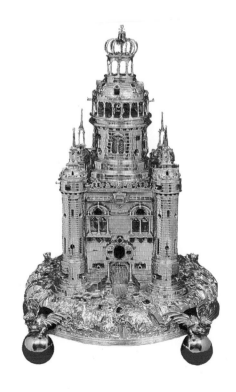

THE
Kings &
Queens
OF
ENGLAND
& SCOTLAND

PLANTAGENET SOMERSET FRY

CEEPI

Project Editor	Simon Adams
Art Editor	Clair Lidzey
Editors	Liza Bruml
	John Wainwright
Designers	Simon Wilder
	Nigel Hazle
Picture Research	Diana Morris
Managing Editor	Vicky Davenport
Managing Art Editor	Nick Harris

First published in Great Britain in 1990
by Dorling Kindersley Limited,
9 Henrietta Street, London WC2E 8PS
Reprinted 1991
Copyright © 1990 Dorling Kindersley Limited, London
Text copyright © 1990 Plantagenet Somerset Fry
This edition specially printed for CEEPI/Dealerfield Ltd in 1992

British Library Cataloguing in Publication Data
Somerset Fry, Plantagenet, 1931 –
    The kings and queens of England and Scotland
    1. Great Britain.   Monarchs, history
    1. Title
    941.00992

    ISBN 0-907305-55-5

Colour reproduction by Scantrans Singapore
Printed and bound in Singapore
by Kim Hup Lee Printing Co PTE Limited

*Page 1: the Exeter Salt; page 2: the Liber Regalis;
page 3: St Edward's Crown; above: ceremonial
trumpets, all part of the Coronation regalia.*

CONTENTS

INTRODUCTION

Whatever else it may be, history is a story, and for a story to be understood and enjoyed it must have a thread. The thread of British history lies in its monarchy. In order to know a little about times past, people like to have some links, the more quickly to identify what happened and why. Kings and queens provide those links, offering a continuity which helps people to remember events, movements, ideas and dates.

Kingship

Kings used at first to be chosen, generally although not always, from a family descending from a powerful leader who happened to be in the right place at the right time. Gradually, the succession of monarchs became more rigidly hereditary, especially when the principle of primogeniture – the right of succession of the first-born – began to be established. This resulted in continuous dynasties, some of whose members turned out to be able and effective rulers, others quite awful. But even bad rulers occasionally did one good thing, and that was to produce an heir who became everything the nation required in a king. In this respect one thinks of Aethelred the Unready, quite the worst of the Anglo-Saxon kings, whose son was the splendid Edmund Ironside, or the hopeless Edward II, father of the great Edward III.

Tyrants Beware!

This book is about the kings and queens of England and Scotland. It looks at their background, weighs up their character as far as can be done from the evidence, and selects some of the principal events of their reign in which they were involved, in many cases decisively. Over the centuries, the changes in the monarchy's power and role have been considerable, yet there are also continuities. From the earliest times, British monarchs have sworn to uphold the constitution, and for at least eight centuries there have been checks to see that they do. Equally, they have sometimes stood between the people and the high-handed policies and actions of over-mighty lords or elected governments. Once, they could dismiss governments and punish their leaders. Now they have no such power, but they do have influence and public support. As one contemporary historian remarked: "Tyrants should beware of kings."

ROYAL PAGEANTRY
The annual procession of the Knights of the Garter at Windsor Castle (left) and the Trooping of the Colour in London (above) are just two of the pageants that illuminate the royal year.

THE
FIRST ENGLISH KINGS
C. 600–1066

When the Romans ended their direct rule of Britain early in the fifth century, they left behind a country under attack from the Angles, Saxons and Jutes of northern Germany. Over the next 200 years, these invaders expelled the native Britons from England and pushed them back into Scotland and Wales. The invaders set up kingdoms of their own, and by the early seventh century England was split into the seven warring kingdoms of the Heptarchy. One of these – Wessex – finally triumphed and produced in Ecgberht, king from 802-39, the first King of England.

Alfred the Great
By the ninth century England was suffering under the onslaught of the Vikings, who first raided the English coast in 787. These raids continued for more than two centuries and considerably disrupted the life of the country. The Vikings were not entirely victorious, however, for they faced powerful opposition from the Anglo-Saxon kings. The greatest of these, and the only one in all English history to be called "The Great", was Alfred who, with his successors, kept the Vikings at bay, consolidated the supremacy of the Wessex kings over the whole of England, and improved the administration of the country. All this changed during the reign of Aethelred II between 979-1016. Faced with an upsurge of Viking activity, he beggared the kingdom to buy the invaders off. By the time of his death, the Vikings were powerful enough to take over the kingdom and install one of their own as king.

Canute
Canute the Dane turned out to be one of the best kings England ever had. He quickly grasped that Anglo-Saxon England was best governed according to a contract between monarch and subject, and he always treated his English advisers as a trusted body of men. The Anglo-Saxon period ended with the reign of the saintly Edward the Confessor who, having spent most of his younger life in exile in Normandy, had become indoctrinated with Norman ways, thus preparing the ground for the conflict between England and Normandy that was to be decisively resolved in 1066.

SAXON ENGLAND
The monastery on Lindisfarne, off the east coast of England, produced gospels famous for their illuminated designs (above). Winchester (left) was the capital of Wessex during the reign of Alfred the Great and for a time capital of all England.

EARLY SAXON KINGS

c. 600–871

THE ANGLO-SAXON occupiers of England had completed the process of driving the Celts out of the country by 613. Thereafter the country was divided into seven kingdoms: Kent, Sussex, Essex, East Anglia, Wessex, Mercia and Northumbria, collectively known as The Heptarchy. All were intent on establishing supremacy over, or defending themselves from, their neighbours. Some, notably Kent and Northumbria, fought to convert their neighbours to Christianity, a religion brought to England by St Augustine in 597. Northumbria was the first to gain the upper hand and then Mercia, but after the death of Offa of Mercia in 796, Wessex established its supremacy and Ecgberht of Wessex (802-39) became, in effect, the first King of England. Meanwhile the seven kingdoms had already turned their attention to fighting off incursions by the Vikings.

SUTTON HOO

In 1939 the remains of the burial ship of Raedwald of East Anglia (c. 600-17) were discovered in a trench near the River Deben at Sutton Hoo, in Suffolk. The vessel contained armour, coins, jewellery and silver, a fabulous treasure revealing the wealth and prosperity of many of the early Anglo-Saxon kings.

VENERABLE BEDE
The English monk and historian, Bede, spent most of his life at the twin monasteries of Monkwearmouth and Jarrow in Durham.

SUNKEN TREASURE
This shoulder clasp (above), exquisitely crafted from precious metals, was once the property of the Anglo-Saxon king, Raedwald, and was discovered in his burial ship at Sutton Hoo.

SCHOLARSHIP

Between 600-1066, Anglo-Saxon England produced a number of brilliant scholars, many of whom enjoyed an impressive reputation throughout Europe. The most notable was Bede, or Baeda (673-735), a monk who lived in the kingdom of Northumbria. His most important work was the *Ecclesiastical History of the English Nation*, which began with a short description of Celtic Britain and outlined the events of the Roman occupation of Britain.

KING OFFA

The kingdom of Mercia rose to prominence under the leadership of Offa (757-96). Offa extended Mercia's boundaries as far north as North Wales and in the south defeated the Wessex army to extend his rule towards Bristol. However, his kingdom was under constant threat from border raids by the Celtic Welsh. To thwart these attacks, Offa constructed a great earthwork dyke, which stretched the length of the Welsh border.

KING ECGBERHT
This silver penny was minted during the reign of King Ecgberht of Wessex, the first effective King of all England.

OFFA'S DYKE
Constructed in the early 780s, much of Offa's Dyke survives today (left).

EARL'S BARTON
Built in the late ninth century, the tower of Earl's Barton Church, Northamptonshire, (below) is a fine example of Anglo-Saxon architecture.

SAXON ARCHITECTURE
It used to be thought that the Saxons did not build in stone. On the contrary, the advance of Christianity throughout England during and after the seventh century was marked by the construction of many churches and some small cathedrals built of stone. Notable examples that have survived include the eighth-century tower and turret of Brixworth Minster in Northamptonshire, and St John's Church at Escomb, County Durham.

THE FIRST KING OF ENGLAND
Ecgberht became King of Wessex in 802, having previously spent some years serving in the army of Charlemagne in Europe. He steadily increased the power and influence of Wessex, and in 825 defeated the Mercians at the Battle of Ellandun. Two years later, Northumbria submitted to him, and from 827 until his death in 839 Ecgberht was recognized by his fellow kings as King of all England. His grandson, Alfred the Great, consolidated these gains.

ALFRED THE GREAT

871–899

THE ONLY ENGLISH KING to be known as The Great, Alfred acceded to the throne of Wessex upon the death of his brother Aethelred in 871. Over the next few years he spent much time fighting off Viking invasions. After routing the Great Army of the Vikings in 878, Alfred signed the Treaty of Wedmore with its leader Guthrum, dividing England along a line running roughly north-west from London to Chester; Alfred ruled to the south of this line and was recognized as overlord of the area to the north, known as the Danelaw. Further Viking incursions followed until, in 886, Alfred captured London and was finally accepted by Saxon and Dane alike as King of all England. Alfred reformed and codified Saxon law, promoted a revival in learning and instigated the compilation of the famous *Anglo-Saxon Chronicle*, a history of the people of England.

ALFRED
This coin from the reign of Alfred bears a likeness of the only English king to be called The Great.

♛ ALFRED

- *Born* Wantage, Oxon, 846/9, fourth son of Aethelwulf, King of Wessex and Osburga of Hampshire.
- *Married* Aethelswitha of Gainas and Mercia, Winchester, 868/9, 6 children.
- *Acceded* 23 April 871.
- *Crowned* (if at all) Kingston-upon-Thames, Surrey.
- *Died* 25/26/28 Oct 899, aged 50/53.

ALFRED'S JEWEL
Set in gold and crystal, this miniature enamel portrait of the King (below) is inscribed Aelfred me ech eh t gewyrcan, which means "Alfred ordered me to be made".

ST CUTHBERT
This medieval manuscript illustration shows St Cuthbert appearing before King Alfred. St Cuthbert was an early English saint much revered during Alfred's reign.

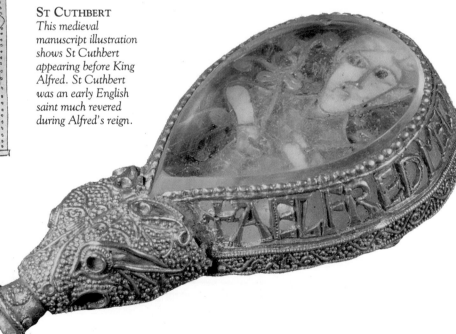

RELIGIOUS INSPIRATION

As a boy Alfred was taken twice to visit the Pope in Rome. He learned to read and write in his teens and he developed a profound interest in learning and a reverence of religion. Thus, when he turned to domestic reconstruction after defeating the Vikings, Alfred devoted much of his energy to reviving the schools and monasteries, and translating important Latin works into Anglo-Saxon himself, notably Bede's *Ecclesiastical History of the English Nation* and St Augustine's *Soliloquies*.

ARTISTIC PATRONAGE

Alfred's biographer, the Welsh scholar Asser, who spent many years at his court, writes of the King's patronage of traditional arts and crafts. Throughout the latter years of Alfred's reign there was a substantial increase in the translation and production of elaborately illustrated manuscripts, and gold and silversmiths throughout England created many items of exquisite jewellery, some of which have survived to this day.

THE GREAT

By the time he acceded to the throne in 871, Alfred had already demonstrated he was a self-confident leader. Healthy, well-educated, decisive and full of initiative, he was not afraid to consult colleagues and seek consensus whenever possible. He was also religious without being obsessed or bigoted, and possessed a strict sense of justice, insisting that even after defeat the Danes should be allowed to remain in their settlements and be treated as equals of the English before the law. As a contemporary stated: "The aim of all his work was to promote the good of his people."

ALFRED
This statue of Alfred stands in his birthplace of Wantage, Oxon.

HISTORY OF ENGLAND
The Anglo-Saxon Chronicle *details 1,200 years of English history from before Julius Caesar's invasion of the British Isles in 55 BC.*

EVENTS OF THE REIGN
871 – 899

◆ **871** Alfred succeeds his brother Aethelred as King of Wessex.
◆ **878** Danes invade Wessex. Alfred takes refuge on the Isle of Athelney and prepares his forces against the Great Army of Guthrum. The apocryphal story about Alfred burning the cakes occurs at this time.
◆ **878** Alfred defeats Guthrum at Ethandune in Wessex.
◆ **878** Treaty of Wedmore divides England into two, and makes Alfred overlord of both halves.
◆ **886** Alfred captures and rebuilds London; he is now recognized as King of all England.
◆ **890s** Alfred builds the first permanent fleet of warships in England, ready to engage Viking invasion ships.
◆ **891** Alfred starts to compile the *Anglo-Saxon Chronicle.*
◆ **894-5** Alfred translates Orosius's world history and Bede's *Ecclesiastical History of the English Nation* into Anglo-Saxon.
◆ **899** Death of Alfred.

THE ANGLO-SAXON CHRONICLE

During the 890s Alfred instigated the compilation of the *Anglo-Saxon Chronicle.* Possibly derived from earlier chronicles, the *Chronicle* was written in Anglo-Saxon, the language spoken by the people, rather than Latin, the language of the Church. It outlined political, social and economic events in England and was continually updated until the 12th century.

SAXONS & VIKINGS

899–1016

FROM THE DEATH OF Alfred the Great in 899 through to the death of Aethelred in 1016, England was frequently at war with Viking invaders from Scandinavia. Wessex was the most powerful English kingdom at this time and led by Alfred's son Edward the Elder and his successors, it managed to recover large areas of central and northern England and expel most of the Danes by 975. But the long reign of Aethelred II (978-1016) weakened the country, for he adopted the policy of timidly buying off the invaders and was powerless to stop the Danish king, Sweyn Forkbeard, pillaging much of the country and seizing the kingdom in 1013.

ONE KINGDOM
Born c. 895 Athelstan succeeded his father Edward the Elder in 925. He was acknowledged as King of all the English, and it can be said that during his reign a unified monarchy was properly established in England. Athelstan is best remembered for his great and bloody victory at Brunanburh, Cumbria, in 937, in which he defeated a confederation of Northumbrian Danes, Scots and Irish.

ATHELSTAN
Crowned in 925, Athelstan (right) came to be recognized as King of all the English until his death in 939.

LONGBOATS
The Viking longboats were about 25 metres (80 feet) long and carried some 50 warriors, who took turns to row (below).

THE VIKINGS
The Vikings were seafaring adventurers from Scandinavia who crossed the North Sea in sail- and oar-powered longboats to invade Britain and Ireland. Their attacks began at the end of the eighth century and continued on and off until the 1060s. Constantly at war with the Anglo-Saxon kings, the Vikings built settlements in many parts of the country, especially in coastal areas. Although they brought terror and violence to Britain they were more than savage and illiterate warriors. They had a strong sense of justice, developed municipal government, produced fine works of art and many were eventually converted to Christianity by the Saxons.

VIKING NORTHUMBRIA

In the 870s the Vikings established their rule over Northumbria, with their capital inside the old Roman walls of York. The last Viking king of Northumbria was Eric Bloodaxe, who had been King of Norway in the 930s but was expelled for his extreme cruelty: he is said to have murdered his seven brothers. In 947 Eric was accepted as king but was expelled by Eadred, King of England, in 949. He returned in 952 but was deposed and killed by Eadred's army in 954, thereby ending Northumbrian independence.

ERIC BLOODAXE
The silver penny (above) of Eric Bloodaxe bears an unsheathed sword, a symbol of his heathen rule in Northumbria.

EADGAR THE PEACEABLE

Eadgar acceded to the throne in 959 and became known as the Peaceable because there were few Viking raids during his reign. Indeed, the *Anglo-Saxon Chronicle* describes the period as a prosperous one in which, with the help of Dunstan, Archbishop of Canterbury, many reforms were introduced. Notable was the Hundred Ordinance, which divided the shires into hundreds, and the introduction of a legal code based on Alfred's laws.

EADGAR
This contemporary manuscript depicts Eadgar (959-75) presenting a charter to Christ for the new minster at Winchester in 966. The illustration reveals the close links between Crown and Church at this time.

- ◆ **899** Edward the Elder accedes to the throne of Wessex on the death of Alfred the Great.
- ◆ **910** Saxons defeat the Danes at the Battle of Tettenhall and advance into East Anglia, the Midlands and Essex.
- ◆ **911** Viking leader, Rollo, is created Count of Normandy by the French king.
- ◆ **918** Edward the Elder subdues the Danes of East Anglia.
- ◆ **919** The princes of West Wales acknowledge Edward as overlord.
- ◆ **925** Edward the Elder dies and Athelstan, his son, becomes King of all England.
- ◆ **927** Athelstan conquers Northumbria and is acknowledged as overlord by the northern rulers.
- ◆ **937** Athelstan defeats a confederation of Danes, Irish and Scots at the Battle of Brunanburh.
- ◆ **939** After death of Athelstan, Edmund I becomes king.
- ◆ **946** Edmund dies and Eadred I becomes King of England.
- ◆ **954** Eric Bloodaxe, Danish King of York, is killed at Stainmore.
- ◆ **959** Eadgar the Peaceable becomes King of England.
- ◆ **960** St Dunstan becomes Archbishop of Canterbury.
- ◆ **973** Eadgar is crowned in a new form of coronation ceremony by St Dunstan.
- ◆ **975** Eadgar dies and Edward the Martyr becomes King of England.
- ◆ **978** Edward is murdered by the agents of Aethelred, who succeeds as Aethelred II.
- ◆ **980** Vikings renew their raids on England.
- ◆ **994** Sweyn Forkbeard, King of Denmark, besieges London but is bribed by Aethelred to withdraw.
- ◆ **1002** Aethelred orders the Massacre of St Brice's Day, during which many Danes living in England are put to death.
- ◆ **1003** Sweyn Forkbeard invades England again.
- ◆ **1008** Aethelred imposes a tax to build a fleet of ships to beat off Danish attacks.
- ◆ **1013** Aethelred flees to Normandy and Sweyn becomes King of England.
- ◆ **1014** Sweyn Forkbeard dies and is succeeded by Canute. Aethelred is then restored to the throne by the southern Saxon nobles.
- ◆ **1016** Aethelred dies, and his son, Edmund Ironside, fights for his inheritance against Canute.

THE AGE OF CANUTE

1016–1066

WHEN AETHELRED DIED IN 1016 there were two claimants to the throne. The Danes chose Canute, son of Sweyn, while the English chose Aethelred's son, Edmund Ironside. Pursuing their claims, Canute and Edmund fought several battles until, after a tremendous struggle in October 1016, they agreed to divide the country between them. However, Edmund died soon afterwards and Canute became king, with England soon to become part of a vast Scandinavian empire encompassing Denmark, Norway and southern Sweden. Canute's reign was marked by good government and great prosperity. After his death in 1035, the throne passed to his two sons and then, in 1042, to Edward the Confessor, who reigned until 1066.

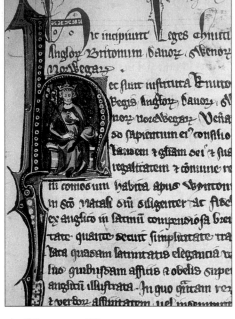

CANUTE
A tall, blond-haired Viking, Canute (above right) became king of England in 1016 and reigned as a strong, fearless and just leader, from 1016 until his death in 1035, when he was mourned by Saxon and Dane.

HEADS OF STATE
Four coins from the 11th century show the heads of (from top left to bottom right) Aethelred II, Canute, Harold Harefoot and Harthacanute, kings of England from 979-1042. Missing is Edmund Ironside, who only ruled for a couple of months.

A VIKING KING
Ruler of England, Denmark and Norway from 1016-35, Canute brought much-needed stability to the affairs of England during his reign. Although a Viking, he treated Dane and Saxon alike and wisely appointed Englishmen to positions of importance in the Church and at court. Indeed, he promised the English people "to be a gracious lord and a faithful observer of secular (and Christian) law", assuring them, in writing, of his devotion to their needs. His modernization of the country's laws bear this out and he may be fairly described as one of the best kings England ever had.

FOUR KINGS
Aethelred II (979-1016), was known as Aethelred the Unready, or, more correctly, the Redeless (rede meant council), because he refused to take advice and his policy towards the Danes proved disastrous. Fortunately, his successor Canute (1016-35) was a wise and just ruler, but Canute's two sons Harold and Harthacanute proved less able. Harold ruled England from 1035-40 with cruelty and abandon, while Harthacanute, his half-brother, who was king until 1042, never, in the words of the *Anglo-Saxon Chronicle*, "did anything worthy of a king while he reigned".

A ROYAL BANQUET
*This 11th century
painting depicts
Edward the Confessor
and his nobles being
waited upon at a royal
banquet. Despite his
Saxon origins, Edward
preferred the company
of his Norman advisers.*

EDWARD THE CONFESSOR

The son of Aethelred II, Edward the
Confessor was born c.1003 and from the
age of 10 until he was 35, lived with his
Norman mother, Emma, in Normandy.
Elected to the throne upon the death of
Harthacanute in 1042, he proved to be a
strong and pious king, determined to
control the growing power of the English
earls and raise a fleet to ward off Viking
assaults on the kingdom. However, he
incurred the displeasure of many
Englishmen by showing a preference for
Norman advisers and by banishing the
rebellious Godwine, Earl of Wessex, from
the kingdom. Although Godwine

returned the next year and forced Edward
to expel many of his Norman friends –
and despite the fact that Godwine's son,
Harold, became Edward's chief adviser for
the rest of his reign – Edward showed his
Norman bias by promising the English
throne to William of Normandy in 1051.

MISSION TO NORMANDY
*In this section of the Bayeux Tapestry,
Edward the Confessor (left) tells Harold
to lead a mission to Normandy in 1064.
Harold and his soldiers ride to church
in Bosham in Sussex to pray before
embarking for Normandy.*

◆ **1016** Aethelred II dies and his
son, Edmund Ironside, is chosen
to succeed by the Saxons, Canute
by the Danes.

◆ **1016** At the Battle of
Ashingdon, in Essex, Canute
defeats Edmund and they agree to
divide the kingdom into two:
Canute controlling the north and
Edmund the south.

◆ **1016** Edmund dies suddenly
and Canute is chosen to rule as
King of all England.

◆ **1017** Canute marries Emma of
Normandy, the widow of
Aethelred II.

◆ **1017** Canute divides England
into four earldoms: Northumbria,
Wessex, Mercia and East Anglia.

◆ **1027** Canute attends the
coronation of the Pope in Rome.

◆ **1035** Canute dies and Harold
Harefoot usurps the throne from
his half-brother, Harthacanute,
the rightful heir.

◆ **1040** Harold Harefoot dies and
Harthacanute accedes to the
English throne.

◆ **1042** Harthacanute dies and is
succeeded by Edward the
Confessor, son of Aethelred II.

◆ **1045** Edward marries Edith,
the daughter of Godwine, Earl
of Wessex.

◆ **1051** Edward banishes the
Godwine family from England.

◆ **1051** William, Duke of
Normandy, pays a visit to
Edward's court and wins a promise
that he should succeed Edward.

◆ **1052** Godwine returns to
England and Edward restores him
to the Earldom of Wessex.

◆ **1052** Construction of
Westminster Abbey begins.

◆ **1053** Godwine dies and his son
Harold becomes Earl
of Wessex and
principal adviser to
the King.

◆ **1064** Harold
Godwineson visits
the court of William
of Normandy and
swears on oath to
support William's
claim to the throne.

◆ **1066** Edward dies
and Harold is chosen
as successor, but
William of Normandy
declares the throne
was promised to him
by Edward before he
died. William
therefore prepares to
invade England.

WESTMINSTER ABBEY

THE ROYAL CHURCH OF ENGLAND

THE ABBEY CHURCH OF WESTMINSTER has played a key role in the history of England's monarchy ever since Edward the Confessor began its construction during the 11th century. With the exception of Edward V and Edward VIII, every English monarch since 1066 has been crowned in the Abbey, most have been married there and, until 1760, many were buried there. The Abbey is also a shrine to numerous British politicians, writers and composers, whose plaques and tombstones fill the aisles and chapels. Among these is the much-visited memorial to Sir Winston Churchill.

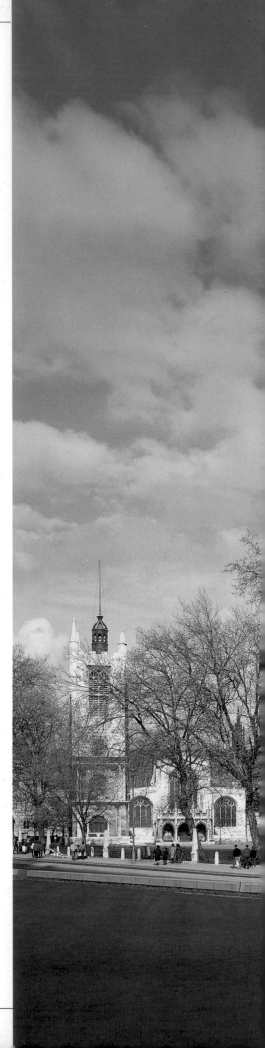

HENRY VII'S CHAPEL
Shortly before he died in 1509 Henry VII began work on a chapel in honour of the Virgin Mary. The chapel (left) which was finished in 1519, contains the tombs of Henry and his wife Elizabeth.

THE WEST FRONT
The final addition to the Abbey was made when the twin towers of the West Front (right), designed by Nicholas Hawksmoor to an original plan by Sir Christopher Wren, were built in 1745.

THE ABBEY'S HISTORY
A place of worship has stood at Westminster on the north bank of the River Thames since the seventh century. Edward the Confessor's building was begun in 1052 and consecrated in 1065, and it remained a Benedictine Abbey until 1540. Of the original building, not a stone remains above ground today, for Edward's abbey was demolished during the reign of Henry III and was largely rebuilt by 1272. Since that time, numerous monarchs have added to and torn down parts of the building, which was finally completed during the 18th century.

THE BATTLE OF HASTINGS

1066

IN JANUARY 1066, Edward the Confessor died without issue. Fifteen years earlier he had promised the succession to William, Duke of Normandy, but on his deathbed he reneged on this and promised the throne to his brother-in-law, Harold Godwineson, who became king as Harold II. Incensed by this betrayal, William launched an invasion fleet across the Channel. On 14 October, some six miles north of Hastings, he engaged Harold's army in battle and won a decisive victory which cost Harold his life and earned William the English crown and the title "the Conqueror". The Battle of Hastings proved to be one of the most decisive events in the history of England. The Anglo-Saxons became subservient to the Normans, who seized total control of every aspect of English society.

HAROLD'S DEATH
The death of Harold at the Battle of Hastings is vividly depicted in the Bayeux Tapestry (right). Struck by an arrow in his right eye, Harold was most probably finished off by the sword of a Norman knight.

A SWORN OATH
In 1064 Harold Godwineson swore an oath to guarantee the succession of William of Normandy, as shown in the Bayeux Tapestry (below).

CLAIMS TO THE ENGLISH THRONE
In 1051 Edward the Confessor promised the throne to William of Normandy. As he lay dying, Edward changed his mind and bequeathed the throne to Harold Godwineson, Earl of Wessex. Harold succeeded on 5 January 1066 and was crowned at Westminster Abbey the following day. William was furious and decided to assert his claim by force of arms.

THE NORMAN INVASION
William prepared an armada of several hundred ships to transport his army – made up of mounted knights and infantry – across the Channel to England. He landed unopposed at Pevensey Bay and moved on to Hastings, where he built a castle and awaited the arrival of the English army, which was in Yorkshire, having just defeated a large Viking army led by Harold Hardrada.

WILLIAM'S FLAGSHIP
In this section of the Bayeux Tapestry, the Norman fleet, grouped around William's flagship, the Mora, is depicted approaching Pevensey Bay.

THE BATTLE

At about 9 am on the morning of 14 October war trumpets were sounded and the Norman army – 7,000 strong, of whom nearly 3,000 were mounted knights in armour – launched an assault on the English lines on the ridge above them but were beaten back and retreated. The English army – also about 7,000 strong and including Harold's crack troops, the housecarls, equipped with deadly two-handed battleaxes – saw the confusion in the Norman lines and broke ranks. Charging down the hill after the Normans, they were met in turn by a vigorous Norman counter-attack.

After a further assault on the ridge had failed to make an impression, William's troops pretended to flee, a clever ruse that once again drew the enemy after them. They then turned about and picked off the pursuers one by one. This tactic proved decisive, and allowed William to employ his archers and knights to finish off the English troops, including Harold, who had remained on top of the ridge.

THE BATTLE GROUND

The English army, led by Harold, engaged William's forces on a ridge six miles inland from Hastings. At the start of the battle the English army lined up 10 to 12 deep on top of the ridge, while William's army assembled 365 metres (400 yards) away at the bottom of the ridge.

THE RIDGE

The ridge on which Harold's main forces were drawn up against the Norman army is shown in the photograph above.

WILLIAM *m* Matilda
THE CONQUEROR   of Flanders
👑 1066-1087

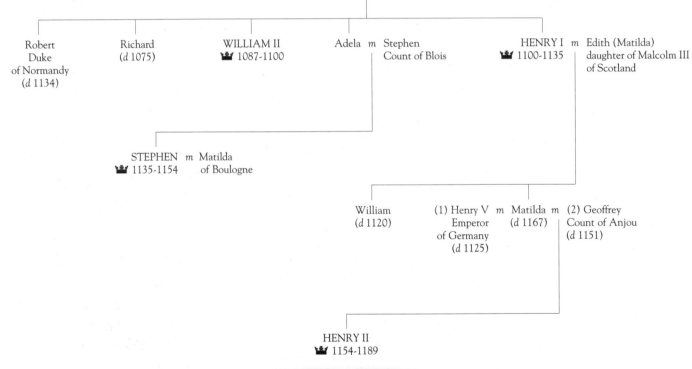

Robert   Richard   WILLIAM II   Adela *m* Stephen   HENRY I *m* Edith (Matilda)
Duke   (d 1075)   👑 1087-1100   Count of Blois   👑 1100-1135   daughter of Malcolm III
of Normandy   of Scotland
(d 1134)

STEPHEN *m* Matilda
👑 1135-1154   of Boulogne

William   (1) Henry V *m* Matilda *m* (2) Geoffrey
(d 1120)   Emperor   (d 1167)   Count of Anjou
                   of Germany   (d 1151)
                   (d 1125)

HENRY II
👑 1154-1189

CHAPTER TWO

THE
NORMANS
1066–1154

The Normans were originally Vikings who settled in north-west France in the early 10th century. Under the leadership of Rollo, they became Counts, and later Dukes, of Normandy and created a powerful state around the mouth of the Seine. In 1035 the Duchy passed to a nine-year-old illegitimate boy and for a time it was in anarchy. The new duke, William, was to become a skilled military commander, and in 1047 he decisively defeated his enemies and united the Duchy behind his rule. From then on William never lost a battle, and by 1066 was the foremost general in Europe.

The Norman Invasion

The Normans never suppressed their restless and adventurous Viking spirit and always felt an irresistible urge to seek new lands to conquer and settle. In the middle of the 11th century, they fanned outwards from Normandy, conquering both Southern Italy and England. William had a claim to the English throne, and in return for military assistance, he offered his land-hungry lords large areas of England in which to settle and construct new feudal lordships once the Anglo-Saxons had been overcome. On 14 October 1066, outside the town of Hastings, William defeated the English king Harold and was himself crowned king on Christmas Day 1066. A new, alien aristocracy was imposed upon more than two million English people and England was given firm, but arrogant government.

THE FOUR KINGS
The four Norman kings of England – William the Conqueror (top left), William Rufus (top right), Henry I (bottom left) and Stephen (bottom right) – are all shown in this 13th-century illustration from Matthew Paris's Great Chronicle.

Norman Rule

The Normans dispossessed many of the Anglo-Saxon landowners, pressed the peasantry into often unpaid service on their new feudal territories, covered the landscape with castles, and treated their Anglo-Saxon subjects with scorn and abuse. On the credit side they taught them better farming, developed the country's economy, put an end to Viking raids, and began to build cathedrals and churches in stone. Historians will always argue whether "Normanization" was good or bad for the Anglo-Saxon inhabitants of England, but few dispute that after the strong rule of the first three Norman kings, the reign of Stephen was disastrous. Not for nothing was it described at the time as a period of "nineteen long winters".

WILLIAM I

1066–1087

THE COAT OF ARMS OF WILLIAM I
There is some confusion as to whether two or three lions were featured on William's coat of arms, but two is the usual number. The use of three lions was not confirmed until the reign of Henry II in 1154.

BORN THE ILLEGITIMATE SON of Robert, Duke of Normandy, William inherited his father's duchy in 1035 at the age of eight. By 1047 he had established a reputation as a brilliant commander, one who was never to fight a battle he did not win nor besiege a castle he did not take. In 1051 he visited Edward the Confessor in England, where he was promised the succession to the English throne. When Edward was succeeded by Harold, Earl of Wessex, in January 1066, William felt cheated, brought a Norman army over to England, defeated Harold at the Battle of Hastings and was crowned King of England. Now known as "the Conqueror", William subdued the local population by confiscating Anglo-Saxon estates and giving them to his Norman followers. William died in 1087 after falling from his horse while besieging the French city of Nantes.

👑 WILLIAM I

- **Born** Falaise Castle, Normandy, 1027/8, illegitimate son of Robert of Normandy and Arlette of Conteville.
- **Married** Matilda of Flanders, Cathedral of Notre Dame d'Eu, Normandy, 1050/52, 10 children.
- **Acceded** 25 Dec 1066.
- **Crowned** Westminster Abbey, 25 Dec 1066.
- **Died** Rouen, Normandy, 9 Sept 1087, aged 59/60.

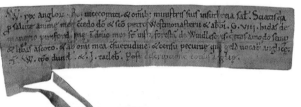

A GREAT SURVEY

In 1085 William sent out commissioners to all the counties of England, except those in the far north, to make a record of the population, extent, value, state of cultivation, ownership and tenancy of the land. The commissioners paid great attention to detail, even recording the numbers of livestock in each shire, and wrote the facts and figures up in what is known as the Domesday Book. One of the most interesting facts to emerge was the size of the population, which stood at some two million.

CONTEMPORARY REFERENCE
The writ above was issued by William I to Ralph, Sheriff of Surrey, concerning the dues owed by Pyrford Manor. Its importance is that it is one of the few contemporary sources to make reference to the great Domesday Book.

DOMESDAY BOOK
Consisting of two volumes – one a survey of the prosperous counties of Essex, Suffolk and Norfolk and the other of the rest of England – the Domesday Book is shown (right) on the replica of the casket in which it was kept upon its completion in 1086.

THE CONQUEROR

William was about 1.8 metres (5 feet 10 inches) tall, thick-set, with a rasping voice, a fist that could fell an ox and "an eye that could quell the fiercest baron". Charismatic and demonstrating considerable powers of leadership from an early age, he became a patient, tactful, courageous, devout, ruthless and sometimes cruel king. Such qualities inspired loyalty among his followers and fear among his enemies, made him constantly victorious in battle and enabled him to introduce the feudal system, strong government and an accompanying political, social and economic stability to England.

WILLIAM I
This portrait of William is unlikely to be realistic, for it was not drawn until the 13th century, when it appeared in the Great Chronicle *of Matthew Paris. The church William holds in his right hand represents his ecclesiastical patronage.*

THE NORMAN NOBILITY

When William landed with his army on the shores of England in 1066, he was accompanied by most of the leading nobles of Normandy and a number of church dignitaries. Among these were two of William's half-brothers (one of whom, Odo, was created Earl of Kent and later became Bishop of Bayeux) and several personal friends, including his childhood friend William FitzOsbern. After William's victory at Hastings, many of his followers were rewarded with huge tracts of land, confiscated from the Anglo-Saxon nobility, and they were licensed to build castles.

WILLIAM AND HIS NOBLES
This manuscript illustration depicts William accompanied by members of the Norman nobility.

EVENTS OF THE REIGN 1066 – 1087

◆ **1066** William and his Norman army defeats Harold II and the Saxons at the Battle of Hastings. Harold is killed and after subduing the rest of the country, William is crowned King of England on Christmas Day.

◆ **1067** William suppresses a Saxon revolt in the southwest of England.

◆ **1068-9** After putting down a revolt led by Edwin and Morcar, grandsons of Leofric of Mercia, William lays waste to the northern counties of England.

◆ **1070** Stigand, the Anglo-Saxon Archbishop of Canterbury is dismissed by William, and the Frenchman, Lanfranc of Bec, is appointed in his place.

◆ **1070** Archbishop Lanfranc lays the foundations of Canterbury Cathedral after the earlier building is destroyed by fire.

◆ **1071** William defeats a revolt led by Hereward the Wake in East Anglia, thus putting an end to Saxon resistance to his rule.

◆ **1072** William invades Scotland and compels Malcolm III to pay homage to him at Abernethy.

◆ **1073** Archbishopric of York subordinated to Archbishopric of Canterbury.

◆ **1078** William begins the construction of the White Tower at the Tower of London.

◆ **1079** William begins the construction of a Norman Cathedral at Winchester.

◆ **1079** Robert, William's eldest son, leads a rebellion in Normandy, but is defeated by his father at the battle of Gerberoi and his life is spared.

◆ **1079** New Forest enclosed by William as a royal hunting area. Severe Forest Laws against trespassing introduced.

◆ **1080** William refuses to pay homage to the Pope.

◆ **1082** Odo, Bishop of Bayeux – William's half-brother – is arrested for conspiracy.

◆ **1085** William orders a survey of the shires of England; the information is recorded in the Domesday Book.

◆ **1086** The Domesday Book is completed and William gathers all the feudal lords and tenants-in-chief of England to renew their oath of fealty to him at Salisbury.

◆ **1087** William dies of his injuries after falling from his horse while besieging the French city of Nantes.

CASTLE BUILDING

THE POWER HOUSES OF THE CONQUERORS

THE CASTLE WAS INTRODUCED TO England in 1066 by William the Conqueror, and during the following six centuries some 2,000 of these fortified residences were erected all over Britain. For much of that time, apart from cathedrals and large churches, castles were the only structures of any size, and they were often feared and resented. Such antipathy was due in no small part to the fact that the castle was both the symbol and the substance of feudal lordship. Fulfilling a defensive and offensive function, it enabled a lord to house his family while providing a secure base from which he could control the surrounding countryside. The castle was also at the heart of local government and within its walls taxes were collected and grievances settled. However, in the 15th century, the decline of feudalism, the banning of private armies and the transfer of power from local lords to central government lessened the need for such structures and castle building went into decline.

DOVER CASTLE
High on a rocky promontory on the south coast of England and dominating the surrounding countryside, Dover Castle (right) was originally an enclosure castle but was later extensively rebuilt.

MOTTE-AND-BAILEY
Raised for a motte-and-bailey castle during the reign of William the Conqueror, the mound at Thetford, in Norfolk (below), is about 25 metres (80 feet) high.

EARLY CASTLES

The first castles were of two kinds, both of simple design. The motte-and-bailey was a raised mound of earth (motte), on top of which was a wooden tower in which the owner lived. Around the mound was a wooden-walled park (bailey), surrounded by ditches. Hundreds of this type were built between 1066-1216. The enclosure castle, of which there were fewer, was a raised platform of earth surrounded by a wooden palisade and then enclosed by a ditch and bank.

THE FIRST ENGLISH CASTLE
This section of the Bayeux Tapestry (left) shows William of Normandy and his followers erecting one of the first motte-and-bailey castles in England, at Hastings, just before the battle of 1066 was fought.

CASTLES OF STONE

Like timber and earth castles, stone castles were of two types, both of which were stone-walled enclosures, often surrounded by a moat, with various buildings inside, but some had a great stone tower at or near their centre, while others did not. Earliest examples include the Tower of London, begun in 1078, and the great hall tower at Chepstow, begun in 1067.

Great towers came in a variety of shapes – rectangular, round, polygonal and D-shaped – and sizes, ranging from about 15-30 metres (50-100 feet) tall and between 10-30 metres (30-100 feet) across. One of the most notable was the great tower at Dover, built by Mauricius Ingeniator in the 1180s. An almost perfect cube of 32.1 by 31.5 by 31.1 metres (98 by 96 by 95 feet), its walls were up to 7 metres (21 feet) thick in places, wide enough to accommodate sizeable rooms.

BUILDING A CASTLE

Timber and earth castles could be built relatively cheaply within a few weeks, but not surprisingly it took a number of years and a considerable sum of money to construct a castle made of stone. The stone had to be quarried and timbers felled before being transported – often over long distances – to the site, and skilled masons, carpenters, blacksmiths and labourers had to be housed, fed and, if they were lucky, paid. All in all, it was a time-consuming and expensive undertaking.

SLOW PROGRESS
It has been estimated that the average construction time for a great tower (right) – including windows, inner walls and chambers and possibly with attendant buildings going up at the same time – may have been around 3 metres (10 feet) of height per year.

WILLIAM II

1087–1100

THE COAT OF ARMS OF WILLIAM II

THE THIRD SON OF William the Conqueror, William II was bequeathed the English throne by his father because he was tougher than his easy-going elder brother, Robert, who received the Duchy of Normandy instead. England needed a strong hand to continue the Conqueror's new order and William began well. In 1088 he put down a baronial revolt with the help of native English lords, but failed to keep his promise to them of good governance in return for their help. William also fell out with the Church over the imposition of heavy taxes, but in his favour did attempt to persuade Robert to govern Normandy more equitably, and repulsed two invasions led by Malcolm III of Scotland.

👑 WILLIAM II

- **Born** Normandy, 1056/60, third son of William I and Matilda of Flanders.
- **Acceded** 9 Sept 1087.
- **Crowned** Westminster Abbey, 26 Sept 1087.
- **Died** New Forest, Hampshire, 2 Aug 1100, aged 40/44.

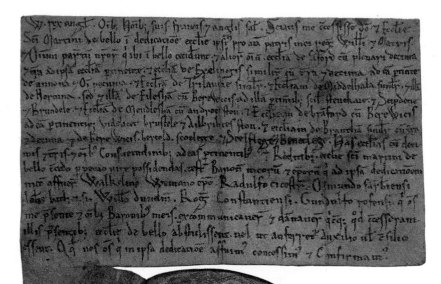

A ROYAL ENDOWMENT
The endowment to the left, affixed with the royal seal, was granted by William to Battle Abbey, founded in 1070 by his father, William I, on the site of the Battle of Hastings.

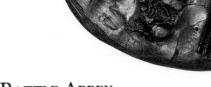

PORTRAIT OF THE KING
This coin minted during his reign is one of the few contemporary portraits we have of William II.

BATTLE ABBEY

Four years after William the Conqueror defeated Harold and the English army near Hastings, he vowed to build an abbey on the site of the battle and to position the high altar on the spot where Harold had fallen. Completed in 1094, the abbey was consecrated on 11 February by Anselm, Archbishop of Canterbury, the Bishop of Chichester – in whose diocese the abbey lay – and six other bishops.

EVENTS OF THE REIGN
1087 – 1100

◆ **1087** William II accedes to the throne on the death of his father, William I.

◆ **1088** With the help of the native English Lords, William crushes a baronial rebellion in Normandy led by his uncle Odo of Bayeux, who supports the claims of William's brother, Robert of Normandy, to the English throne.

◆ **1089** Ranulf Flambard, leading adviser to William, is appointed Justiciar (the King's main judicial officer) and begins to levy heavy taxes on the English church.

◆ **1090** William leads an invasion of Normandy in an attempt to subdue his brother, Robert, Duke of Normandy.

◆ **1091** William defeats an invasion of England led by Malcolm III of Scotland.

◆ **1092** Carlisle is captured from Scotland and Cumberland is annexed to England.

◆ **1093** The foundations of Durham Cathedral are laid down.

◆ **1093** Malcolm III and the Scots invade England again, but they are defeated and Malcolm is killed at the Battle of Alnwick.

◆ **1093** The Benedictine monk and scholar, Anselm, succeeds Lanfranc as Archbishop of Canterbury after an interval of four years when the position was not filled.

◆ **1095** William suppresses a baronial revolt in Northumbria.

◆ **1097** The construction of Westminster Hall begins.

◆ **1097** After a row with William, Anselm is exiled to Rome and William seizes his estates.

◆ **1098** William invades North Wales to suppress a Welsh rebellion against the Norman border lords.

◆ **1100** William is killed by an arrow while out hunting with friends in the New Forest.

RUFUS

William II was short and stout, had fair hair, a fiery red complexion (hence his nickname, Rufus) and suffered from a stutter. Intelligent, witty, generous to his soldiers and unswervingly loyal to his father, he was also cynical, ruthless and no respecter of the Church, which he taxed heavily. He never married, nor produced any offspring, and if the chronicler's descriptions of his court as being licentious are to be believed, then it may well be that he was homosexual.

THE KING'S DEATH

William had a great passion for hunting, and on 2 August 1100, while on the chase in the New Forest, he was killed by an arrow fired by Walter Tyrell, a close friend. Although supposedly an accident, it has been suggested that he was shot at deliberately on the instruction of his younger brother Henry, who was in the vicinity at the time and who, as heir to the throne, succeeded him as king. Henry's removal of the royal treasury at Winchester the next day was suspicious.

WILLIAM II
This contemporary manuscript illustration depicts William with an arrow through his heart, for he was killed by an arrow while out hunting with friends in the New Forest in August 1100.

THE ROYAL HUNT
William enjoyed physical activities, notably hunting. The manuscript illustration below shows William crowned and on horseback pursuing a stag through the forest. He has wounded the stag with one arrow and is preparing to fire the fatal shot.

TOWER OF LONDON

LONDON'S ROYAL FORTRESS

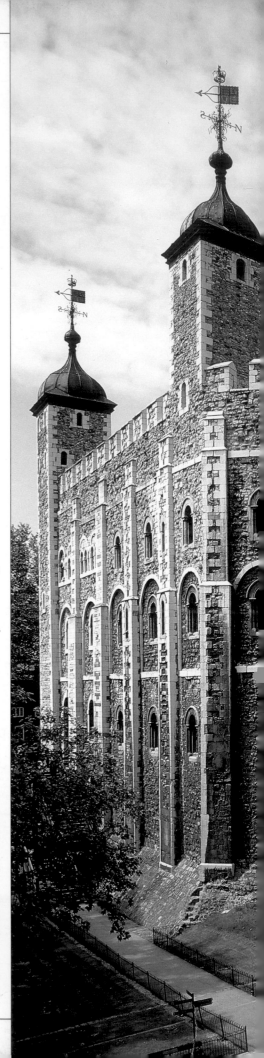

WILLIAM THE CONQUEROR built a simple timber-and-earth castle in London on the north side of the Thames a few months after his victory at Hastings in October 1066. Initially intended to overawe the population of London, by 1100 the structure consisted of a partly-ditched enclosure containing military, administrative and domestic buildings of wood surrounding a large stone tower. Substantial additions were made up to Victorian times, for this famous castle has served as a royal fortress, a palace – the principal residence for all English kings from William II to Henry VII – a royal mint, a royal menagerie, an arsenal, a repository for the Crown Jewels and, most famously, a prison and place of execution.

THE TOWER FROM THE AIR (left)

ESCAPES

The Tower was not built to be a prison, and for centuries was only used to confine the privileged few. Yet if the confinement was not irksome, there were some prisoners who did try to escape. The first successful attempt was by Ranulf Flambard, Bishop of Durham, who escaped in 1101.

ARCHITECTURE OF THE TOWER

At first, the Tower of London consisted of a simple enclosure formed by existing Roman stone and new timber walling. Between 1078 and 1100, the White Tower was erected within the walls, and during the 12th and 13th centuries, the castle area was extended several times to create a much larger stone-walled enclosure. At the end of the 13th century Edward I built a second perimeter wall and added three more towers. No major fortifications were built after this, but several large residential, administrative and ordnance buildings were constructed inside the walls over the next 600 years.

A BROKEN NECK
In 1244 Prince Gruffydd of Wales fell and broke his neck escaping from the Tower.

THE WHITE TOWER

Designed by Gundulf, Bishop of Rochester, the White Tower was built as a royal residence and fortress. Construction began in 1078 and was completed some 20 years later. With walls 3-5 metres (11-15 feet) thick, the tower rises some 30 metres (90 feet) to the top of the battlements and covers an almost rectangular area of 35 by 39 metres (107 by 118 feet). The residential suite for the royal family, as well as a great dining hall and the Chapel of St John, were in the top part of the tower.

STATE ENTRANCE

In 1275 Edward I built a water-gate on the Tower's outer wall to serve as the state entrance from the Thames. During the Tudor period, when the Tower was used primarily as a jail, it became known as Traitors' Gate. Prominent among those prisoners brought to the Tower via this entrance was Princess Elizabeth, later Elizabeth I.

WHITEWASH
The White Tower gained its name not from its distinctive stonework (left) but because it was regularly whitewashed during the Middle Ages.

TRAITORS' GATE
Prominent citizens charged with crimes against the state were ferried along the Thames and into the Tower through Traitors' Gate (above).

HENRY I

1100–1135

THE COAT OF ARMS OF HENRY I

ON HEARING OF THE DEATH of his brother, William II, on 2 August 1100, Henry rode to Winchester, seized the royal treasure and went straight to London, where he was crowned on 5 August. Such indecent haste might indicate that he knew more about William's death in a hunting "accident" than he let on. Certainly, Henry was no fool when it came to placating a predominantly Saxon population. He immediately promised good governance and introduced a number of important reforms, developing the *Curia Regis* (King's Council) to settle disputes between the Crown and its tenants and expanding the system of travelling justices throughout the shires.

 HENRY I

- **Born** Selby, Yorkshire, Sept 1068, fourth son of William I and Matilda.
- **Acceded** 2 Aug 1100.
- **Crowned** Westminster Abbey, 5 Aug 1100.
- **Married** Edith of Scotland, 11 Nov 1100, 4 children; Adela of Louvain, 29 Jan 1121.
- **Died** Rouen, Normandy, 1/2 Dec 1135, aged 67.

NORMAN CATHEDRALS

The Normans built on a grand scale, whether in Normandy, England or Sicily (another one of their conquests). Their stone cathedrals and castles were nearly always constructed in the most imposing positions in order to dominate the surrounding countryside, and many were designed in a distinctive variant of the Romanesque style, loosely called Norman Romanesque.

DURHAM AND ELY
Two of the most notable Norman cathedrals in England are Durham (left), largely completed by 1133, and Ely (below), which was not completed until the 14th century.

HENRY I
This contemporary drawing of Henry I shows a sombre and sad man, for it illustrates a manuscript describing the loss of his only legitimate son, William, who was drowned in 1120.

"BEAUCLERC"

Henry I was a well-built man, of average height and more placid and sober of temperament than his brother William Rufus or his father, the Conqueror. However, he was capable of great cruelty and could be ruthless and unforgiving: he once pushed a man to his death from the top of Rouen Castle for breaking an oath of allegiance to the royal family. Well educated, able to read and write Latin and English, Henry was nicknamed "Beauclerc" and the "Lion of Justice" as he was a lover of legal reform and administrative work. An excellent judge of a man's abilities, he also knew how to generate loyalty among his followers and keep on good terms with his wife Matilda, despite the fact that he had numerous mistresses and illegitimate children by them throughout his 18-year marriage to her.

THE WHITE SHIP
This contemporary illustration (below) depicts the White Ship running aground before sinking while on a voyage from Normandy to England in 1120. Henry's son and heir, William, drowned in the accident.

DEATH OF AN HEIR

Henry's only legitimate son and heir, William – whom he had made Duke of Normandy after Robert (Henry's eldest brother) had been imprisoned for life in 1106 – drowned in November 1120. Returning from Normandy to England aboard the White Ship, William lost his life when the inebriated pilot steered the vessel onto a rock, where it quickly filled with water. Henry's second wife Adela, whom he had married in 1121 after the death of Matilda in 1118, failed to produce another heir, and Henry had to persuade the barons to accept his daughter, Matilda, as heir to the throne.

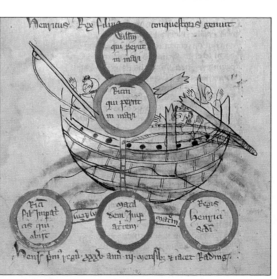

EVENTS OF THE REIGN 1100 – 1135

◆ **1100** Henry I succeeds his brother, William II.

◆ **1100** Henry issues a Charter of Liberties, promising the people good governance.

◆ **1100** Ranulf Flambard, Bishop of Durham and chief adviser to William II, is imprisoned by Henry in the Tower of London but escapes the following year. Archbishop Anselm is recalled from exile.

◆ **1100** Henry marries Edith, daughter of Malcolm III of Scotland and great-grand-daughter of Edmund Ironside. She adopts the extra name of Matilda, which is more acceptable to the Norman barons.

◆ **1101** Robert of Normandy invades England in an attempt to wrest the throne from his brother, Henry. However, after failing, he signs the Treaty of Alton, which confirms Henry as King of England and Robert as Duke of Normandy.

◆ **1101** Henry appoints Roger Salisbury as Chancellor. Salisbury founds the Court of the Exchequer to administer Crown finances and institutes administrative reforms.

◆ **1106** War breaks out between Henry and Robert of Normandy. Henry defeats Robert at the Battle of Tinchebrai, imprisons him in Cardiff Castle for the rest of his life and takes control of Normandy.

◆ **1109** Anselm, Archbishop of Canterbury, dies.

◆ **1110** Pipe Rolls, Exchequer records of the accounts of the sheriffs and other royal officials in each county, are introduced. They remain in force until 1834, and are the longest series of English public records.

◆ **1118** Death of Matilda.

◆ **1120** Henry's 17-year-old son and heir, William, is drowned when the White Ship sinks returning from France. Henry's daughter, Matilda, becomes heir to the throne.

◆ **1121** Henry marries Adela of Louvain.

◆ **1123** St Bartholomew's Hospital is founded in London.

◆ **1126** Henry persuades the barons to accept Matilda as heir to the throne.

◆ **1128** Matilda marries Geoffrey Plantagenet, Count of Anjou.

◆ **1135** Henry I dies of food poisoning near Rouen, in France.

STEPHEN

1135–1154

THE COAT OF ARMS OF STEPHEN
It is not definitely known which coat of arms was used by Stephen, but the archer above usually appeared on his shield.

BEFORE THE DEATH of Henry I, Stephen, the grandson of William the Conqueror, had sworn along with many other barons to accept Henry's daughter Matilda as heir to the throne. However, on Henry's death in 1135, Stephen usurped the throne, but was far too good-natured to control his kingdom. Indeed, historians have described his reign as one of "nineteen long winters" since, for most of the time, there was civil war between Stephen and Matilda. Although Matilda withdrew from the struggle in 1148, order was not restored until 1153 when her son, Henry of Anjou, came over to England and compelled the barons to recognize him as the heir to the throne.

♔ STEPHEN

- **Born** Blois, France, 1096/7, son of Stephen, Count of Blois and Adela of Flanders.
- **Married** Matilda of Boulogne, 1125, 5 children.
- **Acceded** 22 Dec 1135.
- **Crowned** Westminster Abbey, 26 Dec 1135.
- **Died** 25 Oct 1154, Dover, Kent, aged 57/58.

MATILDA
Born in 1102, Matilda (left) was the fiery, arrogant daughter of Henry I. In 1129 she married Geoffrey Plantagenet, Count of Anjou, and their son later became Henry II of England. From 1135-48 she spent much of her time asserting her claim to the English throne and attempting to overthrow her cousin, Stephen, by force of arms. She died in Normandy in 1167.

A RIVAL CLAIM TO THE THRONE

Before his death, Henry I had made the barons swear to recognize his daughter, Matilda, as heir to the throne. However, on his death in 1135 the barons transferred their support to her cousin, Stephen. Partly because of Stephen's misgovernment, Matilda won over a number of the barons to her side and war broke out between the two claimants. In 1141, after defeating and imprisoning Stephen, Matilda declared herself queen, but so alienated the barons that she was forced to relinquish the crown. Seven years of warfare followed until Matilda abandoned the fight and returned to live in France.

EVENTS OF THE REIGN
1135 – 1154

- ◆ **1135** Upon the death of Henry I, Stephen usurps the throne of England from Matilda, Henry's daughter. He does so with the support of the English barons, who renege on their oath to Henry to accept his daughter as queen.
- ◆ **1136** The first baronial revolts against Stephen begin in Norfolk and Devon.
- ◆ **1138** Robert, Earl of Gloucester, an illegitimate son of Henry I, withdraws his support for Stephen and switches allegiance to Matilda.
- ◆ **1138** David I of Scotland invades England to support the cause of his niece, Matilda, but is defeated by Stephen at the Battle of the Standard, near Northallerton in Yorkshire.
- ◆ **1139** Matilda leaves France and lands in England.
- ◆ **1141** Matilda's forces defeat and capture Stephen at Lincoln. Stephen is taken to Bristol Castle and held prisoner, and Matilda is made queen with the support of Stephen's brother, Henry, Bishop of Winchester.
- ◆ **1141** Bishop Henry deserts Matilda and rejoins his brother Stephen's cause.
- ◆ **1141** Earl Robert is captured and exchanged for Stephen.
- ◆ **1142** Matilda escapes the siege of Oxford by crossing the frozen River Thames in her nightgown.
- ◆ **1145** Stephen defeats Matilda's forces at the Battle of Faringdon.
- ◆ **1147** Earl Robert of Gloucester dies.
- ◆ **1148** Matilda abandons the fight and leaves England.
- ◆ **1151** Matilda's son, Henry Plantagenet, succeeds his father, Geoffrey, as Count of Anjou.
- ◆ **1152** Henry of Anjou marries Eleanor, heiress of Aquitaine.
- ◆ **1153** Henry of Anjou lands in England, asserts his claim to the throne and gathers support for further war against Stephen.
- ◆ **1153** Henry and Stephen agree to meet at Wallingford to discuss terms for ending the civil war. A deal is arranged and confirmed in the Treaty of Westminster, by which Stephen is to remain king for the rest of his lifetime, but thereafter the throne passes to Henry, and not Stephen's son, William.
- ◆ **1154** Stephen dies and is buried at the Clunaic monastery in Faversham, Kent.

THE IRRESOLUTE KING

By general consent the chroniclers of the time suggest that Stephen was an attractive personality. Good-natured, courteous, brave as a lion in battle and glad to mix with everybody, he enjoyed a feast with the humblest of his people, whom he treated as his equals. However, he lacked many of the qualities necessary for kingship, being mild and soft, not at all ruthless, lacking in resolution, far too forgiving and easily deceived. He could also be treacherous. The barons soon recognized these weaknesses and exploited them to their own advantage, to the great misery of the country.

STEPHEN
This contemporary manuscript illustration below depicts Stephen wearing a gauntlet and feeding a falcon, hunting being one of his favourite pastimes.

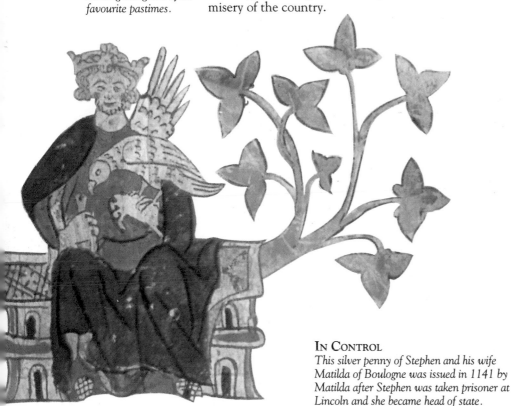

IN CONTROL
This silver penny of Stephen and his wife Matilda of Boulogne was issued in 1141 by Matilda after Stephen was taken prisoner at Lincoln and she became head of state.

CIVIL WAR

In 1136 the Earl of Norfolk led the first rebellion against Stephen. Other revolts broke out and, although they were suppressed, Stephen was lenient with the rebels, a sign of weakness that was to prove disastrous. In 1138 many of the barons deserted the King and transferred their allegiance to Matilda. Over the next few years a state of near-anarchy reigned in England as the two sides fought a series of battles, both suffering fluctuating fortunes. With nobody in effective control, the barons ravaged the countryside and plundered property at will.

THE PLANTAGENETS

1154–1399

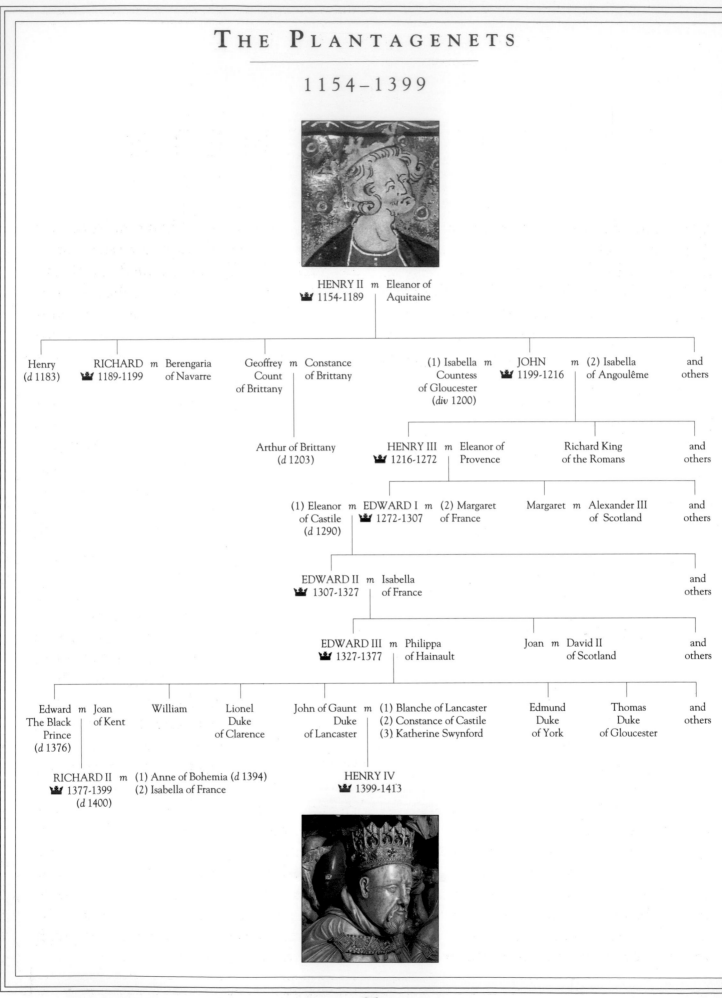

HENRY II *m* Eleanor of
👑 1154-1189   Aquitaine

Henry
(*d* 1183)

RICHARD *m* Berengaria
👑 1189-1199   of Navarre

Geoffrey *m* Constance
Count   of Brittany
of Brittany

(1) Isabella *m* JOHN *m* (2) Isabella
Countess   👑 1199-1216   of Angoulême
of Gloucester
(*div* 1200)

and
others

Arthur of Brittany
(*d* 1203)

HENRY III *m* Eleanor of
👑 1216-1272   Provence

Richard King
of the Romans

and
others

(1) Eleanor *m* EDWARD I *m* (2) Margaret
of Castile   👑 1272-1307   of France
(*d* 1290)

Margaret *m* Alexander III
of Scotland

and
others

EDWARD II *m* Isabella
👑 1307-1327   of France

and
others

EDWARD III *m* Philippa
👑 1327-1377   of Hainault

Joan *m* David II
of Scotland

and
others

Edward *m* Joan
The Black   of Kent
Prince
(*d* 1376)

William

Lionel
Duke
of Clarence

John of Gaunt *m* (1) Blanche of Lancaster
Duke   (2) Constance of Castile
of Lancaster   (3) Katherine Swynford

Edmund
Duke
of York

Thomas
Duke
of Gloucester

and
others

RICHARD II *m* (1) Anne of Bohemia (*d* 1394)
👑 1377-1399   (2) Isabella of France
(*d* 1400)

HENRY IV
👑 1399-1413

CHAPTER THREE

THE PLANTAGENETS

1154–1399

R ichard I, the second Plantagenet king, once said of his family that "from the Devil we sprang and to the Devil we shall go." His family all exhibited the same volatile disposition and demonic energy, whether physical, emotional or intellectual, and almost all were bold, imposing, militaristic, and creative. Largely through their policy of marrying where possible within the family network they passed on strong family likenesses: most of them had reddish hair, breadth of build, great muscular strength and agility, and all displayed courage, foresight, humanity and a sense of justice. Whatever the Plantagenets did, good or evil, they did with all their might.

Yellow Broom

This remarkable family acquired the surname Plantagenet from the nickname borne by Geoffrey, Count of Anjou between 1129-51 and the father of Henry II. Geoffrey used to wear as a badge a sprig of flowering broom (*Planta genista*), a habit said to have originated when, retrieving his hat which fell off one day while out hunting, he scooped up a handful of yellow broom flowers. The name was not formally used until the mid-15th

THE WARRING DYNASTY
The Plantagenet kings were often involved in warfare, either with the French (above), their barons, or rebellious members of their family.

century when Richard, Duke of York, and Protector of England for a few years during the reign of Henry VI, claimed the throne through superior right and called himself Richard Plantagenet to emphasize his claim. The first Plantagenet king of England was Henry II, and he is generally regarded as the greatest. Thirteen more Plantagenet kings followed him in a dynasty that ruled for 331 years, although for the last 86 years, rival families within the dynasty struggling to seize the crown took the names of Lancaster and York, even though all in fact were Plantagenets.

The Plantagenet Era

For much of this long period the kings were involved in costly and on the whole unproductive wars with France and Scotland, and they were also frequently immersed in struggles for power with over-mighty barons at home. As a dynasty, the Plantagenets made their greatest and most permanent contributions in the development of English law, especially the unique Common Law, and by sponsoring a splendid architectural heritage that combined the best of contemporary European styles with distinctive English ideas.

HENRY II

1154–1189

THE COAT OF ARMS OF HENRY II
When Henry became king, he adopted a coat of arms bearing three lions.

HENRY PLANTAGENET was 21 when he became king in 1154. His succession made him lord of an empire which stretched from the Scottish borders down to the Pyrenees, and he was equipped with all the intellectual and physical qualities to rule it well. He began by destroying the castles built by rebellious barons during Stephen's reign, and then set about regulating the power of the Church. He also introduced numerous legal reforms, laying the foundation for the common law, and despite the fact that the latter years of his reign were plagued by family revolts, his substantial empire was intact when he died in 1189.

👑 HENRY II

- ◆ **Born** Le Mans, Anjou, 5 Mar 1133, son of Geoffrey Plantagenet and Matilda.
- ◆ **Married** Eleanor of Aquitaine, Bordeaux Cathedral, 18 May 1152, 8 children.
- ◆ **Acceded** 19 Dec 1154.
- ◆ **Crowned** Westminster Abbey, 19 Dec 1154.
- ◆ **Died** Chinon Castle, France, 6 July 1189, aged 56.

THOMAS À BECKET

In 1162 Henry appointed Thomas à Becket Archbishop of Canterbury, to reform the abuses of the Church. Becket quarrelled with the King in 1164 and again in 1170. In exasperation, Henry cried out: "Will not someone rid me of this turbulent priest?" Four of Henry's knights took him literally and murdered Becket in his cathedral.

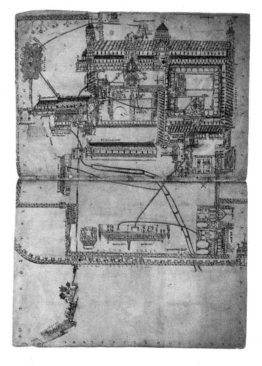

CANTERBURY CATHEDRAL
The extent of Canterbury Cathedral while Becket was Archbishop can be gauged from these contemporary plans.

THE MURDER OF BECKET
The illustrated manuscript above depicts the murder of Thomas à Becket by four of Henry's knights in Canterbury Cathedral in 1170.

ROYAL SEAL
The royal seal of Henry II shows the King on horseback.

LEGAL REFORMS

In 1164 Henry set out various Church reforms in the Constitutions of Clarendon. Notable proposals were that the clergy or others associated with the Church, if charged with a criminal offence, should be tried in the civil courts, and that no appeal should be made to Rome without the king's consent. Despite fierce opposition from the Church, the proposals were adopted. At the Assize of Clarendon in 1166, the right to trial by jury was established.

A LION OF A KING

Henry II was strongly built, with a leonine head, freckled face, red hair and a cracked voice. Tough and athletic, he possessed immense energy, which enabled him to travel ceaselessly about his extensive domains. Generous to the poor, a pillar of justice and an intellectual giant, Henry was the greatest of the Plantagenets and arguably the most able English king since Alfred.

HENRY II

ORFORD CASTLE
Built between 1166-73, only the unique 21-sided great tower of Orford Castle in Suffolk remains standing today.

IN STONE

To strengthen his position in England, Henry destroyed the warring barons' wood and earth castles, and replaced them with stone castles of his own. He also extended and repaired many existing structures.

EVENTS OF THE REIGN
1154 – 1189

◆ **1154** Henry II accedes to the throne upon the death of his second cousin, Stephen.

◆ **1155** Henry appoints Thomas à Becket Chancellor of England.

◆ **1155** Pope Adrian IV issues the papal bull *Laudabiliter*, which gives Henry authority to invade Ireland and bring its Church under the control of Rome.

◆ **1162** Henry appoints Thomas à Becket Archbishop of Canterbury in the hope that he will help introduce church reforms.

◆ **1164** Henry introduces the Constitutions of Clarendon, which place limitations on the Church's jurisdiction over crimes committed by the clergy. This leads to a violent quarrel between Henry and Thomas à Becket and the latter goes into exile in France.

◆ **1166** The Assize of Clarendon establishes trial by jury for the first time.

◆ **1166** Dermot McMurrough, King of Leinster in Ireland, appeals to Henry to help him oppose a confederation of other Irish kings. In response, Henry sends a force led Richard de Clare, Earl of Pembroke, thereby beginning the English settlement of Ireland.

◆ **1168** English scholars expelled from Paris and settle in Oxford, where they found a university.

◆ **1170** Henry and Becket are reconciled, but the two of them quarrel again. Becket is killed by the high altar in Canterbury Cathedral on 29 December.

◆ **1171** Henry invades Ireland and receives homage from the King of Leinster and the other Irish kings. Henry is accepted as Lord of Ireland.

◆ **1171** At the Council of Cashel, Henry makes the Irish clergy submit to the authority of Rome.

◆ **1173** Becket is canonized.

◆ **1173-4** Henry's sons, Henry, Richard and Geoffrey, lead a rebellion against him.

◆ **1189** Henry dies at Chinon Castle in Anjou.

HENRY II

THE ANGEVIN EMPIRE

WHEN HENRY II became King of England in 1154 he was already Count of Anjou and of Touraine, and Duke of Normandy and of Aquitaine. As such he was lord of an empire that stretched from the Cheviot Hills down to the Pyrenees, his territories in France exceeding even those of the French king. Known as the Angevin Empire (because the county of Anjou lay at its heart), this vast domain was held together by diplomacy and force of arms. For both Henry and his son Richard I, preserving the geographic and political integrity of the empire against the encroachments of Philip II of France was of the utmost importance, and in that sense, their position as kings of England, which was but one part of the empire, was in many respects a secondary consideration.

ELEANOR OF AQUITAINE
Eleanor, the wife of Henry II, was buried in Fontevrault Abbey, France. Her imposing tomb effigy is shown on the left.

CHATEAU-GAILLARD
The medieval illustration on the right depicts a French army besieging Château-Gaillard in 1204.

HENRY'S QUEEN

In May 1152 Henry married Eleanor of Aquitaine, as rich, passionate, charismatic and energetic as her husband. Their marriage was an unhappy one, and after the couple fell out she constantly encouraged her sons to rebel against their father. Although his family never succeeded in overthrowing him, Henry felt sufficiently threatened to keep Eleanor in a state of virtual imprisonment for the last 15 years of his reign. She outlived him and died in 1204, aged 82.

DECLINE AND FALL

The Angevin Empire remained intact up to the death of Richard I in 1199, but began to break up thereafter. This was largely due to the aggressive policies pursued by Philip II of France, who was intent on restoring France to the greatness it had enjoyed under Charlemagne. Philip had seized some of the Angevin domains in 1193, when Richard I was imprisoned in Germany, only to lose them again after Richard's release. However, during John's reign from 1199-1216, Philip renewed his efforts with spectacular success, and by the time of his death in 1223, he had restored most of the Angevin territories and properties to France, including the supposedly impregnable Château-Gaillard.

THE ROCK OF CASHEL
In 1171 the bishops of Ireland assembled at the cathedral on the Rock of Cashel (above), in County Tipperary, to submit to Henry II. The bishops agreed to a number of reforms to bring the Irish Church into line with the Roman Church.

THE CONQUEST OF IRELAND
The Irish Church had consistently declined to follow the doctrines of the Church of Rome. In 1155 the Pope gave dispensation to Henry II to bring them into line. Henry assembled an invasion force and in 1171 accepted the submission of his nobles in Ireland and the Irish kings and bishops. Although not a conquest of the whole country, this marked the beginning of more than 700 years of English rule in Ireland.

CHINON CASTLE
The castle of Chinon was begun in the late 10th century and is situated on a spur overlooking the River Vienne near Tours in France. A key administrative centre of the Angevin Empire, the castle was where Henry confined his wife for long periods during their protracted quarrelling.

RICHARD I

1189–1199

RICHARD I
- *Born* Beaumont Palace, Oxford, 8 Sept 1157, third son of Henry II and Eleanor of Aquitaine.
- *Acceded* 2 Sept 1189.
- *Crowned* Westminster Abbey, 2 Sept 1189.
- *Married* Berengaria of Navarre, Chapel of St George, Limassol, Cyprus, 12 May 1191.
- *Died* Chalus, France, 6 April 1199.

THE COAT OF ARMS OF RICHARD I

RICHARD I CAPTURED the imagination of his time and has been one of history's heroes ever since. His crusading zeal, his chivalry, even the manner of his dying – when he pardoned the archer who fired the fatal arrow – all have left behind a seemingly imperishable reputation as the typical "parfit gentil knight" of Chaucer. But the England whose throne he inherited saw him for only seven months of a 10-year reign, and Englishmen paid dearly to support a campaign more than 2,000 miles away in a land that they knew nothing about, paid up again for a huge ransom for his return from captivity in Germany, only to see him disappear to fight in France, where he was mortally wounded.

CHATEAU-GAILLARD
Built between 1196-8 by Richard, Château-Gaillard in France was an enormous and sophisticated concentric castle far in advance of its time. Protected by a complex system of ditches, banks, gates and additional walls, the castle (below) seemed virtually impregnable.

JERUSALEM
This contemporary illustration (above) depicts Christian forces of the Third Crusade laying siege to the holy city of Jerusalem.

A FRENCH FORTRESS

One of the greatest castles that Richard built during his campaigns in France was Château-Gaillard. Standing high on a rocky escarpment overlooking the Seine, the castle dominated the frontier between Normandy and the territories of Philip of France. Richard claimed he could hold it "even if the walls were made of butter", but in 1204, Philip's men gained access via the drainage system.

THE CRUSADES

Richard reigned for 10 years, but spent only seven months in England. Half of that was in 1189, the year of his accession, when he raised money to finance the Third Crusade, which lasted until 1192. Richard accumulated the money by selling state and Church offices and lands, and charters of self-government to the towns. He even offered to sell London if a buyer could be found. Once in the Holy Land, Richard captured Acre and defeated Saladin in 1191. He then secured a treaty to guarantee Christians safe pilgrimage to Jerusalem.

THE LIONHEART

Richard was tall, long-legged, athletic and powerful. Well educated, he was also musical, wrote verses and could speak and make jokes in Latin. But like his father he spoke little English. Brilliant at the martial arts, he showed tremendous personal courage in battle, was justifiably known as the Lionheart (*Coeur de Lion*) and often did penance for the cruelty and vengeance that sometimes marked his military campaigns.

RICHARD I
An effigy of Richard I of England (left) marks his tombstone at Fontevrault Abbey in France.

THE KING'S HEIR

At the end of his reign, Richard designated as his heir his youngest brother John, rather than the boy prince Arthur, who was the son of his next brother, Geoffrey. John cared deeply for England, and would do what was needed for a country Richard knew he had neglected in his reign.

RICHARD COEUR DE LION
A suitably heroic and war-like Richard is represented in this equestrian statue (above) erected to his memory outside the Houses of Parliament.

EVENTS OF THE REIGN 1189 – 1199

◆ **1189** Richard I becomes King of England upon the death of his father, Henry II.
◆ **1189** William Longchamp is appointed Chancellor of England and governs the country during Richard's absence abroad.
◆ **1189** Richard sets out with Philip of France on the Third Crusade to the Holy Land.
◆ **1191** William Longchamp falls from power and Richard's brother, John, takes over the government.
◆ **1191** Richard captures the city of Acre, in Palestine, and defeats Saladin at Arsouf, near Jaffa.
◆ **1192** Richard reaches an agreement with Saladin, whereby Christians can make pilgrimages to Jerusalem without fear of assault.
◆ **1192** On his way back to England from Palestine Richard is captured by the Duke of Austria, who hands him over to Henry VI, Emperor of Germany. Henry demands a ransom of 100,000 marks from England for Richard's release from prison.
◆ **1194** The ransom is raised in England and paid to Henry.
◆ **1194** Richard is released from captivity. He returns home for a brief period, before leaving to fight in France, never to return.
◆ **1199** Richard is mortally wounded at Chalus, in France.

JOHN

1199–1216

THE COAT OF ARMS OF JOHN

THE YOUNGEST SON OF HENRY II, John inherited from his brother Richard the throne of England, as well as the Plantagenet dominions in France, which he lost to the French by 1204. John's failure to recapture these territories, his dispute with Rome over the Pope's choice of a new Archbishop of Canterbury, and a high level of taxation had the English nobility up in arms against him. In 1215 they forced the King to agree to the Magna Carta, guaranteeing their rights in relation to those of the crown. This led to civil war, which only ended with John's death in 1216. Yet despite these disasters, it is now known that John was a much better king than history has usually portrayed him.

♛ JOHN

◆ **Born** Beaumont Palace, Oxford, 24 Dec 1166, fourth son of Henry II and Eleanor.
◆ **Married** Isabella of Gloucester, 29 Aug 1189, no children; Isabella of Angoulême, 24 Aug 1200, 5 children.
◆ **Acceded** 27 May 1199.
◆ **Crowned** Westminster Abbey, 27 May 1199.
◆ **Died** Newark Castle, Lincolnshire, 18 Oct 1216, aged 49.

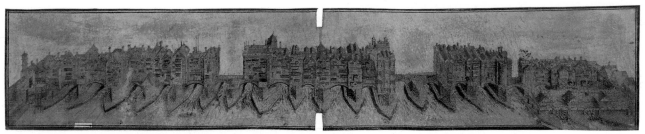

OLD LONDON BRIDGE
Completed during the reign of John, London Bridge (above) remained standing until its demolition 600 years later.

BRIDGE OVER THE THAMES
There has been a bridge across the Thames on or around the site of the present London Bridge since Roman times. The construction of the first stone bridge was begun by Henry II in the 1170s, but progress was slow until the French engineer, Isambert of Saintes, was employed by John to complete the project. The bridge, which included a drawbridge, a double row of houses and some 140 shops, all resting on 19 arches, was finally opened in 1206. It remained the only stone bridge across the Thames in London until 1750.

LOVE OF LEISURE
Despite a reputation for hard work, John always found time for leisure. Chief among his recreations was hunting, but he also enjoyed his comforts and is said to have particularly relished taking a bath, an extremely uncommon practice at that time.

HUNTING
John's favourite pastime was hunting, as shown in this 14th-century illustration.

JOHN
King John in a castle, as depicted (right) in this contemporary manuscript illustration.

JOHN

Despite his problems with France and the English barons, recent historical research suggests that John was an energetic administrator, a good general, an astute diplomat, and a hard-working and keenly intelligent ruler with a strong sense of justice. In that respect he was one of the ablest of the Plantagenet monarchs. However, a chronicler writing only a decade after his death said that while he was a great prince, he was hardly a happy one.

EVENTS OF THE REIGN
1199 – 1216

◆ **1199** John accedes to the throne on the death of Richard.
◆ **1204** England loses almost all its possessions in France.
◆ **1206** John refuses to accept Stephen Langton as Archbishop of Canterbury.
◆ **1208** Pope Innocent III issues an Interdict against England, banning all church services except baptisms and funerals.
◆ **1209** Pope Innocent III excommunicates John for his confiscation of ecclesiastical property.
◆ **1212** Innocent III declares that John is no longer the rightful king of England.
◆ **1213** John submits to the Pope's demands.
◆ **1214** Philip Augustus of France defeats the English army at the Battle of Bouvines.
◆ **1214** The English barons gather at Bury St Edmunds to discuss the demands they wish to make on the King.
◆ **1215** John meets the barons at Runnymede, near Windsor, and finally agrees to their demands and seals Magna Carta.

ROCHESTER CASTLE
Throughout his reign John spent huge sums of money on the construction and maintenance of castles. He was also experienced in conducting siegeworks, capturing Rochester Castle (above) in 1216 by undermining the east corner of the tower.

◆ **1215** The Pope decrees that John need not adhere to Magna Carta and civil war breaks out.
◆ **1216** The barons seek French aid in their fight against John; Prince Louis of France captures the Tower of London.
◆ **1216** John loses his war chest of cash and jewels in the Wash.
◆ **1216** John dies at Newark and is buried in Worcester Cathedral.

MAGNA CARTA

1215

ON 15 JUNE 1215 KING JOHN sealed the draft of Magna Carta (the Great Charter). The document was drawn up by senior representatives of the English nobility and clergy in an attempt to curtail what they considered to be an abuse of royal power in matters of taxation, justice, religion and foreign policy. The Charter laid down the respective rights and responsibilities of citizens and the church in relation to the power of the crown. Over the next two centuries regular references were made by those questioning the royal prerogative, but as feudalism died out, much of the Charter's relevance evaporated. Under the Tudors it was forgotten. Today, however, it is seen as a milestone in English constitutional history.

THE BARONS MEET
Prior to the negotiations at Runnymede, the barons drafted their final demands of the King in the abbey of Bury St Edmunds in Suffolk, the ruins of which are shown on the right.

THE BARONS' QUARREL

The barons' sense of grievance towards John had been brewing since the start of his reign. Heavy taxation, the loss of English territories in France, culminating in a disastrous defeat at Bouvines in 1214, and a dispute with Rome over the Pope's choice of Archbishop of Canterbury which resulted in a papal Interdict banning many church services in England, were all attributed to the abuse of royal power.

By 1215 the barons had had enough and, led by Stephen Langton, Archbishop of Canterbury, drew up a list of demands in Bury St Edmunds, threatening civil war if John did not agree to them. John asked for time to consider the demands and a truce was arranged for a year to Easter 1216.

THE RUNNYMEDE MEMORIAL
Paid for by the American Bar Association and dedicated in 1957, the Magna Carta Memorial commemorates the sealing of the Great Charter in 1215. It stands next to the Thames at Runnymede.

SEALING THE CHARTER

Before the Charter was sealed, there was much haggling between the King, who was in residence at Windsor, and the barons, who had moved to nearby Staines. Finally, after protracted negotiations, John agreed to meet the barons midway between the two towns in a field at Runnymede on 15 June 1215. After a short ceremony the barons' demands were presented for agreement and the royal seal was duly affixed to the Charter. Over the next four days, copies were made and despatched around the kingdom, and those barons who had earlier renounced their allegiance now renewed their homage to the king.

WHAT THE CHARTER SAID

In its original draft, Magna Carta contained 63 clauses defining the rights and responsibilities of the crown and its subjects. Notably, it limited the King's powers to tax the barons, guaranteed the rights of the church and the city corporations, and held that no free man should be arrested or imprisoned except by the lawful judgement of his equals or by the laws of the land. The "Great" in its title refers to the unusual scope of the charter, and not its length.

FOUR VERSIONS
The Charter of 1215 is not the version with which we are familiar today. It was reissued in 1216 with some of the clauses removed, and reissued again in 1217 with more revisions. The final version, and the one that has been cited ever since, was agreed by Henry III in 1225 (right).

HENRY III

1216–1272

THE COAT OF ARMS OF HENRY III

HENRY III WAS ONLY NINE at his accession in 1216, and during his minority England was ruled wisely by two Regents. In 1227 Henry took over the government himself, and years of misrule followed. After he married Eleanor of Provence in 1236, many foreigners obtained leading positions in the government. This provoked an angry response from the English barons, led by Simon de Montfort, and civil war eventually broke out. In 1265 de Montfort summoned the first English parliament but the barons soon quarrelled among themselves. Henry's son, Prince Edward, defeated de Montfort and the King reassumed control of the government until his death in 1272.

👑 HENRY III

- **Born** Winchester, 1 Oct 1207, first son of John and Isabella.
- **Acceded** 28 Oct 1216.
- **Crowned** Gloucester Cathedral, 28 Oct 1216; Westminster Abbey, 17 May 1220.
- **Married** Eleanor of Provence, 14 Jan 1236, 9 children.
- **Died** Westminster, 16 Nov 1272.

THE REGENCY

Before his death, John willed that his nine-year-old son Henry should have as his Regent William the Marshal, Earl of Pembroke. A wise counsellor, William managed the government of England with Hubert de Burgh until his death in 1219, leaving de Burgh as sole Regent. Henry later dismissed de Burgh, despite years of loyal service, on a trumped-up charge of treason, and decided to rule with the help of French advisers.

WILLIAM THE MARSHAL
Regent for Henry III for the first three years of his reign, William the Marshal was renowned as a fearless warrior and knight (above).

THE CORONATION

Prince Henry was in Gloucester when his father, John, died during the war with his barons in 1216. The rebel barons offered the throne to Louis, Dauphin of France, but Henry was crowned at Gloucester Cathedral within 10 days of his father's death. The speed with which the coronation took place threw the barons into disarray, and after a series of defeats at the hands of the King's forces their revolt collapsed.

MAKESHIFT CEREMONY
This contemporary illustration shows Henry being crowned with his mother's gold chaplet in a makeshift ceremony at Gloucester Cathedral in October 1216. He was crowned again formally in Westminster Abbey in May 1220.

THE STATE OF ENGLAND

Despite a long period of misrule and extravagance, Henry III presided over an age of great advance in ecclesiastical and educational building, scholarship and artistic achievement. The first three colleges were established at the University of Oxford, which had been founded in the late 12th century, while at Cambridge University, founded in 1209 during the reign of John, foreign students were encouraged to make their homes there. In the monasteries, the skills of writing and illustrating chronicles were developed, and delicate drawings and graceful lettering came into fashion. The leader of this new style was the scholar-monk, Matthew Paris, who was an illuminator and a goldsmith as well as the leading historian of his time.

THE UNKINGLY KING

Henry III had few of the personal qualities required to command respect or guarantee the smooth functioning of the apparatus of state. Unmartial, untrustworthy, childishly fickle and prone to petulance, he alienated enemies and advisers alike. However, in some respects he redeemed himself as a ruler by patronizing the arts, and inspiring the improvements to Westminster Abbey and the construction of Salisbury Cathedral.

HENRY III

HENRY'S REALM

The map of England above comes from the Chronica Majora, *a history of the world from the beginning of time written by Matthew Paris.*

A PEACEFUL END

Despite all the difficulties he faced during his reign, notably from the English barons, Henry died in 1272 leaving behind a kingdom that was prosperous, united and prepared to accept the rule of his son, Edward I. Henry's effigy on his tomb in Westminster Abbey is shown above.

EARLY PARLIAMENTS

1265

THE IDEA OF PARLIAMENT did not emerge as a result of a single, dramatic change in England's system of government but evolved over centuries. Parliament's roots lie in three royal councils, the earliest of which was the Anglo-Saxon Witenagemot, or Witan. The council comprised landowners, bishops, abbots and royal officials. A similar Norman body, known as the Great Council (*Magnum Concilium*), gave rise to the *Curia Regis*, or King's Court, which acted as an advisory body to the king, who could summon or dismiss it at will. Gradually, official records began to refer to "Parliament" rather than "council", but it was some time before Parliament came to mean those actively involved in government. A major development took place in 1265 when Simon de Montfort summoned representatives from the boroughs as well as lords, clergy and knights. Before a century had passed, parliament had the right to make laws and levy taxation, and the knights and borough representatives had begun to sit as a separate body, the Commons.

DE MONTFORT
An Anglo-French lord, Simon de Montfort married Henry III's sister Eleanor and carried out important foreign assignments on the King's behalf until he fell out of royal favour. De Montfort later became the leader of barons bent on reforming England's government. Simon de Montfort's seal is shown below.

MEDIEVAL PARLIAMENT
This 16th-century illustration (left) shows Edward I presiding over a parliamentary session, probably in 1278. The justices and law officers in the centre sit on woolsacks and are surrounded by lords (right) and bishops and abbots (left). Two clerks seated on one of the woolsacks note the proceedings.

SIMON DE MONTFORT

Simon de Montfort was determined to open up government to a wider range of consultation. In 1254 he declared war on Henry III and captured the King at Lewes. In January 1265, with the King still his prisoner, de Montfort summoned a parliament to include not only lords, bishops and abbots, but also four knights from each shire and two burgesses (citizens) from the main cities and towns. This was the first time that all classes, with the exception of villeins (serfs), were represented in Parliament.

PARLIAMENT BUILDINGS

Simon de Montfort's first Parliament of 1265 met in London, most probably in the royal Palace of Westminster. In the 14th century the House of Lords and House of Commons began to meet separately, the Lords in the Palace's White Chamber, situated between Westminster Hall and the Thames, and the Commons, after an initial meeting in the White Chamber in 1341, in Westminster Abbey's Chapter House or the Refectory. From 1548 until 1834, the House of Commons convened in the Palace's Chapel of St Stephen.

In 1834 fire destroyed Westminster Palace, sparing only Westminster Hall. The present Houses of Parliament were built by Sir Charles Barry and Augustus Pugin in the middle of the 19th century to house both Commons and Lords. The Commons' Debating Chamber was gutted by fire following an air raid in 1941 and was reconstructed by Giles Gilbert Scott.

HOUSES OF PARLIAMENT
Situated beside the River Thames, the present Houses of Parliament were built between 1840 and 1860 and incorporate part of the medieval Palace of Westminster.

STATE OPENING OF PARLIAMENT
The Speaker leads the members of the House of Commons (below) to the House of Lords, where the Queen outlines the government's legislative proposals for the forthcoming year. The state opening is one of the few occasions when both Houses of Parliament meet with the sovereign.

PARLIAMENT TODAY

The British Parliament at Westminster comprises the sovereign, the House of Lords and the House of Commons, which is a representative body made up from 650 members elected from all sections of the community in English, Welsh, Scottish and Northern Irish constituencies. The principal functions of Parliament are to pass laws to regulate the life of the community, to agree taxation to provide the resources for carrying on the business of government, and to scrutinize the policies and the administration of the government, especially its spending proposals.

EDWARD I

1272–1307

THE COAT OF ARMS OF EDWARD I

A RENOWNED WARRIOR, Edward I is best remembered for his attempt to unite the kingdoms of England and Scotland under his personal rule, earning the nickname "Hammer of the Scots". He successfully conquered Wales, incorporating the Principality into England in 1284, and made his own son Prince of Wales in 1301. As a legal reformer, he reorganized the law courts, clarified much of the law and dismissed corrupt judges. In summoning a partly elected Parliament in 1295 – the so-called Model Parliament – Edward attempted to ensure that "what touches all should be approved by all", an early attempt at representative democracy.

♛ EDWARD I

- *Born* Westminster, 17/18 June 1239, son of Henry III and Eleanor of Provence.
- *Married* Eleanor of Castile, Burgos, Spain, Oct 1254, 16 children; Margaret of France, Canterbury, 8/10 Sept 1299, 3 children.
- *Acceded* 20 Nov 1272.
- *Crowned* Westminster Abbey, 19 Aug 1274.
- *Died* Burgh-on-Sands, Cumbria, 7 July 1307, aged 68.

REFORMING THE SYSTEM

Between 1275 and 1290, Edward instituted a series of reforms aimed at remedying long-standing grievances. He checked who owned what lands by means of writs of *Quo Warranto* in 1278; dealt with the prevalence of highway robbery and violence in the Statute of Winchester of 1285 by appointing the first Justices of the Peace; and gave local residents the responsibility of policing their own communities. And in 1295 he summoned a Parliament that, because of its composition of lords, clergy, knights and elected burgesses, came to be known as the Model Parliament.

IN MEMORIAM
Eleanor's body was brought from Nottinghamshire to London for burial in Westminster Abbey (her effigy is shown above). At each of the 12 places the cortège stopped, Edward erected a memorial (left).

ELEANOR OF CASTILE
Edward's first wife Eleanor was a dark-haired, beautiful woman. She accompanied Edward on Crusade in 1270-73, giving birth to at least two of their 16 children while abroad. When she died in 1290, aged 54, Edward was heartbroken.

ON CRUSADE

In 1267 the Eighth Crusade was launched by Louis IX of France to expel the infidel Muslims from Palestine. Edward, who was Louis's nephew, agreed to join the Crusade and set out from Dover in 1270. Louis died of plague soon after and his successor was not interested in continuing the Crusade. Edward decided to carry on and eventually arrived at Acre in 1271. There, a year was wasted by squabbles between the various Christian armies and Edward left Palestine in 1272, returning to England in 1274.

THE KING RETURNS
Edward was still heir to the throne when he went on Crusade in 1270. He returned to England in 1274 a king in his own right, for Henry III had died in 1272. The contemporary manuscript illustration above shows Edward entering London as its new king.

"LONGSHANKS"

At two metres (six feet) tall, Edward was called "Longshanks" because he stood head and shoulders above his fellow Englishmen. He had black hair, which in later life turned snowy white, and was regarded as handsome, despite a drooping eyelid. Edward was once considered the greatest of our medieval kings, although his reputation has recently undergone a reappraisal and he has emerged a little less unblemished. He could be a bully, was ambitious and devious, often capricious – he sacked a number of top officials for still undiscovered reasons – and could be ruthlessly cruel. Like so many of the Plantagenets, he had a violent temper: he once clouted a page at a royal wedding so hard that he agreed to pay him damages. Yet allowing for contemporary exaggeration, his reputation for chivalry and fearlessness remains unscathed, and he was a brave fighter and an able administrator.

EDWARD
In 1274 Edward was crowned in Westminster Abbey, as shown in this contemporary illustration.

EVENTS OF THE REIGN
1272 – 1307

◆ 1272 On his way home from Crusade, Edward hears that, on the death of his father Henry III, he has become King.

◆ 1274 Edward arrives back in England and is crowned in Westminster Abbey.

◆ 1277 Edward invades North Wales to compel Prince Llywelyn to pay homage to him.

◆ 1278 Writs of *Quo Warranto* issued to end the quarrels over land ownership.

◆ 1279 Statute of Mortmain stops landowners giving land to the Church to avoid feudal dues.

◆ 1282 Edward invades North Wales again and defeats Llywelyn, who is killed later in the year.

◆ 1284 Welsh independence ended by Statute of Rhuddlan.

◆ 1285 Statute of Winchester controls highway robbery and violence, and institutes the first Justices of the Peace.

◆ 1290 Edward expels all Jews from England.

◆ 1290 Margaret, Maid of Norway, heir to the Scottish throne, dies on way home to claim her inheritance.

◆ 1290 Death of Eleanor of Castile at the age of 54.

◆ 1292 Edward chooses John Balliol to be King of Scotland.

◆ 1295 Model Parliament is summoned with lords, clergy and representatives from each shire, city and borough.

◆ 1295 Balliol summoned to join Edward on a campaign in France; he refuses and forms the Auld Alliance with France.

◆ 1296 Edward invades Scotland and defeats and deposes Balliol. He then takes over the throne of Scotland and removes the Stone of Scone to Westminster.

◆ 1297 Scots rise against English rule and under William Wallace defeat Edward at the Battle of Stirling Bridge.

◆ 1298 Edward invades Scotland again and defeats William Wallace at the Battle of Falkirk.

◆ 1299 Edward marries Margaret of France.

◆ 1301 Edward creates his son Prince of Wales.

◆ 1305 Wallace is betrayed, tried and executed in London.

◆ 1306 Robert Bruce takes over leadership of Scottish resistance to English rule and is crowned King of Scotland at Scone.

◆ 1307 Edward invades Scotland again, but dies on his way north.

THE CONQUEST OF WALES

1277–1284

WALES HAS A HISTORY much older than that of England. Driven out of England by the Anglo-Saxons in the fifth and sixth centuries, the Celts formed a number of small princedoms in Wales that were united in the early 13th century. After Edward I came to the English throne, he summoned the Welsh prince, Llywelyn Yr Ail, to pay him homage. Llywelyn refused, whereupon Edward invaded Wales in 1277 and exacted the homage. In 1282 Edward invaded again and by 1284 Wales was finally incorporated into England.

WELSH INDEPENDENCE

In the first decades of the 13th century Wales enjoyed a period of near total unification under Llywelyn Fawr (the Great). The Welsh began to build stone castles as bases for their forces to resist continual raiding and more serious invasions by Norman-English lords, who erected numerous castles on the borders. Some of these Welsh-built castles, notably Castell-y-Bere in North Wales, were captured by Edward I during his invasion of Wales and used to consolidate his power over the rebellious principality.

THE COMING OF CHRISTIANITY

Christianity came to Wales in the early fourth century and Welsh churches remained bastions of the faith in the years following the departure of the Romans in the fifth century. In the sixth century St David founded monasteries throughout the country, and after the Norman invasion of England in the 11th century, when some parts of east and south Wales were occupied by Norman marcher lords, there was a spate of ecclesiastical building.

STRATA FLORIDA
Regarded as the Westminster Abbey of Wales, the abbey of Strata Florida in central Wales (left) was founded in 1164 by Rhys ap Gruffydd, Prince of South Wales. Its reputation as a centre of Welsh nationalism led Edward I to burn it down in 1294.

DOLBADARN
The castle of Dolbadarn in North Wales (above) was one of several castles built during the reign of Llywelyn Fawr in the early 13th century.

IN MEMORIAM
This slate monument stands outside Builth, in mid-Wales, in memory of Llywelyn Yr Ail, the last independent Prince of Wales, who was ambushed and killed on a bridge near the town on 11 December 1282.

LLYWELYN

Llywelyn Yr Ail (the Last) was Prince of independent Wales from 1246-82. In 1274 he refused to pay homage to Edward I, who invaded Wales in 1277 to enforce his homage. Llywelyn was defeated, as he was in 1282 when he declared war again.

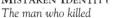

MISTAKEN IDENTITY
The man who killed Llywelyn, Adam Frankton (right), did not realize that the man he had killed was the last independent Prince of Wales.

THE ENGLISH OCCUPATION

After Edward's successful invasion of Wales, the English king sought to maintain his control over Wales, particularly North Wales which had given him the most trouble, by constructing 10 substantial new castles. These were to be administrative centres as well as army quarters and were strategically sited to command the coast, river crossings or key roads. Among these great buildings, which in some cases took nearly 40 years to complete, were Beaumaris, Caernarfon, Conwy, Fflint, Harlech and Rhuddlan.

HARLECH
Completed in 1290, Harlech Castle is sited on a crag commanding views over the Lleyn peninsula and Snowdonia. In 1404 it was captured by Owain Glyndwr and was used as a base for his lengthy rebellion against Henry IV.

THE PRINCE OF WALES

1301

IN 1284 EDWARD I was in Wales following his successful conquest of the country. His wife, Eleanor, gave birth to a son and heir, Edward, while they were staying at some hastily built lodgings at Caernarfon. There has long been a tradition, unsupported by any evidence, that Edward held up his baby son at a gathering of Welsh nobles and said: "Here is your new Prince of Wales." In reality it was not until Edward was 17, in 1301, that he was created Prince of Wales. Ever since, it has been customary for the monarch to create his or her eldest son Prince of Wales.

THE INVESTITURE
Although Caernarfon Castle was the birthplace of the first Prince of Wales, the castle has only been associated with two investitures, both in this century. In 1911 George V invested his eldest son Edward (later Edward VIII) in a ceremony devised by David Lloyd George, the Chancellor of the Exchequer and Caernarfon's Member of Parliament. It was the first time that a monarch had visited the castle since 1400. The second ceremony took place in 1969, when Elizabeth II invested her son Charles as the new Prince of Wales.

THE CHARTER OF APPOINTMENT
When James I's eldest son Henry Frederick was created Prince of Wales in 1610, he was given a Charter of Appointment (below). In the left-hand corner, Henry can be seen kneeling before his father, who is handing the charter to him.

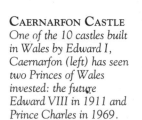

CAERNARFON CASTLE
One of the 10 castles built in Wales by Edward I, Caernarfon (left) has seen two Princes of Wales invested: the future Edward VIII in 1911 and Prince Charles in 1969.

THE CHARTERED PRINCE
Until 1911 the title of Prince of Wales was bestowed in Parliament by the monarch, who issued a Charter of Appointment to the new Prince. There was a ceremony of investiture, but it was held in London, not Wales, and followed the order of events set out in the charter which created the Black Prince, Edward III's son, Prince of Wales in 1343. This charter listed the insignia as "a coronet around his head ... with a gold ring in his finger ... and with a silver rod."

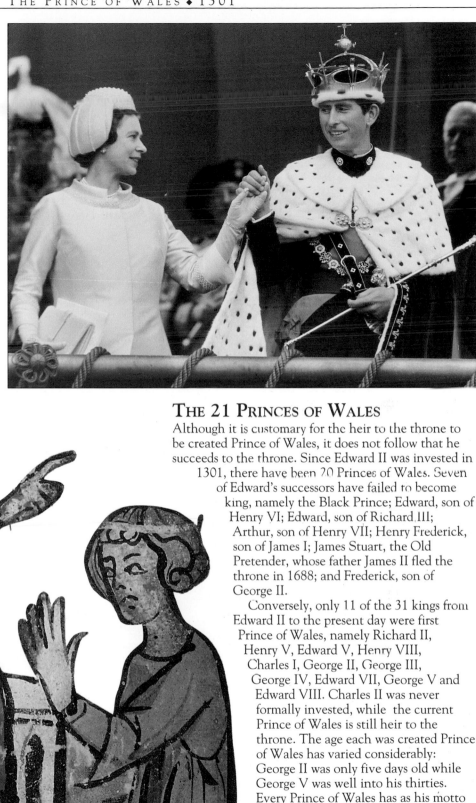

THE CURRENT PRINCE
Prince Charles was invested by Elizabeth II on 1 July 1969 (right). The ceremony was the first to be televised and was broadcast worldwide.

THE 21 PRINCES OF WALES

Although it is customary for the heir to the throne to be created Prince of Wales, it does not follow that he succeeds to the throne. Since Edward II was invested in 1301, there have been 20 Princes of Wales. Seven of Edward's successors have failed to become king, namely the Black Prince; Edward, son of Henry VI; Edward, son of Richard III; Arthur, son of Henry VII; Henry Frederick, son of James I; James Stuart, the Old Pretender, whose father James II fled the throne in 1688; and Frederick, son of George II.

Conversely, only 11 of the 31 kings from Edward II to the present day were first Prince of Wales, namely Richard II, Henry V, Edward V, Henry VIII, Charles I, George II, George III, George IV, Edward VII, George V and Edward VIII. Charles II was never formally invested, while the current Prince of Wales is still heir to the throne. The age each was created Prince of Wales has varied considerably: George II was only five days old while George V was well into his thirties. Every Prince of Wales has as his motto the words adopted by the Black Prince from the King of Bohemia at the Battle of Crécy: *Ich Dien*, "I serve".

THE FIRST PRINCE
This illustration from a contemporary manuscript records the creation of the first Prince of Wales in 1301. Prince Edward kneels before his father, Edward I, to receive the title.

EDWARD II

1307–1327

THE COAT OF ARMS
OF EDWARD II

ONE OF THE SADDER PERSONALITIES among English monarchs, it is hard not to feel sorry for Edward II, not only for the terrible manner of his death but also for the difficulties that beset him during his 20-year reign. The only surviving son of Edward I and his first wife Eleanor, Edward was born into a family of girls. He grew up dominated by female company as his father was frequently absent, yet he had a poor relationship with his mother. As a result, Edward was very reliant on his friends and was fiercely loyal to them, sticking to Piers Gaveston and then the Despensers long after it was clear to everyone else that they were bad for him and for the country. He was eventually deposed and murdered on his wife's orders in 1327.

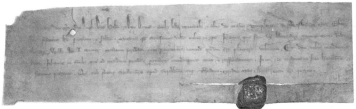

THE PRIVY SEAL OF
EDWARD II

EDWARD II

- ◆ **Born** Caernarfon Castle, 25 April 1284, fourth son of Edward I and Eleanor of Castile.
- ◆ **Acceded** 8 July 1307.
- ◆ **Married** Isabella of France, Boulogne, France, 25/28 Jan 1308, 4 children.
- ◆ **Crowned** Westminster Abbey, 24/25 April 1308.
- ◆ **Deposed** 25 Jan 1327.
- ◆ **Murdered** Berkeley Castle, 21 Sept 1327, aged 43.

REBELLION

Edward's reign was plagued by rebellion, largely because of his poor choice of advisers and the arrogant and inefficient way in which they governed in his name. Twice his nobles rebelled against him, murdering Piers Gaveston in 1312 and Sir Hugh Despenser and his son in 1326.

A PROSPEROUS REIGN

Although Edward had little interest in administration, his reign has gone down in history as one of increasing prosperity, for there was less taxation than under either his father or his son.

DEPOSING THE KING
In 1326 Isabella and her lover Roger Mortimer, who had both been living in France, landed in Suffolk (left) and marched against the King. Edward was deposed in favour of his 14-year-old son in 1327. For the next three years, Isabella and Roger ruled in the name of the young Edward III, but in 1330 Edward seized power. Mortimer was tried and executed and Isabella forced to retire from public life.

DEATH OF A FAVOURITE
Isabella and her lover Roger Mortimer can be seen in the foreground in this contemporary illustration, while Edward's favourite, Sir Hugh Despenser, is brutally murdered in the background.

ISABELLA OF FRANCE

Edward married Isabella in 1308 and the couple had four children. It is difficult to assess the nature of their marriage because Edward was almost certainly homosexual and his relationship with Gaveston was of that kind. Isabella thus had to accept considerable humiliation, which she endured until she fell in love with Roger Mortimer, an opponent of the King.

THE LOYAL FRIEND

Blessed with good health, good looks and a good brain, Edward was physically strong and enjoyed a variety of sporting interests. He was amiable, fond of good conversation, artistic and had a strong sense of humour. But many of his agreeable traits usually militated against him: although he was generous, he was unable to be severe when the occasion demanded, and his loyalty to his friends, one of his greatest virtues, led to his downfall, for he was a poor judge of character.

EDWARD II
After his death in 1327, Edward was buried in Gloucester Cathedral. His imposing tomb effigy is shown on the left.

EVENTS OF THE REIGN
1307 – 1327

◆ **1307** Edward II accedes to the throne on the death of his father Edward I.
◆ **1308** Edward's favourite, the Gascon noble Piers Gaveston, is exiled for misgovernment.
◆ **1309** Gaveston returns from exile in France.
◆ **1310** Parliament sets up a committee of Lords Ordainers to control the King and improve administration. The King's cousin, Thomas, Earl of Lancaster, takes control.
◆ **1312** Gaveston is kidnapped by the King's opponents and is beheaded.
◆ **1314** Edward and the English army are routed at the Battle of Bannockburn by Robert Bruce. Scottish independence is assured.
◆ **1320** Edward takes two new favourites, Sir Hugh Despenser and his son Hugh.

EDWARD'S DEATH

The circumstances of Edward's death were horrible. After his deposition in January 1327, he was eventually imprisoned in Berkeley Castle in Gloucestershire, from where it was announced on 21 September that he had died. Isabella and Mortimer had ordered that he be put to death but with no external marking on his body to betray the violence. The only way to do this was by disembowelling: *cum vero ignito inter celanda confossus* – with a red hot iron inserted into the rectum – which was a conventional but gruesome death for homosexuals at this time.

BERKELEY CASTLE
Edward languished in Berkeley Castle for six months during 1327. At one point, with the help of friends, he escaped and hid but was recaptured and returned to his cell at Berkeley.

◆ **1322** Barons' rebellion, led by Thomas, Earl of Lancaster, is crushed at the Battle of Boroughbridge in Yorkshire.
◆ **1326** Edward's wife Isabella abandons him and with her lover Roger seizes power and deposes Edward. The Despensers are both put to death.
◆ **1327** Edward is formally deposed by Parliament in favour of his son Edward III, and is murdered in Berkeley Castle.

EDWARD III

1327–1377

THE COAT OF ARMS OF EDWARD III
When Edward claimed the French throne in 1337, he quartered the fleurs-de-lys of France with the lions of England on his shield.

ONLY 14 WHEN HE came to the throne, Edward ruled for 50 years, a reign dominated by the 100 Years' War with France. Edward started the war in 1337 to further his claim to the French throne, playing a major role in the early stages and then handing over to his son Edward, the Black Prince. His principal aim was to unite the nobility into a cohesive class of public servants, motivated by chivalry, enriched by the wealth he enabled them to win, and tied to the crown by marriage to one of his many relatives. In this he succeeded magnificently, his reputation abroad enhanced by sound administration and reforms at home.

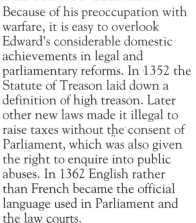

REFORM OF THE LAW

Because of his preoccupation with warfare, it is easy to overlook Edward's considerable domestic achievements in legal and parliamentary reforms. In 1352 the Statute of Treason laid down a definition of high treason. Later other new laws made it illegal to raise taxes without the consent of Parliament, which was also given the right to enquire into public abuses. In 1362 English rather than French became the official language used in Parliament and the law courts.

EDWARD III

- *Born* Windsor Castle, 13 Nov 1312, son of Edward II and Isabella of France.
- *Acceded* 25 Jan 1327.
- *Crowned* Westminster Abbey, 1 Feb 1327.
- *Married* Philippa of Hainault, York, 24 Jan 1328, 13 children.
- *Died* Surrey, 21 June 1377, aged 64.

THE YOUNG KING
Edward was only 14 when he was crowned (above), and for three years power lay with his mother, Isabella of France, and Roger Mortimer.

THE PUBLIC POET

Born about 1340, Geoffrey Chaucer became page to Edward's son Lionel, Duke of Clarence, and was brought into Court. He worked for Edward in a variety of capacities, eventually becoming Comptroller of Customs for London in 1374. Chaucer began to write poetry in the early 1360s, and wrote his most famous work, *The Canterbury Tales*, between 1387-98.

GEOFFREY CHAUCER (*right*)

THE BLACK PRINCE

Edward III's eldest son, also called Edward, was known as the Black Prince because of the colour of his armour. He was born in 1330 and won his spurs at the Battle of Crécy in 1346. The victor of Poitiers in 1356, he became the most feared military commander in Europe, but while fighting in Spain, he caught an infection that slowly debilitated him and he predeceased his father by one year, in 1376.

FATHER AND SON
Edward III and the Black Prince (above) were both able military commanders, winning several battles in the 100 Years' War.

THE HEROIC KING

Tall, handsome, with gold-red hair and penetrating eyes, Edward was a flamboyant, affable and generous man. He excelled in all the knightly arts, loved hunting and falconry, and was astute in choosing advisers whose loyalty he always kept: in his long reign, Edward never had to deal with a rebellion, and was much loved by his people, who thought him immortal. His wife, Philippa of Hainault, was a tallish, comely woman to whom Edward was devoted. She was a wise counsellor, perhaps the wisest he had, and was much respected.

EDWARD AND PHILIPPA *(left)*

THE SHIP OF STATE
In the 1340s Edward III introduced a gold coinage on which he was depicted as commander of the ship of state (above). The ship evoked memories of his great naval victory over the French at Sluys in 1340 during the 100 Years' War, while his shield included the arms of France in recognition of his claim to the French throne.

THE 100 YEARS' WAR

1337–1453

BETWEEN 1337 AND 1453 England and France engaged in a series of battles that have become known as the 100 Years' War. The prolonged but intermittent struggle began with Edward III's claim to the French throne through his French mother Isabella. The claim was strengthened by grievances between the two countries and in 1337 Edward III declared war on France. The war brought considerable wealth to England at the expense of France, but from 1431 the French began to win back the territory lost to the English, and by 1453 had ousted them from all France except for Calais.

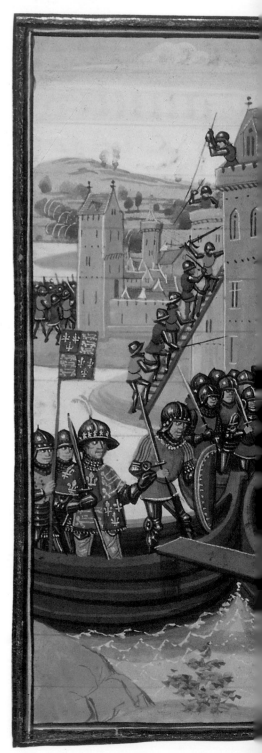

SIEGE OF TOURNAI
After his victory at Sluys, Edward attempted but failed to capture the city of Tournai (below).

THE WAR'S PROGRESS

The 100 Years' War can be divided into three phases. The first lasted from 1337-60 and was marked by Edward III's military successes at Crécy (1346) and Poitiers (1356), culminating in an advantageous treaty at Brétigny in 1360. Between 1360-1415 there was a period of desultory warfare, in which the Brétigny gains were largely lost, while the final phase, which began with Henry V's success at Agincourt in 1415, was reversed by 1453 when the English were finally driven out of France.

BATTLE OF CRECY
On 26 August 1346 the English army scored a great victory over the French at Crécy (above). The French lost over 10,000 men, while English deaths were less than 200.

LOOTING
During the War much of France was ruined as the English armies raided towns (right).

THE EFFECT OF THE WAR

The 100 Years' War swept away the great prosperity France had enjoyed for more than two centuries. Merchants would not risk travelling through the war-stricken countryside and the Champagne Fairs, which were renowned for their oriental luxuries, English wool and Flemish cloth, collapsed. Local industry suffered as well: in Provins, there had been 3,000 looms at work in 1340; by 1399 there were only 32.

To make matters worse, civil war broke out in France in the 1380s between two royal factions and lasted well into the next century. As early as 1360 the Italian poet Petrarch wrote that France was " a heap of ruins". England, on the other hand, enjoyed immense prosperity, although the country was weakened by the impact of the Black Death in 1348-50.

METHODS OF WARFARE

Castles became a prime target for attack during the 100 Years' War because of their strategic location. Besieging a castle usually involved two tactics: some of the attacking army scaled the walls with the use of ladders, while the remainder directed missiles at the castle from below. A bow-like firing device known as a ballista and stone-hurling machines called mangonels and trebuchets were used to catapult objects such as stone blocks, stone and iron balls and iron bolts. Most other encounters took place in the open field, where battles were usually won as a result of superior archery skills.

WINDSOR CASTLE
THE ROYAL FAMILY'S OLDEST RESIDENCE

PRIOR TO THE 14TH CENTURY, the Royal Palace of Windsor was a relatively simple structure. Erected soon after the Norman Conquest of England in 1066, one of the first royal associations with the castle was recorded in 1110, when Henry I's court assembled there. Over the years, successive monarchs, particularly Edward III and George IV, have enlarged and rebuilt the castle to the point where its great complex of palatial apartments, chapels, towers, turrets and curtain walls now occupies no less than 12 acres on the banks of the River Thames. Today the castle is one of the principal residences of the royal family and the oldest royal residence in regular use.

EARLIER BUILDINGS

The first castle at Windsor was erected by William the Conqueror after the Battle of Hastings in 1066. A timber and earth structure sited on a natural mound carved out of a chalk cliff by the Thames, it remained as such until the reign of Henry I, who converted the wooden tower and fortifications into stone. The fortifications were strengthened over the next century, so that by the middle of the 13th century, a chronicler could report that there was "no finer castle in the whole of Europe".

THE ROUND TOWER
The large circular tower (below) at the heart of the castle was built during the reign of Henry II in the late 12th century and is one of the oldest surviving parts of the building.

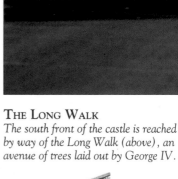

THE LONG WALK
The south front of the castle is reached by way of the Long Walk (above), an avenue of trees laid out by George IV.

DEVELOPMENT OF THE CASTLE

Windsor Castle first became a permanent residence of the royal family during the long reign of Edward III, who began rebuilding the castle after 1346. The works, which cost the then massive sum of £50,000 and took a quarter of a century to complete, were so extensive that a contemporary chronicler reported that "almost all the masons and craftsmen throughout England were brought to that building". Work continued on the castle in a spasmodic fashion until the reign of George IV, whose programme of modernization was the last substantial work to be carried out on the buildings.

THE WATERLOO CHAMBER
Built by George IV to commemorate the Battle of Waterloo in 1815, the Waterloo Chamber (below) is filled with the portraits of contemporary sovereigns, statesmen and generals who had distinguished themselves in the struggle against Napoleon.

THE INTERIOR

Until the reign of Edward III, the interior of the castle had always been somewhat spartan. Edward transformed the living quarters, turning them into a palatial royal home. Subsequent monarchs refurbished the royal apartments in accordance with the dictates and styles of contemporary fashion, notably George IV, whose extravagant reconstruction was designed to "sweep away the last traces of the medieval fortress". By 1830 the transformation of Windsor Castle from a fortified military installation into a comfortable country house was complete.

THE ORDERS OF CHIVALRY

THE REWARDS OF VIRTUE

DURING THE MIDDLE AGES, the word chivalry originally referred to the knightly class, who were called The Chivalry. In time, the word came to be associated with such attributes as courtesy, bravery, honour, and the protection of women, and knights began to form themselves into various secular and religious orders to uphold these virtues. In 1348 Edward III founded a chivalric order designed to embody the ideals of King Arthur's legendary Round Table. Since then, a number of chivalric orders have emerged, admission to which is usually earned by outstanding public services or as a mark of royal favour.

THE GARTER SERVICE
Every year the Queen and the Duke of Edinburgh (left) lead their fellow knights in a procession through Windsor Castle to a service in St George's Chapel to celebrate the Order of the Garter. Each member of the Order wears the Garter Star, bearing the cross of St George and the Order's famous motto (below).

THE GARTER

The Most Noble Order of the Garter was founded in 1348 by Edward III. The idea for the Order is believed to have originated at a dance, when the King picked up a garter lost by the Countess of Salisbury, tied it round his leg, and cried out *"Honi soit qui mal y pense"* (Shame on him who thinks evil of it). Edward restricted the Order to a membership of 24 people, in addition to himself and his eldest son, the Black Prince. In the past, Knights of the Garter have traditionally been members of the British or foreign royal families or peers of the realm, but in recent years commoners have been included, most notably Sir Winston Churchill.

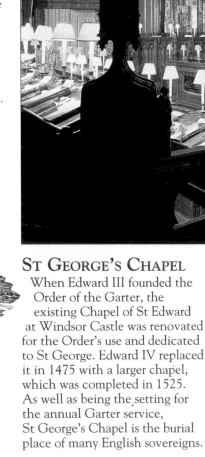

ST GEORGE'S CHAPEL
When Edward III founded the Order of the Garter, the existing Chapel of St Edward at Windsor Castle was renovated for the Order's use and dedicated to St George. Edward IV replaced it in 1475 with a larger chapel, which was completed in 1525. As well as being the setting for the annual Garter service, St George's Chapel is the burial place of many English sovereigns.

ORDERS OF CHIVALRY

Apart from the Garter, there are other orders of chivalry that carry knighthoods with them. Scotland's equivalent to the Garter, the Most Ancient and Most Noble Order of the Thistle, limits its membership to 16 knights, all of whom must be Scottish. Founded in 1687, the Order holds an annual service in the Thistle Chapel of St Giles's Cathedral, Edinburgh, which takes place on St Andrew's Day, 30 November.

Other orders include the Order of the Bath (founded in the 15th century), the Order of St Michael and St George (1818), the Royal Victorian Order (1896) and the Most Excellent Order of the British Empire, the lower ranks of which carry no knighthood. Established by George V in 1917, its membership now numbers more than 100,000. The Order of Merit (OM), founded by Edward VII in 1902, is one of the most prestigious honours of all, even though its 24 members receive no title with their award.

ORDER OF THE BATH
Founded in about 1400 by Henry IV and then reconstituted in 1725, the Order of the Bath is the second oldest chivalric order in England. In 1975, 250 years after George I revived the Order, Prince Charles, the Prince of Wales, was installed as Grand Master. Each year, its members meet for a service in Westminster Abbey, an event depicted in 1749 by the Venetian artist Giovanni Antonio Canaletto (below).

THE KNIGHTS' BANNERS
Each Knight of the Garter has an emblazoned banner bearing his coat of arms that hangs above his personal stall in St George's Chapel (above).

RICHARD II

1377–1399

THE COAT OF ARMS OF RICHARD II
Richard incorporated the arms of Edward the Confessor into the left of his coat of arms as a personal tribute to the saintly king.

WHEN RICHARD came to the throne in 1377, he was the 10-year-old child of a popular father, the Black Prince, who had died the year before. For the first 10 years of his reign, the country was ruled by his advisers and was troubled by internal revolt, notably the Peasants' Revolt of 1381 and a rising by discontented nobles in 1387. In 1389 Richard took over the government himself, informing his uncle, the Duke of Gloucester, that "I am now old enough to manage my own affairs." At first Richard ruled well and presided over a period of prosperity, but in 1394 his beloved wife Anne died and his behaviour changed. By 1399, after some years as a tyrant, he had become a mumbling melancholic, and was forced to abdicate in favour of his cousin Henry Bolingbroke, Duke of Lancaster.

👑 **RICHARD II**

◆ *Born* Bordeaux, France, 6 Jan 1367, son of Edward the Black Prince and Joan of Kent.
◆ *Acceded* 22 June 1377.
◆ *Crowned* Westminster Abbey, 16 July 1377.
◆ *Married* Anne of Bohemia, Westminster, 14/20/22 Jan, 1382; Isabella of France, France, 4 Nov 1396.
◆ *Deposed* 19 Aug 1399.
◆ *Died* 6 Jan or 14 Feb 1400, aged 33.

WILLIAM OF WYKEHAM

Born in Winchester in 1324, William of Wykeham rose to become Bishop of Winchester in 1366 and Chancellor of England in 1367. He fell into disgrace in 1372 but was restored to favour by Richard, serving once again as Lord Chancellor from 1389. In 1382 he founded a school in his home town with the intention that its pupils should come from poor homes. The school later became known as Winchester College.

WINCHESTER COLLEGE
Originally called St Mary's College, the school (left) William of Wykeham founded in Winchester is today one of the major public schools in England.

ABDICATION
In the illustration below, Richard (on the right) can be seen yielding the throne to Henry Bolingbroke (on the left) in 1399.

ROYAL ABSOLUTISM

In 1387 a number of barons, including the King's uncle, Thomas, Duke of Gloucester, and his cousin, Henry Bolingbroke, rebelled against the unpopular government of Richard's advisers. Calling themselves the Lords Appellant, they held a parliament which ordered the killing or banishing of many of the King's friends.

In 1389 Richard took over the reins of government himself but in 1397, without warning and clearly after nursing deep grievances against the Lords Appellant, he rounded on them, murdering Gloucester and banishing Bolingbroke. When Bolingbroke's father, John of Gaunt, died in 1399, Richard then seized his possessions.

His Father's Shadow

Richard always suffered in comparison with his famous father, the Black Prince, for he was too frail and slight to be a gallant knight. This problem racked Richard all his life, yet he did not lack bravery, as he demonstrated during the Peasants' Revolt. A connoisseur of the arts, in particular music, Richard took an interest in jewellery and has been credited with the invention of the handkerchief.

RICHARD II

This portrait of Richard, which is displayed in Westminster Abbey, is the earliest known painted portrait of an English sovereign. It is thought to be the work of André Beauneveu of Valenciennes, a painter at the English court during the 1390s.

EVENTS OF THE REIGN 1377 – 1399

◆ 1377 Richard II succeeds his grandfather, Edward III; the kingdom is ruled at first by the King's uncles, John of Gaunt and Thomas of Gloucester.

◆ 1380 John Wycliffe begins to translate the New Testament from Greek into English.

◆ 1381 Poll Tax leads to the Peasants' Revolt.

◆ 1382 William of Wykeham founds Winchester College.

◆ 1382 Richard marries Anne of Bohemia.

◆ 1387-9 Led by the Duke of Gloucester, the Lords Appellant control the government.

◆ 1389 Richard takes control of the government; William of Wykeham is Lord Chancellor.

◆ 1394 Death of Anne of Bohemia, Richard's first wife.

◆ 1394 Richard leads army to reconquer west of Ireland.

◆ 1396 Richard marries Isabella, daughter of the King of France.

◆ 1397 Richard takes revenge against Lords Appellant and exiles Henry Bolingbroke.

THE EXILE RETURNS

In 1399 Richard set out on his second expedition to Ireland (left), determined to receive the submission of the Gaelic leaders who ruled the west of the country. It was while he was fighting in Leinster that he heard the news that his cousin, Henry Bolingbroke, had returned from exile to claim his birthright. Ironically, among Richard's retinue was Bolingbroke's son Henry, later to become Henry V.

IRELAND

In 1394 and again in 1399, Richard led an army to Ireland, the first English king for almost a century to go there. The whole of Ireland was nominally under English rule but in reality much of the country was independent.

◆ 1398 Geoffrey Chaucer completes *The Canterbury Tales*.

◆ 1399 On the death of John of Gaunt, Bolingbroke becomes Duke of Lancaster, but Richard seizes his possessions. Bolingbroke returns from exile to claim his inheritance and seizes the throne. Richard returns from fighting in Ireland but is deposed and imprisoned in Pontefract Castle, where he dies in 1400.

THE PEASANTS' REVOLT

1381

IN 1381 WIDESPREAD DISCONTENT among the peasantry erupted in large-scale rebellion. Triggered by a government poll tax, a number of uprisings occurred spontaneously in many parts of the country and more than 100,000 men converged on London. Richard II and his government were taken completely by surprise and at first agreed to the peasants' demands. Once the rebels had been appeased and left London, however, the King reneged on his promises to redress their grievances.

DEATH AT SMITHFIELD
The King met the Kentish peasants at Smithfield, near the City of London, on 15 June. Encouraged by Richard's promise the previous day to redress the rebels' grievances, Wat Tyler made further demands. In doing so, he provoked the Mayor of London, who struck him a fatal blow (below). With great presence of mind, the King gained the peasants' confidence by declaring himself their leader (below right).

THE REBEL LEADERS
John Ball (in the centre of the picture above), a priest and follower of the religious reformer John Wycliffe, emerged as a leader of the Essex rebels along with Jack Straw. He led some of them to Kent, where they converged with Wat Tyler (on the left above). Both groups carried the King's flag in the misguided belief he would champion their cause.

SEEDS OF REBELLION

Short of finance, the government of Richard II imposed a poll (or head) tax in 1377 and again in 1379. The poll tax was levied on the person and was not proportionate to individual wealth. It therefore weighed most heavily on the poor. Peasants were already hard-pressed at this time, for their wages were held down by law, and many evaded paying the taxes. The introduction of another, higher poll tax in 1380 and the despatch of officials to collect outstanding arrears led to widespread violence against the collectors and caused the peasants to revolt against the government in 1381.

STATUTE OF LABOURERS

One of the main causes of the Peasants' Revolt was the Statute of Labourers of 1351. This law set labourers' wages at the level existing before the Black Death, which between 1348-9 had reduced England's population by more than a third. The law prevented workers changing jobs in search of higher pay, but it also proved unpopular with landowners, who were unable to offer high wages to attract good workers.

THE PEASANTS' LOT
Hard work was the lot of every peasant in the 14th century, for they had to work on their landlord's fields as part of their feudal obligations as well as on their own land.

THE REVOLT

In June 1381 angry peasants set off from Essex and Kent towards London. By the time they reached the city on 13 June, they numbered more than 100,000. En route, the rebels burned the court rolls on which people were registered for poll tax. Great houses were pillaged and the Archbishop of Canterbury and the King's treasurer were both murdered in the Tower of London.

The 14-year-old King faced Jack Straw and the Essex rebels on 14 June at Mile End, to the east of London. He agreed to each one of the peasants' demands: an end to serfdom, the fixing of a low rent for all land, and an unconditional pardon. The next day, the King met the Kentish rebels and repeated his promises.

THE AFTERMATH

Once the immediate threat posed by the Peasants' Revolt had been lifted, Richard withdrew his promises and revoked his pardon. One by one, uprisings in other parts of the country were suppressed, some with considerable violence: in St Albans, 15 rebels, including John Ball, were hanged. In all, perhaps 200 people are estimated to have died as a result of the Revolt.

Although the Revolt failed in the short term, frightened landowners became reluctant to enforce feudal duties over their peasants and before long serfdom died out. The Revolt also resulted in the abolition of the poll tax, at least until the last years of this century, when it has appeared to be just as unpopular because it, too, is not related to the ability or otherwise to pay.

THE HOUSE OF LANCASTER

1399–1461

EDWARD III *m* Philippa
♔ 1327-1377 | of Hainault

Edward *m* Joan   William   Lionel *m* Elizabeth   John *m* (1) Blanche   Edmund *m* Isabella   and
The   of Kent   Duke   of Gaunt of Lancaster Duke   of   others
Black   of Clarence   of York   Castile
Prince
(*d* 1376)

RICHARD II   Edmund *m* Philippa of   HENRY IV *m* Mary Bohun   Anne *m* Richard
♔ 1377-1399   Mortimer   Clarence   ♔ 1399-1413   Mortimer Earl
(*d* 1400)   Earl of March   of Cambridge

Roger *m* Eleanor   HENRY V *m* Catherine   John   Humphrey   Richard *m* Cecily
Earl of   of Kent   ♔ 1413-1422 of France   Duke   Duke   Duke   Neville
March   of Bedford   of Gloucester   of York

Edmund   Anne   Margaret *m* HENRY VI   EDWARD IV
Earl of   Mortimer   of Anjou   ♔ 1422-1461   ♔ 1461-1470
March   ♔ 1470-1471   ♔ 1471-1483
(*d* 1425)

Anne *m* Edward
Neville Prince
of Wales
(*d* 1471)

CHAPTER FOUR

THE HOUSE OF LANCASTER

1399–1461

A branch of the Plantagenet family, the House of Lancaster was a short dynasty of three kings, all named Henry. The first, Henry IV, was the Duke of Lancaster and the eldest son of John of Gaunt, the fourth son of Edward III. Gaunt had obtained the dukedom through his marriage to Blanche, the daughter of the first duke, who was the great-grandson of Henry III. Henry IV's claim to the throne was a good one, but it was far from watertight: he had deposed his cousin, Richard II, in 1399 but there were others closer to Richard in strict hereditary order. One of these was Richard's heir, Edmund Mortimer, who was descended from Lionel, third son of Edward III. Henry won the support of most barons and his claim was reinforced by Parliament.

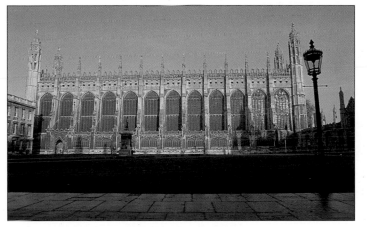

PERPENDICULAR STYLE
During the 15th century, the Perpendicular style of Gothic found its triumphant expression in England. It is epitomized in King's College Chapel (above), begun in the reign of Henry VI, and in several English cathedrals.

A Time of War

The Lancastrian period was marked by almost continual warfare. Baronial revolt and war with Welsh patriots broke out in the first decade, and dynastic war during the last, with prolonged warfare in France occupying most of the remaining four decades when Henry V re-opened the 100 Years' War. He recovered many English possessions but they were all lost during the reign of his son, Henry VI, and by 1453 only the port of Calais remained in English hands.

The Dynastic Squabble

The loss of the French possessions, together with the weak government of Henry VI, led to the outbreak of the Wars of the Roses, a campaign led by the supporters of Richard, Duke of York and Protector of England during the illness of his cousin, Henry VI, to place him on the throne instead of Henry. Richard was descended from Edward III's fifth son, while his mother, Anne Mortimer, was descended from Edward's third son. Richard's claim to the throne was a strong one, and, by strict hereditary succession, better than Henry VI's. Despite these dynastic squabbles, the Lancastrian period was a time of growing prosperity for the country. There was a marked improvement in the social conditions of farmers, labourers, townsfolk and merchants, and it was a great period in English architecture.

HENRY IV

1399–1413

ALTHOUGH HENRY'S SEIZURE of the throne from Richard II in 1399 was in dispute, it was never questioned by Parliament, for many people welcomed the accession of this strong and able ruler. Yet throughout his reign, Henry was troubled by risings against him from some of those who had once been his most loyal supporters, notably the Percy family of Northumberland. His reign was disrupted by a major national revolt of the Welsh under Owain Glyndwr, a descendant of the ancient Welsh princes, and he was also challenged by his son, Henry of Monmouth, who set up his own court in competition with his father's. The constant revolts and his continual shortage of money wore out this once vigorous man, and he died a shadow of his former self.

THE COAT OF ARMS OF HENRY IV
Following the lead of the French king, whose throne he claimed, Henry IV reduced the number of fleurs-de-lys in the coat of arms to three.

👑 HENRY IV

- *Born* 3 Apr 1367, son of John of Gaunt and Blanche of Lancaster.
- *Married* Mary de Bohun, 1380/81, 7 children; Joan of Navarre, 7 Feb 1403.
- *Acceded* Sept 1399.
- *Crowned* Westminster Abbey, 13 Oct 1399.
- *Died* London, 20 Mar 1413, aged 56.

THE OFFER OF THE THRONE
When his father, John of Gaunt, died early in 1399, Henry was in exile in France, banished by Richard II. The King seized Henry's inheritance, whereupon Henry returned to England, stating that he had come back to claim his rightful estates. He found, however, that the country had had enough of Richard's autocratic rule, and so made a bid for the throne. His claim was based on his father being the fourth son of Edward III, but the eight-year-old Edmund Mortimer, Richard's heir, had a stronger claim through Edward III's third son. Parliament backed Henry, and so he became king as Henry IV.

AN EMPTY THRONE
When Henry returned from exile in 1399, Richard was in Ireland, leaving the throne empty. In this illustration, Henry Bolingbroke, wearing the tall black hat, is contemplating whether to become king.

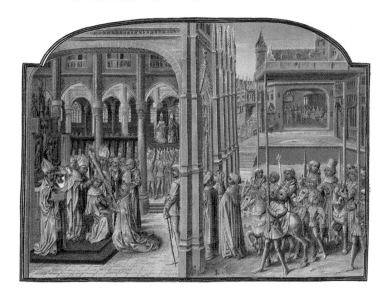

THE CORONATION

Thirteen days after Parliament offered him the throne, Henry Bolingbroke was crowned as Henry IV in Westminster Abbey. His predecessor, Richard II, had been deposed and was to be imprisoned in Pontefract Castle.

HENRY AND JOAN

The gilt and painted effigies (below) of Henry and his second wife Joan stand above their tombs in Canterbury Cathedral.

THE CORRESPONDENT

Short, stocky and with red hair, Henry was brave, energetic, had good health (until his last years), enjoyed sports and excelled in martial arts. He was also well read, an accomplished musician and encouraged the arts: one of his first acts as king was to increase Geoffrey Chaucer's pension. Henry was also an inveterate correspondent, keeping in touch with many heads of state, including the emperors of Byzantium and Abyssinia and even the Mongol leader Tamerlane. As a youth he had travelled widely, fighting with the Teutonic Knights in Lithuania, making a pilgrimage to Jerusalem, and visiting Cyprus, Prague, Rhodes and Venice.

OWAIN GLYNDWR

Soon after Henry became King, the Welsh rose in revolt under Owain Glyndwr, a descendant of the last independent Prince of Wales. Seeking full independence for the principality, Glyndwr marshalled his forces in North Wales and opened a guerrilla campaign against the English in 1401. In 1404 he made a treaty with the French, who sent an army to help him, and for the next 10 years defeated all attempts to subdue him.

WELSH INDEPENDENCE

In 1404 Owain Glyndwr set up an independent Welsh parliament at Machynlleth (below), where it is believed that he was crowned Prince of Wales. A second parliament was held in Harlech Castle in 1405, captured from the English the previous year.

HENRY V

1413–1422

THE COAT OF ARMS OF HENRY V

WITHIN MONTHS OF SUCCEEDING his father at the age of 25, Henry V re-opened the 100 Years' War with France in order to win back territories in France lost by his ancestors. After taking an army across the Channel in mid-1415, Henry defeated a French army three times the size of his own at the Battle of Agincourt. Henry's reign was marked by further victories against the French, and by 1420 he had forced the French king Charles VI to accept him as his heir – a pact sealed by Henry's marriage to Charles's daughter, Catherine. Unfortunately, Henry died before he could become King of France, and his military conquests were all lost in the reign of his son, Henry VI.

👑 HENRY V

- **Born** Monmouth Castle, 9 Aug or 16 Sept 1387, son of Henry IV and Mary de Bohun.
- **Acceded** 21 Mar 1413.
- **Crowned** Westminster Abbey, 9 April 1413.
- **Married** Catherine of France, Troyes, France, 2/3 June 1420, 1 son.
- **Died** Vincennes Castle, France, 1 Sept 1422, aged 34 or 35.

THE WAR IN FRANCE

Henry's military campaign in France revived the English claim to the French throne and aimed to recapture previously held English territories, notably Normandy and part of the Duchy of Aquitaine, which had fallen under French control. However, the campaign also had the effect of uniting the previously feuding English nobles in a common cause and thus diverting them from plotting against Henry.

Nearly the whole of the English nobility accompanied the King to France in 1415, and the success of the undertaking served to strengthen Henry's position as king. Henry captured Harfleur, the leading port in north-west France, after a five-week siege and then won the Battle of Agincourt a few weeks later. In 1417 he returned to France and conquered Normandy.

TREATY OF TROYES

In 1420 Charles VI of France signed a treaty with Henry V by which Charles made Henry his heir and regent of France and betrothed him to his daughter Catherine. Henry can be seen kneeling in front of his father-in-law in the contemporary illustration above.

THE BATTLE OF AGINCOURT

On 25 October 1415 an exhausted English force of 9,000 soldiers, consisting mainly of foot-soldiers and archers, destroyed the superior might of the French cavalry at the Battle of Agincourt (left). In a strategically brilliant operation, 6,000 Frenchmen were killed, while less than 400 English soldiers lost their lives.

THE CHIVALRIC KING

As a boy Henry loved outdoor activities. By the age of 10 he could ride, swim, bend a bow and hunt. He was also a fine scholar and an accomplished musician. Imbued with the ideals of chivalry, he grew up strong, bold and skilled at arms, proving himself in campaigns against the Welsh. Once king, Henry pursued his policies with zeal and revealed himself to be a shrewd tactician – both militarily and politically – merciful to his enemies and devoutly religious.

HENRY V

This portrait of Henry by an unknown artist shows a sensitive and thoughtful young man, although history recalls him as an adventurous, even headstrong leader.

EVENTS OF THE REIGN
1413 – 1422

◆ **1413** Henry accedes to the throne upon the death of his father, Henry IV.
◆ **1415** Henry thwarts the Cambridge plot, an attempt by a group of nobles to replace him on the throne with his cousin, Edmund Mortimer, Earl of March.
◆ **1415** Henry renews the war against France, captures Harfleur and wins the Battle of Agincourt.
◆ **1416** Death of Owain Glyndwr, leader of the Welsh revolt against the crown.
◆ **1420** Under the Treaty of Troyes, Henry becomes Regent of France and heir to the French King Charles VI.
◆ **1420** Henry marries Catherine, daughter of Charles VI.
◆ **1421** Birth of Prince Henry, later Henry VI.
◆ **1422** Henry V dies in France before he can succeed to the French throne.

HENRY'S TOMB

Henry's tomb in Westminster Abbey is marked by an imposing effigy of the King.

EARLY DEATH

Before Henry could succeed to the French throne he died of dysentery in September 1422. Charles VI, the French king, died the following month, leaving Henry's 10-month-old son, Henry VI, as king of both countries. For a while Henry managed to hold on to the territories his father had gained in France, but by the early 1450s the English had been expelled completely.

HENRY VI

1422–1461, 1470–1471

THE COAT OF ARMS
OF HENRY VI

HENRY VI SUCCEEDED to the thrones of England and France when he was less than a year old. His rule in France was soon undermined by the campaigns of Joan of Arc and within a generation all his father's conquests were lost. During his long reign, his own mind failed him more than once and he had to submit the kingdom to the rule of a Protector, Richard, Duke of York. This led to civil war and his throne was taken away from him by the Protector's son, Edward IV, in 1461, given back briefly in 1470, and finally taken away in 1471. Weeks later Henry was murdered in the Tower, only days after his only son was killed in battle. It was an ignominious end to an inglorious reign.

♔ HENRY VI

- *Born* Windsor Castle, 6 Dec 1421, son of Henry V and Catherine of France.
- *Acceded* 1 Sept 1422.
- *Crowned* Westminster Abbey, 5/6 Nov 1429.
- *Married* Margaret of Anjou, Titchfield Abbey, Hants, 23 April 1445, 1 son.
- *Deposed* 4 Mar 1461.
- *Restored* 30 Oct 1470.
- *Deposed* 11 Apr 1471.
- *Murdered* Tower of London 27 May 1471, aged 49.

JOAN OF ARC

In 1422 Henry was king of a French people who had lost faith in their leaders and themselves. Their pride was restored by Joan of Arc, a peasant girl from Domremy in eastern France. In 1429 Joan claimed to have had a vision telling her to drive the English out of France and began a campaign that was to see the English expelled from all but Calais by 1453. In 1431 the English captured and burned Joan at the stake in Rouen.

FAN VAULTING
The fan vaulting in the ceiling of King's College Chapel (left) is a fine example of this decorative style.

ROYAL BLESSING
In 1429 Joan of Arc visited the French king Charles VII at Chinon (above) to gain his help against the English.

KING'S COLLEGE

In 1441 Henry conceived the idea of a new college at Cambridge. It was originally intended for 12 scholars but the plans were extended to accommodate 70 scholars, 10 priests and 16 choir boys. The college chapel was begun in 1445 and was designed in the Perpendicular style. Work continued on it spasmodically until its completion in 1515.

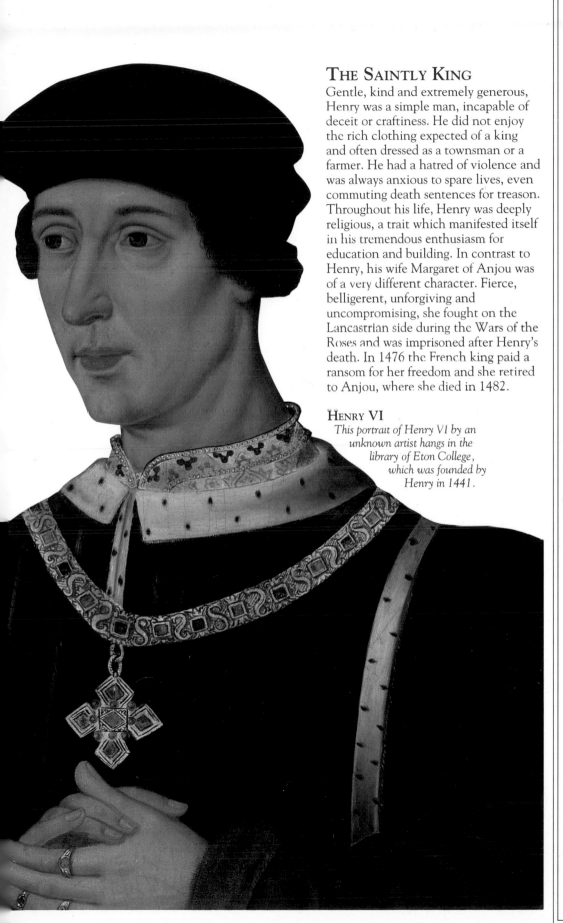

THE SAINTLY KING

Gentle, kind and extremely generous, Henry was a simple man, incapable of deceit or craftiness. He did not enjoy the rich clothing expected of a king and often dressed as a townsman or a farmer. He had a hatred of violence and was always anxious to spare lives, even commuting death sentences for treason. Throughout his life, Henry was deeply religious, a trait which manifested itself in his tremendous enthusiasm for education and building. In contrast to Henry, his wife Margaret of Anjou was of a very different character. Fierce, belligerent, unforgiving and uncompromising, she fought on the Lancastrian side during the Wars of the Roses and was imprisoned after Henry's death. In 1476 the French king paid a ransom for her freedom and she retired to Anjou, where she died in 1482.

HENRY VI
This portrait of Henry VI by an unknown artist hangs in the library of Eton College, which was founded by Henry in 1441.

EVENTS OF THE REIGN
1422 – 1471

◆ **1422** Henry becomes King of England on the death of his father Henry V, and then, two months later, King of France on the death of his grandfather Charles VI.
◆ **1422** John, Duke of Bedford, is appointed Regent of France; Humphrey, Duke of Gloucester, is Regent of England.
◆ **1429** Joan of Arc begins to expel the English from France.
◆ **1431** Joan of Arc is burned at the stake by the English.
◆ **1437** Henry assumes personal rule of England.
◆ **1453** End of 100 Years' War: English driven out of France.
◆ **1454** Richard, Duke of York, Henry's cousin, is made Protector during Henry's mental illness.

COURT OF EXCHEQUER
The Court of Exchequer existed to settle disagreements over taxation and other financial affairs. In this contemporary illustration from Henry's reign, the judge, who is wearing a red robe, is presiding over a session of the court.

◆ **1455** Duke of York is dismissed: he rebels against the King and takes over the government. Start of the Wars of the Roses.
◆ **1461** Henry is deposed by Richard's son Edward, Duke of York, who is then crowned Edward IV.
◆ **1470-71** Henry is briefly reinstated on the throne.
◆ **1471** Henry is murdered in the Tower of London.

WARS OF THE ROSES

1455–1485

THE WARS OF THE ROSES can be seen quite simply as the military expression of an on-going family quarrel between two branches of the royal house of Plantagenet, the houses of Lancaster and York. The Lancastrian branch provided the kings from 1399 to 1461, and the Yorkist branch from 1461 to 1485, with a brief interlude in 1470-71. The wars broke out in 1455 as a result of Yorkist exasperation with the weak and inefficient government of the Lancastrian Henry VI, and lasted with lengthy intervals for 30 years. Each side had its own supporters in the nobility, but the wars themselves cannot be described as a civil war, for the divisions between Lancaster and York did not filter down to all classes. Merchants were unaffected, trade expanded and agriculture was untouched.

THE DYNASTIC QUARREL

The quarrel between Lancaster and York arose after the deposition in 1399 of Richard II by Henry, Duke of Lancaster. Henry was the son of John of Gaunt, Edward III's fourth son. However, the Yorkists were descended from both the third and fifth sons of Edward, giving them a prior claim to the throne.

TAKING SIDES

The essentially arbitrary line-up of the protagonists in the Wars of the Roses is depicted in this 19th-century painting by Henry Payne (below), which shows the nobles choosing sides by picking different coloured roses.

JOHN OF GAUNT

THE ROSES

The Wars of the Roses take their name from the emblems used by each royal house. The Lancastrians sported the Red Rose of Lancaster, the Yorkists the White Rose of York. When the Lancastrian Henry Tudor brought the wars to an end in 1485 by marrying Elizabeth of York, he adopted the Tudor Rose – a combination of red and white roses – to mark the personal union of the two royal houses.

CANNON
The first cannons to be made in Britain, such as the one above, were manufactured in Scotland during the 1470s.

CONTEMPORARY WARFARE

By the time of the Wars of the Roses warfare was no longer a succession of lengthy sieges of castles with just an occasional battlefield skirmish. Gunpowder, first tried out in Europe at the end of the 13th century, had been slow to prove its effectiveness. But by the middle of the 15th century, siege engines such as ballistae, mangonels and trebuchets, which hurled large rocks, bags of small stones or even rotting animal carcasses at castle walls, had given way to rudimentary cannons and hand-guns aimed at troops on a battlefield. These new weapons allowed armies increasing mobility, and in the 16th century even heavily fortified castles were vulnerable.

FIGHTING THE WARS

In the 30 years of fighting that constitute the Wars of the Roses, there were 10 major battles and a handful of lesser engagements. But the total period of campaigning, from the first Battle of St Albans in 1455 to the Battle of Bosworth in 1485, amounted to less than 13 weeks, an average of one week every two and a half years. The armies on both sides were composed largely of nobles, their sons and retainers, together with foreign mercenaries, which accounts for the high total of nobles – more than 80 – who lost their lives during the wars.

DEATH OF THE KINGMAKER
In 1470 the Yorkist Edward IV was deposed in favour of the Lancastrian Henry VI following a coup staged by Richard Neville, Earl of Warwick. Known as "The Kingmaker", Warwick had earned his title for his role in placing Edward on the throne in 1461, and then for engineering his removal in 1470. In early 1471 Edward and Warwick met at the Battle of Barnet (left), where Warwick was slain.

WARS OF THE ROSES 1455 – 1485

◆ **1454** Richard, Duke of York is appointed Protector of England during the mental incapacity of Henry VI.

◆ **1455** Duke of York dismissed. He raises an army and defeats the King's Lancastrian forces at the first Battle of St Albans. The Lancastrian leader, the Duke of Somerset, is killed. York takes over government of England.

◆ **1459** War is renewed and the Lancastrians are defeated at Bloreheath; the Yorkists are then defeated at Ludford. Parliament holds a session at Coventry and declares York a traitor.

◆ **1460** Yorkist army led by Richard Neville, Earl of Warwick – "The Kingmaker" – defeats Lancastrians at the Battle of Northampton. Henry VI is captured, his wife Margaret escapes to Scotland. York is again Protector and claims the throne for himself as true heir.

◆ **1460** Margaret raises an army in the north, defeats and kills Richard of York at Wakefield.

◆ **1461** Edward, son of Richard, defeats Lancastrian army at Mortimer's Cross, but Warwick loses to Margaret at second Battle of St Albans. Warwick declares Edward king. He is crowned Edward IV after Warwick defeats Margaret at Battle of Towton.

◆ **1462-3** Lancastrian revolts are suppressed.

◆ **1464** Warwick defeats Lancastrians at Battle of Hexham; Henry VI is captured and brought to the Tower of London.

◆ **1469-70** Warwick falls out with Edward IV, defeats him at Edgecote. They are later reconciled but Warwick is banished. He makes peace with Margaret, returns to England with an army and Edward flees to Flanders. Henry VI is restored to the throne.

◆ **1471** Edward returns to England, defeats and kills Warwick at Battle of Barnet. Margaret is defeated at the Battle of Tewkesbury; her son Edward, Prince of Wales, is killed in the battle. Henry VI is captured and murdered in the Tower of London.

◆ **1485** Richard III, brother of Edward IV, is defeated at Bosworth Field by Henry Tudor, the Lancastrian heir and claimant to the throne. The Wars of the Roses come to an end.

THE HOUSE OF YORK

1461–1485

Elizabeth *m* EDWARD IV
Woodville   👑 1461-1470
  👑 1471-1483

Richard Neville
Earl of Warwick
"The Kingmaker"
(*d* 1471)

George *m* Isabel   Anne *m* RICHARD III   and
Duke   👑 1483-1485   others
of Clarence
(*d* 1478)

Edmund Tudor *m* Margaret Beaufort
Earl   great-granddaughter
of Richmond   of John of Gaunt
             and Katherine Swynford

EDWARD V   Richard   Elizabeth *m* HENRY VII   Edward   Margaret   Edward
👑 1483   (*d* 1483?)   👑 1485-1509   Earl   Countess   Prince
(*d* 1483?)   of Warwick   of Salisbury   of Wales
                                                  (*d* 1499)   (*d* 1541)   (*d* 1484)

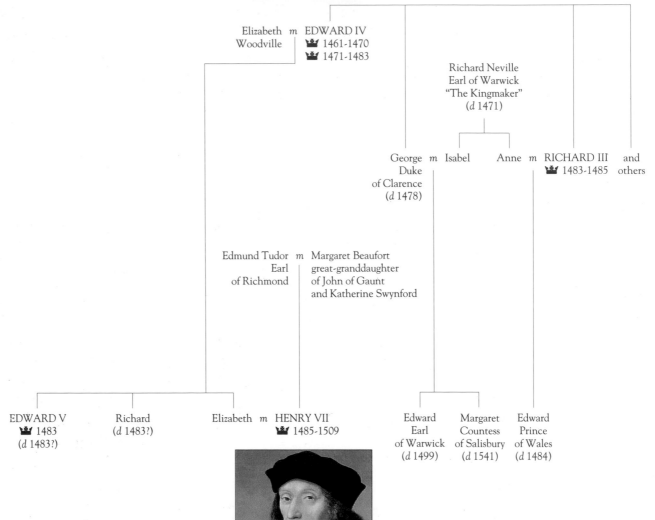

CHAPTER FIVE

THE
HOUSE OF YORK
1461–1485

The House of York was another branch of the House of Plantagenet, and although this dynasty ruled briefly after the House of Lancaster, it had a stronger claim to the throne. It was descended from two of Edward III's sons, Lionel of Clarence and Edmund of York, one of them senior to John of Gaunt, ancestor of the Lancastrians.

from the succession, the clamour mounted. York was appointed Protector while the King remained ill, but was dismissed at Christmas 1454 when Henry recovered. Richard then took up arms against the King and defeated a Lancastrian army at St Albans in what was to be the first of many battles of the Wars of the Roses.

The Protector

When the Lancastrian Henry VI had his first bout of mental disorder in 1453, he had no children. His heir was Richard Plantagenet, Duke of York, whose descent from Edward III was much stronger than anyone else's, even of the King himself. Richard had not pressed his claim to the throne while the King remained childless, but he was popular in England, more so than the King's advisers. As the government of Henry VI became more inefficient and its conduct of the war with France more deplorable, there was a growing clamour for Richard Plantagenet to be brought in to govern the country. At first Henry's supporters resisted, but when the Queen, Margaret of Anjou, gave birth to a son, Edward, in 1454, thus excluding Richard

EDWARD IV
In this contemporary illustration, Edward is shown sitting on his throne with his wife, Elizabeth Woodville, kneeling to his left.

The Yorkist Dynasty

In 1460 Richard of York formally claimed the throne but he was defeated and killed in battle at Wakefield by Margaret. The following spring, his son Edward, aided by the great Richard Neville, Earl of Warwick, was proclaimed the first Yorkist king. The Yorkist dynasty only lasted until 1485, but in that short time England enjoyed a leap forward in national prosperity. Much of this was stimulated by the Edward IV, who gave as much attention to developing his personal business enterprises as to matters of state. There was also a flourishing of architecture, music and literature, and in 1476 William Caxton set up England's first printing press, which "quickened the production of books beyond all medieval dreams."

EDWARD IV

1461–1470, 1471–1483

THE COAT OF ARMS
OF EDWARD IV

BARELY 19 WHEN HE DEFEATED the Lancastrian Henry VI in battle, Edward IV came to the throne with two aims: to restore the system of justice and to improve royal finances, both of which had suffered during the reign of Henry VI. At first Edward allowed his cousin Richard, Earl of Warwick to govern the kingdom, using the time profitably to enrich himself in commercial activities in order to reduce Crown debts. His marriage to Elizabeth Woodville, the widow of a commoner, upset Warwick, who briefly deposed Edward in favour of Henry VI. Once restored in 1471, Edward proved himself an able ruler in his own right; the country enjoyed a well-deserved period of peace.

👑 EDWARD IV

- **Born** Rouen, France, 28 April 1442, first son of Richard Plantagenet, Duke of York, and Cecily Neville.
- **Acceded** 4 Mar 1461.
- **Crowned** Westminster Abbey, 28 June 1461.
- **Married** Elizabeth Woodville, 1 May 1464, 10 children.
- **Died** Westminster, 9 April 1483, aged 40.

ENCOURAGING PROSPERITY

Edward's own success in the wool and cloth trade led him to do much to foster the development of English trade. He recognized the value of merchant companies by giving them a direct role in the election of the Lord Mayor of London, and actively worked to keep the country out of disruptive foreign entanglements.

ENGLISH TRADE
During Edward's reign, cloth exports rose to their highest ever (right), while trade doubled in the 50 years after 1430.

THE QUEEN
The nobility resented Edward's marriage to Elizabeth (left).

ELIZABETH WOODVILLE

In 1464 Edward announced that he had married the widow of an English commoner. His marriage to Elizabeth Woodville, the daughter of a knight, was very happy, but it led to a major rift between Edward and Warwick, who felt his dominant position to be threatened.

ADMINISTRATION

Edward took a close interest in government and justice. He was the first king to address the House of Commons, and introduced the Court of Requests for poor peasants to bring complaints of overcharging by greedy landlords.

IN COUNCIL
Edward's Royal Council was small in number and consisted of men he knew he could trust (left).

AN ABLE RULER

When Edward became king at the age of 19, he was described by many as a beautiful young man, about two metres (six feet) tall, with polished manners and a genial disposition. He had an excellent memory and is said to have known the name and wealth of every important person in his kingdom. Although described as lazy and easy-going, Edward was in fact a very hard worker, busying himself with government, military matters, commerce, law, diplomacy, and family life. He wore himself out to die aged only 40.

EDWARD IV
This portrait, painted by an unknown artist, shows Edward to be a handsome, dark-haired young man.

EVENTS OF THE REIGN 1461 – 1483

◆ **1461** Edward defeats the Lancastrian army at Mortimer's Cross and is proclaimed king by his cousin Warwick, "The Kingmaker", in succession to Henry VI.

◆ **1464** Edward marries Elizabeth Woodville, offending Warwick and other lords.

◆ **1469** Warwick breaks with Edward and joins Henry VI's wife Margaret to usurp Edward.

◆ **1470** Edward is briefly driven out of England to exile in Flanders when Henry VI is restored to the throne.

◆ **1471** Edward returns to England and defeats and kills Warwick at the Battle of Barnet.

◆ **1471** Margaret is defeated at the Battle of Tewkesbury; soon after, Henry VI is murdered in the Tower of London.

◆ **1474** Edward grants privileges to the Hanseatic League of North German trading cities to conduct trade in England.

◆ **1476** William Caxton sets up a printing press in England.

◆ **1478** Edward falls out with his brother George, Duke of Clarence, who is then murdered in the Tower, supposedly in a butt of malmsey wine.

◆ **1483** Death of Edward.

THE BOOK TRADE
Although Caxton's printing press was slow, reproduction was good, as can be seen from the pages of one of his books illustrated below.

PRINTING PRESS

In 1476 William Caxton set up Britain's first printing press, which used movable wooden type, at Westminster. Caxton had learned his trade in Flanders, and was to produce about 80 titles in England before his death in 1491.

EDWARD V

1483

THE COAT OF ARMS
OF EDWARD V

ON THE DEATH OF EDWARD IV in April 1483, the crown passed to his young son Edward V. In his will, Edward IV appointed his brother Richard, Duke of Gloucester, as Protector. But in June Edward was declared illegitimate and deposed in favour of Richard. Together with his younger brother, Edward was moved into the Tower of London, and after a few months the princes were never seen again. Their deaths are one of the great mysteries of English history, and it is unlikely that we will ever know what happened to the two princes, or who, if anyone, killed them.

👑 EDWARD V

◆ *Born* Westminster Abbey, 1/2/4 Nov 1470, son of Edward IV and Elizabeth Woodville.
◆ *Acceded* 9 April 1483.
◆ *Deposed* 25 June 1483.
◆ *Died* Sept 1483?, aged 12.

THE BRIEF REIGN

Edward and his brother Richard arrived in London from their home in Ludlow Castle on 4 May. Arrangements were made for Edward's coronation on Sunday 22 June, and Parliament was summoned to meet on 25 June. On or about 10 June, however, Edward and Richard were declared illegitimate. The Bishop of Bath and Wells revealed to the Protector that when Edward IV had married Elizabeth Woodville, he was already betrothed to Lady Eleanor Butler.

A betrothal constituted the same commitment as marriage in those days, and so Edward IV's marriage was invalid and his sons were illegitimate. When Parliament met, it felt it had no option but to approve a proposal that Richard of Gloucester should succeed to the throne as Richard III.

PRINCES IN THE TOWER

Soon after his arrival in London, Edward and his brother Richard were lodged in the royal apartments of the Tower. During the summer of 1483 they were seen at "sundry tymes" and then they disappeared. Two skeletons of what appeared to be two boys were found in the White Tower in 1674, but despite a detailed forensic examination of the bones in 1933, the skeletons have never been properly identified. Although it has been repeated over the centuries that they were murdered by their uncle, Richard III, no evidence has been produced to prove the case either way.

PRINCE EDWARD

The manuscript above contains one of the few known contemporary portraits of Edward, standing between his parents.

BLOODY TOWER

It is thought that the two princes were killed in the Bloody Tower (the square tower in the picture to the left) and then buried in the Wakefield Tower (the round tower) before reburial next to the White Tower.

THE TWO PRINCES
This famous portrait of Edward and his younger brother Richard was painted by Sir John Everett Millais in the late 19th century, some 400 years after their death.

EDWARD V

Of the character of Edward V, we know very little. When he was three, he was taken with his infant brother to Ludlow Castle to live with his uncle Earl Rivers, brother of his mother Elizabeth. Edward's life in Ludlow was sheltered, and with a heavy emphasis on study in his routine, he soon began to show signs of a scholarly bent. He was shielded from the political goings-on in London and saw little of his father and even less of his father's relatives.

EVENTS OF THE REIGN 1483

◆ Edward V succeeds his father Edward IV in April and makes his way with his brother Richard to London. Richard of Gloucester becomes Protector.
◆ The two princes arrive in London in early May and lodge with the Bishop of London before moving to royal apartments in the Tower of London.
◆ In June Edward is declared illegitimate by Parliament, which declares Richard of Gloucester king as Richard III.
◆ Last sighting of the two princes in the grounds of the Tower of London in September.

HISTORIC DOUBTS

In 1768 Horace Walpole, son of the former Prime Minister Robert Walpole, wrote Historic Doubts on the Life and Reign of King Richard The Third, *in which he acquitted Richard of the two murders. Since then, numerous books have appeared on the subject, but none has solved the controversy surrounding the disappearance of the two princes.*

HISTORIC DOUBTS
ON THE
LIFE AND REIGN
OF
King RICHARD the Third.

By M. HORACE WALPOLE.

L'Hiftoire n'eft fondée que fur le témoignage des Auteurs qui nous l'ont tranfmife. Il importe donc extremement, pour la fçavoir, de bien connoître quels étoient ces Auteurs. Rien n'eft à negliger en ce point ; le tems où ils ont vecû, leur naiffance, leur patrie, la part qu'ils ont eue aux affaires, les moyens par lefquels ils ont été inftruits, et l'intérêt qu'ils y pouvoient prendre, font des circonftances effentielles qu'il n'eft pas permis d'ignorer : delà depend le plus ou le moins d'autorité qu'ils doivent avoir : et fans cette connoiffance, on courra rifque très fouvent de prendre pour guide un Hiftorien de mauvaife foi, ou du moins, mal informé.

Hift. de l'Acad. des Infcript. Vol. X.

LONDON:

THE CULPRIT?

When Henry VII defeated Richard III in 1485, he went to great lengths to blacken his name, although nothing was said then about Richard having murdered his nephews. But within a few years this became the accepted interpretation of events. That Henry might have ordered their deaths to remove any rivals for his throne was never discussed then, but it has been argued since.

RICHARD III

1483–1485

THE COAT OF ARMS OF RICHARD III

PROBABLY THE MOST MALIGNED of English kings, Richard III has stimulated more speculation and enquiry into his character and motivation than any of his predecessors or successors. Few contemporaries had either good or bad to say about him, although the chronicler John Rous called him a "mighty prince and a special good lord". Richard was king for barely two years, but once he was dead, historians, clerics, even playwrights fell over themselves to blacken his name. Most propaganda was designed to serve the Tudor dynasty, which began when Henry VII defeated Richard in battle, but in more recent times, historians have questioned whether Richard has deserved his evil reputation.

♛ RICHARD III

- **Born** Fotheringhay Castle, Northants, 2 Oct 1452, third son of Richard Plantagenet, Duke of York, and Cecily Neville.
- **Married** Anne Neville, Westminster Abbey, 12 July 1472, 1 son.
- **Acceded** 26 June 1483.
- **Crowned** Westminster Abbey, 6 July 1483.
- **Died** Bosworth Field, Leicestershire, 22 Aug 1485, aged 32.

ANNE NEVILLE

In 1472 Richard married Anne Neville, daughter of Richard Neville, Earl of Warwick. By all accounts it was a happy union: they had known each other since they were small children. They both enjoyed music and took an interest in education, endowing colleges at Cambridge University.

COLLEGE OF ARMS

For more than 500 years the royal heralds have controlled the issuing of coats of arms from headquarters in the City of London. Their building below dates from the 1670s.

RICHARD AND ANNE *(left)*

COLLEGE OF ARMS

Heralds were first employed by kings as messengers. They also arranged coronations and state funerals, and read out royal proclamations. When it became necessary to control the use of coats of arms identifying each noble family, the heralds carried out the regulating. By the reign of Richard III, 10 different types of herald were in existence. All were incorporated in 1483 into a single college, which still controls the issuing of all coats of arms today.

RICHARD III

RICHARD III'S
GREAT SEAL

A MUCH-MALIGNED KING

Tall, lean and with slender limbs, Richard was
once described by a woman who danced with
him as the handsomest man in the room,
excepting his brother Edward, who was widely
regarded as beautiful. Contrary to
Shakespeare's portrayal, there is no evidence
that Richard was a hunchback, although he
might have had one shoulder slightly higher than
the other. Devoted to his brother Edward and
reliable in all the many tasks Edward asked him
to do Richard was undoubtedly courageous and
proved in his short reign to be an energetic,
painstaking and just ruler.

BOSWORTH

On 22 August 1485 the
8,000-strong army of Henry
Tudor faced Richard's
12,000-strong army at
Bosworth. Richard's support
ebbed away but he dived
into the thick of battle,
coming within a sword's
length of Henry Tudor
before he was cut down.

BATTLE ROYAL
*The fields outside the
Leicestershire town of
Market Bosworth were
the site of one of the
most important battles
in English history, a
battle that decided the
fate of a royal dynasty.*

THE TUDORS

1485–1603

HENRY VII *m* Elizabeth of York
1485-1509 (*d* 1503)

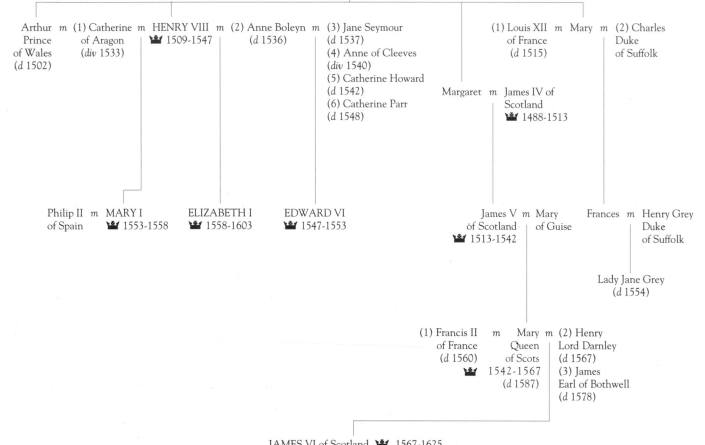

Arthur *m* (1) Catherine *m* HENRY VIII *m* (2) Anne Boleyn *m* (3) Jane Seymour
Prince of Aragon 1509-1547 (*d* 1536) (*d* 1537)
of Wales (*div* 1533) (4) Anne of Cleeves
(*d* 1502) (*div* 1540)
(5) Catherine Howard
(*d* 1542)
(6) Catherine Parr
(*d* 1548)

(1) Louis XII *m* Mary *m* (2) Charles
of France (*d* 1515) Duke
of Suffolk

Margaret *m* James IV of
Scotland
1488-1513

Philip II *m* MARY I   ELIZABETH I   EDWARD VI
of Spain 1553-1558   1558-1603   1547-1553

James V *m* Mary   Frances *m* Henry Grey
of Scotland of Guise   Duke
1513-1542   of Suffolk

Lady Jane Grey
(*d* 1554)

(1) Francis II *m* Mary *m* (2) Henry
of France Queen Lord Darnley
(*d* 1560) of Scots (*d* 1567)
1542-1567 (3) James
(*d* 1587) Earl of Bothwell
(*d* 1578)

JAMES VI of Scotland 1567-1625
JAMES I of England 1603-1625

CHAPTER SIX

THE
TUDORS
1485–1603

The Tudor dynasty got its name from Henry Tudor (or Tudur, to give it its Welsh spelling). Henry was the grandson of Owain Tudor, a Welsh squire who claimed descent from the ancient independent princes of Wales. Henry's mother was Margaret Beaufort, great-granddaughter of John of Gaunt, the ancestor of the Lancastrian dynasty, which made Henry the Lancastrian heir. Henry defeated the last Yorkist king, Richard III, at the Battle of Bosworth in 1485, where Richard was slain, and he became Henry VII. There is a story, which we need not doubt, that the English crown was worn by Richard during the battle. It fell off his head during his fight to the death and rolled into a bush, from where it was retrieved by Lord Stanley and placed on Henry's head. Once king, Henry married Elizabeth of York, the daughter of Edward IV, and through their marriage they united the two royal houses into the new House of Tudor.

THE TUDOR ROSE
Incorporating both the white rose of York and the red rose of Lancaster, the Tudor Rose symbolized the union of the two royal houses in the new dynasty.

The Tudors

The accession of Henry as the first Tudor monarch marked the end of the Middle Ages in England. The nobility had so weakened themselves in the Wars of the Roses that the Tudors were able to wield far more power than their Plantagenet predecessors. The five Tudor monarchs were not always popular – indeed in some instances they were detested – but none was either murdered or deposed. Except in the short reign of the boy king, Edward VI, no lord was ever allowed to become so mighty as seriously to undermine royal power, and Parliament was always kept under firm control. Curiously, English people tolerated an absolutism that would have been unthinkable in the previous century. Terrible injustices were done, and the horrors of religious persecution of both Protestants and Catholics make particularly gruesome reading.

National Pride

The Tudors did an enormous amount to generate national pride, chiefly by ensuring the involvement of far more sectors of the population in the development of national institutions and the growth of national aspirations. Henry VII stimulated a further leap forward in economic activity, favouring the merchant and manufacturing classes, and the whole period was illuminated by the flowering of the English Renaissance in architecture, literature and the theatre, reaching its apogee in the unique genius of William Shakespeare.

HENRY VII

1485–1509

THE LEADING LANCASTRIAN CLAIMANT to the crown, Henry acceded to the throne after defeating Richard III of York at Bosworth in 1485. In 1486 Henry married Elizabeth, daughter of Edward IV, thereby uniting the warring houses of York and Lancaster. He then set about breaking the power of the English barons – the source of so much conflict – by reviving the Court of Star Chamber to try the barons if they broke the law, and banning them from raising private armies. Financially astute, Henry pursued peaceful and commercially orientated policies for most of his reign. By his death in 1509 Henry's policies had paid off and the royal exchequer was handsomely in credit.

THE COAT OF ARMS OF HENRY VII

♛ HENRY VII

- **Born** Pembroke Castle, Wales, 28 Jan 1457, son of Edward Tudor and Margaret Beaufort.
- **Acceded** 22 Aug 1485.
- **Crowned** Westminster Abbey, 30 Oct 1485.
- **Married** Elizabeth of York, Westminster, 18 Jan 1486, 8 children.
- **Died** Richmond Palace, Surrey, 21 April 1509, aged 52.

THE KING'S RULE

Henry was determined to control the power of the nobility both to secure his position on the throne and to bring to an end the military conflict that had ravaged England during the Wars of the Roses. After investing the Court of Star Chamber with the power to try and punish the nobility who broke the law, Henry banned their private armies. During a visit to Hedingham Castle, Henry found the Earl of Oxford's servants dressed in military uniforms, and fined the Earl, telling him "I cannot have my laws broken in my sight".

HEDINGHAM CASTLE
Built in the 1130s, Hedingham Castle was the baronial seat of one of Henry's friends, the Earl of Oxford.

THE ROYAL UNION

On 18 January 1486 Henry married Elizabeth of York in Westminster Abbey. The couple had lived together prior to the ceremony, and the marriage effectively ended the feud between the houses of York and Lancaster. Elizabeth was considered beautiful by her contemporaries and their marriage was a happy one.

TOMB EFFIGIES
The Italian Pietro Torrigiano carved the figures of Henry and Elizabeth on their tomb in Henry VII's chapel in Westminster Abbey.

THE ASTUTE KING

Henry spent much of his early life in exile in Brittany. His family were poor and a tough upbringing taught him the value of money. He also learnt that subtle statecraft and fiscal manipulation – policies he pursued rigorously – were often better than fighting as a way to defeat one's enemies. Some considered him mean, but his generosity to the church, the sick and the poor proves otherwise. A cultured man, Henry patronized the printer William Caxton and brought over French and Italian scholars to teach in England as part of the Revival of Learning.

HENRY VII
In appearance, Henry was tall, dark, blue-eyed, well-built and athletic. This portrait by Michiel Sittow, painted in 1505, shows a man of tough, reserved character.

EVENTS OF THE REIGN 1485 – 1509

◆ **1485** Henry accedes to the throne after defeating Richard III at the Battle of Bosworth.

◆ **1485** Henry forms the Yeomen of the Guard.

◆ **1486** Henry marries Elizabeth of York, thereby uniting the houses of York and Lancaster.

◆ **1487** Henry revives the Court of Star Chamber, giving it powers to try nobility who break the law.

◆ **1487** Henry crushes a revolt by the Earl of Lincoln on behalf of Lambert Simnel, a claimant to the throne, at Stoke.

◆ **1491** Henry invades France but at the Treaty of Étaples agrees to withdraw English forces in return for a large sum of money.

◆ **1492** Perkin Warbeck claims the throne and attempts to overthrow Henry, but is defeated and put to death in 1499.

A LIKENESS OF SORTS
The portrait of Henry on this contemporary Italian milk-glass vase depicts him with a characteristically Tudor head of red hair. Henry, however, was dark!

◆ **1492** Christopher Columbus discovers America.

◆ **1497** Henry sponsors the voyages of John and Sebastian Cabot to North America.

◆ **1502** Prince Arthur, Henry's eldest son, dies and Prince Henry (the future Henry VIII) becomes heir to the throne, later marrying Arthur's widow Catherine of Aragon.

◆ **1502** Princess Margaret, Henry's eldest daughter, marries James IV of Scotland.

◆ **1503** Death of Elizabeth of York, Henry's wife.

◆ **1509** Henry VII dies at Richmond Palace.

HENRY VIII

1509–1547

THE COAT OF ARMS OF HENRY VIII

IN THE EARLY YEARS of his reign, Henry pursued private pleasures and left the government in the capable hands of his Chancellor, Cardinal Wolsey. However, in 1529, when the latter failed to secure from the Pope the King's divorce from Catherine of Aragon, he was charged with treason. In 1534 Henry declared himself Supreme Head of the English church and broke off relations with Rome. Excommunicated by the Pope, Henry became increasingly autocratic and set about consolidating the spiritual and political independence of England from Rome. By his death he was much hated and the exchequer was bankrupt.

HENRY VIII

- **Born** Greenwich, 28 June 1491, second son of Henry VII and Elizabeth.
- **Acceded** 22 April 1509.
- **Crowned** Westminster Abbey, 24 June 1509.
- **Married** Catherine of Aragon, 1509, 1 daughter; Anne Boleyn, 1533, 1 daughter; Jane Seymour, 1536, 1 son; Anne of Cleves, 1540; Catherine Howard, 1540; Catherine Parr, 1543.
- **Died** Whitehall, 28 Jan 1547, aged 55.

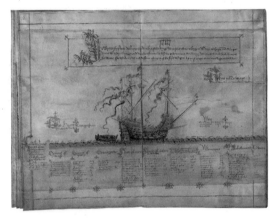

THE ENGLISH NAVY

In order to strengthen his hand in European diplomacy and deter any invasion, Henry embarked on a ship-building programme to increase the size and fire-power of the English navy.

THE GREAT HARRY
Shown at sea in 1546, the Great Harry (above) was one of the largest warships to set sail in Europe.

THE KING'S DIPLOMAT
Thomas Wolsey was born in 1475. The son of an Ipswich butcher, he entered the church and became Archbishop of York in 1514. A year later he received his Cardinal's hat and became the Chancellor of England. After failing to secure Henry's divorce from Catherine of Aragon, Wolsey fell from grace in 1529.

CARDINAL WOLSEY
Although well-educated, Henry at first had no enthusiasm for statecraft or personal rule, entrusting the business of government during the first two decades of his reign to Cardinal Wolsey. Wolsey administered England's affairs at home and abroad with great skill, presiding over a period of growing prosperity.

FIELD OF THE CLOTH OF GOLD
In 1520 Cardinal Wolsey organised a summit meeting near Calais between Henry VIII and Francis I of France. Wolsey hoped the two kings would sign a treaty to guarantee peace in Europe, but nothing was achieved and England and France were soon at war again.

"KING HAL"

When Henry acceded to the throne at the age of 18, he was tallish, handsome and of fair complexion. He spoke several languages, played musical instruments and was adept at dancing, hunting, womanizing and sport. However, when older, Henry became grossly overweight, riddled with disease and displayed a cruel and tyrannical streak. By the time of his death, some 50,000 families, including those of two of his wives, had reason to mourn at least one member whom Henry had put to death.

HENRY VIII
This portrait of the King, painted by Hans Holbein in 1537, shows him at the height of his power and prestige.

PLAYING THE HARP
In his youth Henry learned to play several musical instruments, including the organ, the virginals and the harp (above), to quite a high standard. He also composed songs and masses, and it has been suggested that he wrote the famous air, Greensleeves.

EVENTS OF THE REIGN 1509 – 1547

◆ 1509 Henry accedes to the throne on the death of his father Henry VII.
◆ 1509 Henry marries Catherine of Aragon, daughter of the King and Queen of Spain and widow of his brother Arthur.
◆ 1513 English army defeats the Scots at the Battle of Flodden, killing James IV of Scotland.
◆ 1515 Thomas Wolsey becomes Chancellor of England.
◆ 1516 Catherine gives birth to Princess Mary (later Mary I).
◆ 1517 Martin Luther publishes his 95 theses against the abuses of the Roman Catholic Church.
◆ 1518 The Pope and the kings of England, France and Spain pledge peace in Europe.
◆ 1520 Henry holds peace talks with Francis I of France at the Field of the Cloth of Gold.
◆ 1529 Cardinal Wolsey is accused of high treason, but dies before he can be brought to trial.
◆ 1529 Sir Thomas More becomes Chancellor of England.
◆ 1532 Sir Thomas More gives up the Chancellorship.
◆ 1533 Henry's marriage to Catherine is annulled by Archbishop Thomas Cranmer.
◆ 1533 Henry marries Anne Boleyn; Princess Elizabeth (later Elizabeth I) is born.
◆ 1533 Henry is excommunicated by the Pope.
◆ 1534 The Act of Supremacy is passed, establishing Henry as head of the Church of England.
◆ 1535 Sir Thomas More is executed after refusing to accept Henry as supreme head of the Church of England.
◆ 1535 Thomas Cromwell made Vicar-General of England.
◆ 1536 Anne Boleyn is executed and Henry marries Jane Seymour.
◆ 1536 Act of Union between Wales and England.
◆ 1536 Cromwell begins the dissolution of the monasteries.
◆ 1537 Jane Seymour gives birth to Edward (later Edward VI), but dies after childbirth.
◆ 1540 Henry marries and divorces Anne of Cleves.
◆ 1540 Thomas Cromwell is executed on a charge of treason.
◆ 1540 Henry marries Catherine Howard, his fifth wife.
◆ 1542 Catherine Howard is executed for treason.
◆ 1543 Henry marries Catherine Parr, his sixth wife.
◆ 1547 Henry VIII dies.

EARLY TUDOR PALACES

BUILDING A NEW DYNASTY

THE BUILDING OF ROYAL RESIDENCES flourished under Henry VII and Henry VIII as both kings sought to celebrate the splendour of the Tudor dynasty. Towards the end of Henry VII's reign large palaces were built at Richmond and Greenwich and Henry VIII's love of ostentatious display resulted in even more lavish spending, so that by the end of his reign he had more than 40 houses at his disposal. Some of these were constructed by his courtiers and later acquired by Henry VIII, notably Cardinal Wolsey's palace at Hampton Court, while others, such as Nonsuch Palace, were built by Henry for his own use.

THE PALACE CLOCK
The clock dominating Anne Boleyn's gateway in Hampton Court Palace (right) is purported to stop when any long-standing resident of the Tudor palace dies.

THE ROYAL FAVOURITE
Constructed during the reign of Henry VIII – his initials can be seen intertwined on the Clock Tower (right) with those of Anne Boleyn – St James's Palace has always been a favourite residence of the royal family and numerous royal births and marriages have taken place within its red-brick walls.

ST JAMES'S PALACE
Built between 1532-6, St James's Palace was constructed on the site of a leper hospital. It became one of the main royal residences in London following the destruction of Whitehall in 1698 and remained so until George III moved to Buckingham Palace in 1762. Today the palace is the centre of diplomatic London: a foreign diplomat is accredited to the Court of St James.

ROYAL LONDON
This early 17th-century drawing by Leonard Knyff (below) shows the centre of London dominated by the palaces of Whitehall in the foreground and St James's in the background.

WHITEHALL PALACE
The official residence in London of the Archbishop of York, Whitehall Palace was confiscated in 1529 by Henry VIII from its then incumbent, Cardinal Wolsey. The palace, which was originally known as York Place, was used as the London residence of Anne Boleyn and witnessed her secret marriage to Henry in 1533. Most of the building was destroyed by fire in 1698 and only the early 17th century Banqueting House, which was designed by Inigo Jones, survives today.

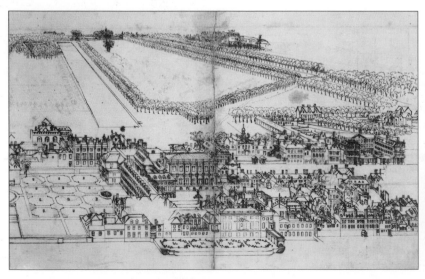

HAMPTON COURT

Built in 1514 for Cardinal Wolsey, more than 2,500 men were employed in the construction of the 1,000-room palace of Hampton Court. In a desperate bid to retain royal favour, Wolsey gave the palace to Henry VIII in 1525, although he continued to live there for some years. After he gained possession in 1529, Henry enlarged the palace, as did William III, who hired Sir Christopher Wren to redesign the East Front at the end of the 17th century. Legend has it that two of Henry VIII's wives, Jane Seymour and Catherine Howard, haunt the palace to this day.

RICHMOND PALACE

Built in 1500 by Henry VIII on the site of an early royal palace, Richmond Palace was designed in the Gothic style around a central courtyard and it was one of the most imposing of the Tudor palaces. Situated in Surrey near the River Thames, the palace took its name from the title held by Henry VII's father, Edmund Tudor, whose earldom was named after the Yorkshire town of Richmond.

ROYAL RUIN
Richmond Palace (above) fell into disrepair during the mid-17th century and only the gatehouse survives today.

THE SIX WIVES OF HENRY VIII

THE MUCH-MARRIED KING

HENRY VIII HOLDS THE RECORD as the most married of English kings. His first three marriages were love matches fuelled not only by his lusty disposition and roving eye but also by a fervent desire to produce a male heir to the throne. Indeed, Henry's desire for a son was so great that he was prepared to annul his first marriage – risking excommunication by the Pope – and execute his second wife in order to achieve his dynastic ambitions. His third wife Jane Seymour, whom he genuinely loved, died giving him the son he craved, and his subsequent three marriages were motivated more by the search for a suitable step-mother for his children and for companionship than by his need for sexual gratification.

CATHERINE
Catherine of Aragon was an attractive woman with red-brown hair, a pretty mouth and nose and lovely eyes.

ANNE
As this portrait (above right) reveals, Anne Boleyn possessed raven hair, an almond-shaped mouth and black eyes, which captivated the King.

ANNE BOLEYN
Anne was already pregnant with Elizabeth (later Elizabeth I) when she married Henry in 1533. After Elizabeth's birth and a subsequent miscarriage and two still-births, the King lost interest in Anne. He turned his attentions to Jane Seymour and in May 1536 had Anne executed on a charge of high treason.

CATHERINE OF ARAGON
In 1509 Henry married Catherine of Aragon, the widow of his older brother, Arthur. The couple had eight children, but only Mary survived infancy. Desperate for a male heir, Henry had the marriage annulled in 1533 after falling for Anne Boleyn.

JANE SEYMOUR

Even as Anne Boleyn was pregnant with her second child, Henry was casting his eyes in other directions. He fell in love with Jane Seymour, one of Anne's ladies-in-waiting, but she only responded to his overtures after Anne had been executed. Within 18 months of their marriage in 1536, Jane bore him a son, Edward, but died soon after childbirth.

ANNE
Described by Henry as the "Mare of Flanders", Anne of Cleves (left) was ugly, dull and unable to speak English.

CATHERINE HOWARD

After the annulment of his marriage to Anne of Cleves, Henry made overtures to Catherine Howard. They were married on 28 July 1540, but Catherine maintained liaisons with younger lovers and when Henry found out she was executed for high treason in February 1542.

CATHERINE
A far from virtuous woman, Catherine Howard (left) was plumpish, vivacious, of sensuous disposition and unfaithful to her husband Henry.

ANNE OF CLEVES

Devastated by Jane Seymour's death, Henry undertook an arranged marriage with the German princess, Anne of Cleves. The couple were married in January 1540, but Henry refused to consummate the relationship, and the marriage was annulled in July.

JANE SEYMOUR
Pictured immediately to the right of Henry, and attended by his children Mary (left), Edward (centre) and Elizabeth (right), Jane Seymour was fair, pale-faced, of medium height, "full of goodness", modest and even-tempered.

CATHERINE
Catherine Parr (above) was well-educated, agreeable and a not-unattractive woman who knew how to handle the King during his disease-ridden old age.

CATHERINE PARR

In 1543, having recovered from his betrayal by Catherine Howard, Henry married the twice-widowed Catherine Parr. The King saw her as an ideal step-mother for his three children and a woman who would show due consideration to him during his few remaining years. Both expected few if any physical demands of each other. In all this he was to be proved correct. A year after Henry's death in 1547, Catherine married Thomas Seymour, uncle to the new king Edward VI, but she died in childbirth the following year.

THE REFORMATION
THE BREAK WITH ROME

IN 1517 MARTIN LUTHER, a German theologian, published 95 theses or arguments attacking corruption in the Roman Catholic Church. As his ideas spread, reformers, who became known as Protestants, emerged throughout Europe. A theological debate ensued that eventually erupted into religious warfare that was to last for well over a century. In England, Henry VIII initially defended the Catholic church. However, when the Pope refused to grant him a divorce from his first wife, the King broke with Rome and declared himself Supreme Head of the Church of England.

DEFENDER OF THE FAITH
In 1521 Pope Leo X invested Henry VIII with the title Fidei Defensor – *Defender of the Faith – after the King published a pamphlet,* Assertio Septem Sacramentorum, *defending the Catholic church in the face of Protestant attack. English monarchs have borne this title ever since, even though the faith to be defended is now Protestant.*

SUPREME HEAD
This gold medal struck after the Reformation to celebrate Henry VIII's position as Supreme Head of the Church of England bears the inscription Fidei Defensor.

SIR THOMAS MORE
Sir Thomas More had trained as a lawyer and was one of Europe's leading intellectuals. Four centuries after his execution in 1535, he was canonized by Pope Pius XI.

THE KING'S SERVANTS

Throughout the stormy years of the English Reformation in the 1530s, two men guided the ship of state. The first, Thomas More, became Henry's Lord Chancellor in 1529, the first layman to hold the office. However, when Henry insisted that More take the Oath of Supremacy to acknowledge the King as head of the English Church, he refused. After resigning his office in 1532, More was imprisoned in the Tower and finally beheaded in 1535.

More's successor as the King's principal servant was Thomas Cromwell, who had worked under Cardinal Wolsey. Cromwell was ordered by the King to enforce the 1534 Act of Supremacy and strip the monasteries of their power and wealth. But in 1540, having arranged an unsuitable marriage between Henry and Anne of Cleves, Cromwell was arrested and put to death on a trumped-up charge of treason.

*Built in 1090, Castle
Acre Priory in Norfolk
was dissolved in 1539.
This view down the
nave shows the west
front of the building,
which originally
featured Romanesque-
style twin towers.*

DISSOLUTION OF THE MONASTERIES

After Henry VIII's break with Rome,
Cromwell set up a commission to examine
the state of the English monasteries.
Many were found to be racked with
corruption. The King, who urgently
needed money to finance his extravagant
lifestyle, ordered their dissolution. In
1536 the smaller monasteries were closed
and their property confiscated. The
remaining monasteries were similarly
dealt with in 1539.

THOMAS CROMWELL
*Born in 1485
the son of a
blacksmith,
Thomas
Cromwell became
a member of the
Privy Council in
1531, rising to
become Lord Privy
Seal in 1536.
Cromwell was the
administrative genius
behind the English
Reformation,
dissolving the
monasteries and
reforming the
workings of English
government.*

THE GREAT BIBLE

THE BIBLE IN ENGLISH

The first complete translation of the
Bible into English was completed in 1535
by Miles Coverdale and published in
Zurich. In 1537, Henry VIII licensed for
publication in England a translation by
Thomas Matthew for general reading in
churches; it was this translation that
formed the basis of the Great Bible
that was issued in 1539. Again
translated by Miles Coverdale, the
Great Bible went through numerous
editions – the 1540 edition bearing a
foreword by Thomas Cranmer,
Archbishop of Canterbury, after
whom it is often named – and became
the authorized Bible for use in the
Anglican church until it was
replaced in 1571.

EDWARD VI

1547–1553

THE COAT OF ARMS OF EDWARD VI

EDWARD VI ASCENDED the throne at the age of nine in 1547, but because he was a minor the government was managed by two Protectors throughout his six-year reign. The first Protector was Edward's uncle, Edward Seymour, Duke of Somerset, the second, from 1550, John Dudley, Earl of Warwick, later Duke of Northumberland. Under their guidance, measures were introduced to consolidate the Reformation in England: the Catholic mass was declared illegal and a new Book of Common Prayer was introduced. These reforms were barely in place when, in late 1552, Edward caught tuberculosis, dying the following year.

EDWARD VI

- **Born** Hampton Court Palace, Surrey, 12 Oct 1537, son of Henry VIII and Jane Seymour.
- **Acceded** 28 Jan 1547.
- **Crowned** Westminster Abbey, 20 Feb 1547.
- **Died** Greenwich Palace, 6 July 1553, aged 15.

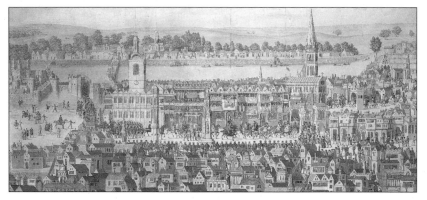

A ROYAL PROCESSION
On the eve of his coronation Edward was carried in a procession (above) from the Tower of London through the streets of the city to Westminster. The procession took most of the day, for there were countless stops for him to enjoy musical recitals and to receive gifts from a loyal and excited populace.

EDWARD'S CORONATION

On 20 February 1547 the nine-year-old Edward VI underwent a coronation ceremony in Westminster Abbey that lasted nearly seven hours, some five hours less than that for an adult king. The coronation was followed in the evening by an elaborate banquet and lavish reception for the assembled nobility and other dignitaries.

THE REFORMATION

During Edward's reign the religious reformation that had begun under his father was consolidated. An Act of Uniformity was passed in 1549 which prohibited the use of the Catholic mass, and the clergy were ordered to remove statues of the saints and icons in churches and to whitewash over all wall paintings. This caused great offence in many districts, and in Devon and Cornwall it led to a revolt, which was put down with severity, using German mercenary troops.

IN VICTORY
This piece of Tudor propaganda, painted by an unknown artist in 1548-9, combines portraits of, from left to right, Henry VIII (in bed), Edward VI, the Dukes of Somerset and Northumberland, and Thomas Cranmer, Archbishop of Canterbury, as well as other lords. At their foot lies a defeated Pope, the whole painting being an allegory of the triumph of the English Protestant Reformation over the Catholic Church.

EDWARD VI
Despite attempts by the unknown artist of this painting (right) to portray Edward in the same light as his father, the reality of the King as a small, pale child who suffered from poor health for much of his life is painfully evident.

THE BOY KING

Until the age of six, Edward was brought up with his half-sister Elizabeth (the future Elizabeth I). From then on he was groomed for kingship by his tutor, John Cheke. Edward was a precocious child who could be somewhat priggish at times, yet he was also tolerant and kind-hearted, loathing the practice of burning Catholic heretics at the stake.

EVENTS OF THE REIGN 1547 – 1553

◆ 1547 Edward VI accedes to the throne after the death of his father Henry VIII.

◆ 1547 Edward Seymour, Earl of Hertford, Edward VI's uncle, is invested as Duke of Somerset and Protector of England.

◆ 1547 The English army defeats the Scots at the Battle of Pinkie as part of an attempt to force a marriage between Mary, Queen of Scots, and Edward VI.

◆ 1549 The First Act of Uniformity is passed, making the Roman Catholic mass illegal.

◆ 1549 The First Book of Common Prayer is issued, which changes the Church service from Latin to English.

◆ 1550 The Duke of Somerset is deposed as Protector of England and replaced by John Dudley, Earl of Warwick, who creates himself Duke of Northumberland.

◆ 1552 Somerset is executed.

◆ 1553 The Duke of Northumberland persuades Edward to nominate Lady Jane Grey as his heir in an attempt to secure the Protestant succession.

◆ 1553 Edward VI dies at Greenwich Palace.

BOOK OF COMMON PRAYER
Officially known as the First Prayer Book of Edward VI, the Book of Common Prayer was first issued in 1549.

A NEW SERVICE

In order to bring the English church services in line with the teachings of the Reformation, Thomas Cranmer, Archbishop of Canterbury, wrote a new prayer book in sonorous and beautiful language. First issued in 1549, it is still used by many Anglicans today.

MARY I

1553–1558

THE DAUGHTER OF HENRY VIII and his first wife, Catherine of Aragon, Mary was, like her mother, a fervent Catholic. She suffered years of humiliation after her parents' divorce in 1533, and was then denied the succession by her brother Edward VI, who left the throne to the Protestant Lady Jane Grey in 1553. However, a few days into Jane's reign, Mary advanced on London and claimed the throne. Once crowned, Mary burned numerous Protestants at the stake for heresy, repealed Protestant legislation and restored Papal supremacy in England. However, her marriage in 1554 to the Catholic Philip of Spain failed to produce an heir and Mary died embittered in 1558.

THE COAT OF ARMS OF MARY I

👑 MARY I

- ◆ *Born* Greenwich Palace, 18 Feb 1516, daughter of Henry VIII and Catherine of Aragon.
- ◆ *Acceded* 19 July 1553.
- ◆ *Crowned* Westminster Abbey, 1 Oct 1553.
- ◆ *Married* Philip of Spain, Winchester Cathedral, 25 July 1554.
- ◆ *Died* St James's Palace, London, 17 Nov 1558, aged 42.

A CATHOLIC HUSBAND

Early in 1554 Mary announced her intention to marry Philip of Spain. The nation was appalled at the prospect of a Catholic foreigner sharing the English throne, but a revolt against the union was quickly put down. Mary married Philip in July 1554. However, their four-year marriage was an unhappy one, they had no children and Philip spent hardly any time with Mary in England.

BETROTHAL
A shilling coin (above) and a portrait (below) show the royal couple.

QUEEN JANE

On the instigation of Edward VI's Protector, Lady Jane Grey was proclaimed queen upon the death of Edward VI in an attempt to secure a Protestant succession. Jane reigned for nine days before she was deposed by Mary; she was then imprisoned and executed on Tower Green in 1554.

LADY JANE GREY
Shown here in a portrait by Master John, Lady Jane Grey embraced wholeheartedly her responsibilities as queen during her nine-day reign.

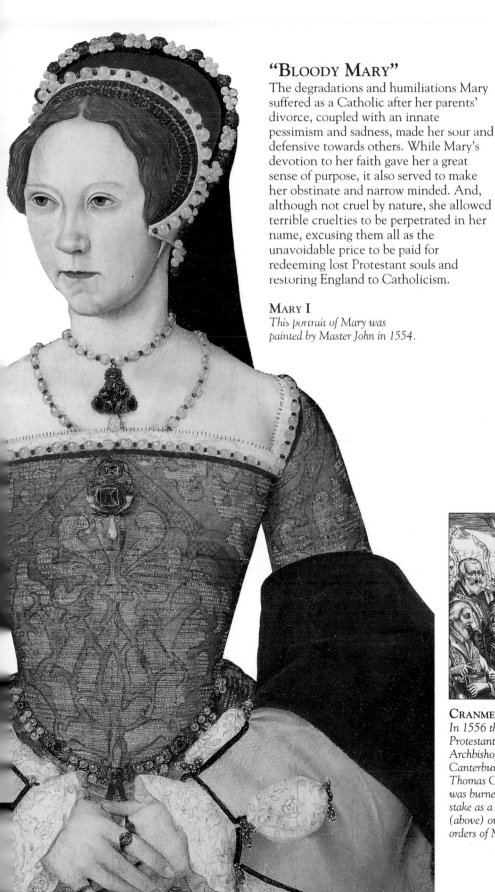

"BLOODY MARY"

The degradations and humiliations Mary suffered as a Catholic after her parents' divorce, coupled with an innate pessimism and sadness, made her sour and defensive towards others. While Mary's devotion to her faith gave her a great sense of purpose, it also served to make her obstinate and narrow minded. And, although not cruel by nature, she allowed terrible cruelties to be perpetrated in her name, excusing them all as the unavoidable price to be paid for redeeming lost Protestant souls and restoring England to Catholicism.

MARY I
This portrait of Mary was painted by Master John in 1554.

EVENTS OF THE REIGN
1553 – 1558

◆ **1553** Lady Jane Grey is proclaimed Queen by the Protector, Northumberland. After nine days, Mary arrives in London, Lady Jane Grey is arrested and Mary is crowned.
◆ **1554** After Mary declares her intention to marry Philip of Spain, Sir Thomas Wyatt leads a revolt to depose her.
◆ **1554** Wyatt's rebellion is crushed; Wyatt, Lady Jane Grey and her husband are executed.
◆ **1554** Mary marries Philip of Spain in Winchester Cathedral.
◆ **1554** The persecution of Protestants begins, the heresy laws are revived and England is reconciled to Papal authority.
◆ **1555** Three Protestant bishops are burned at the stake for heresy.
◆ **1556** Cardinal Reginald Pole is made Archbishop of Canterbury.
◆ **1556** Thomas Cranmer, former Archbishop of Canterbury, is burned at the stake for heresy.
◆ **1556** Philip becomes King of Spain; he leaves England, never to return.
◆ **1557** England declares war on France.
◆ **1558** The port of Calais – the last English possession in France – is captured by the French.
◆ **1558** Mary dies at St James's Palace in London.

CRANMER
In 1556 the Protestant former Archbishop of Canterbury, Thomas Cranmer, was burned at the stake as a heretic (above) on the orders of Mary.

RESTORATION OF CATHOLICISM

In order to return England to the Catholic fold, Mary ordered the dismissal and execution of many leading Protestant bishops and the appointment of reliable Roman Catholics to replace them. In 1554 all anti-Catholic laws passed during the reign of Edward VI were rescinded.

ELIZABETH I

1558–1603

THE COAT OF ARMS OF ELIZABETH I

DESPITE A TRAUMATIC EARLY LIFE – her mother was executed when she was only three and her half-sister Mary had her imprisoned during her brief reign – Elizabeth displayed strength of purpose and prudence as queen. Strong-willed and imperious like her father Henry VIII, but unlike him fair and grateful to devoted servants, she picked advisers who proved able and loyal. Throughout her 45-year reign Elizabeth showed considerable political acumen in defying a predominantly Catholic Europe intent on overturning the Protestant faith, while presiding over a period of adventure that saw a vast expansion of English trade and prosperity and significant developments in the arts.

👑 **ELIZABETH I**

◆ **Born** Greenwich Palace, 7 Sept 1533, daughter of Henry VIII and Anne Boleyn.
◆ **Acceded** 17 Nov 1558.
◆ **Crowned** Westminster Abbey, 15 Jan 1559.
◆ **Died** Richmond Palace, Surrey, 24 Mar 1603, aged 69.

HATFIELD HOUSE
Elizabeth was given a house at Hatfield (right) in 1533 after she was born, and lived there most of the time until 1558.

MATTHEW PARKER
Appointed Archbishop of Canterbury by Elizabeth in 1559, Matthew Parker introduced measures that created a compromise between Catholicism and Calvinism in the church.

WILLIAM CECIL
In 1558 Elizabeth appointed William Cecil (later Lord Burghley) Chief Secretary of State. In 1572 he became Lord Treasurer, an office he held until he died in 1598.

CROWN SERVANTS

Of the many fine servants of the crown who held office during Elizabeth's reign, William Cecil and Matthew Parker stand out as particularly astute appointments. Cecil served Elizabeth with the highest distinction for 40 years as principal adviser and minister, introducing important financial reforms, countering plots, and arranging support for the Protestant cause in Europe. Parker, as Archbishop of Canterbury, helped to establish a moderate Church of England after the excesses of Mary's persecution of Protestants.

ELIZABETH I
This portrait of the Queen by Marcus Gheeraerts the Younger was painted in about 1592, when the Queen was nearly 60.

LONDON
Between 1530 and 1600, a period of increasing prosperity, the population of London grew rapidly from some 50,000 to over 200,000.

ELIZABETH

Red-headed and of average height, Elizabeth I was handsome rather than beautiful, proud, wise, brave, affable, gracious and tolerant, all characteristics that helped her to overcome the many difficulties she faced during her reign. The fact that she was also vain, mean, imperious, impulsive and sarcastic never seemed to put off the numerous suitors who courted her up to the age of 60. Elizabeth never married.

EVENTS OF THE REIGN 1558 – 1603

◆ **1558** Elizabeth accedes to the throne on the death of her half-sister Mary.
◆ **1559** Act of Supremacy makes Elizabeth head of the Church of England.
◆ **1562** John Hawkins and Francis Drake make first slave-trading voyage to America.
◆ **1562** Elizabeth gives aid to the Protestant Huguenots in the French Wars of Religion.
◆ **1563-4** 17,000 die of the Plague in London.
◆ **1568** Mary Queen of Scots flees to England from Scotland and is imprisoned by Elizabeth.
◆ **1577-80** Francis Drake sails round the world.
◆ **1586** Mary Queen of Scots is sent to trial.
◆ **1587** Mary Queen of Scots is executed.
◆ **1587** Drake attacks the Spanish fleet in Cadiz Harbour.
◆ **1588** The English navy and bad weather defeat Spanish Armada.
◆ **1590** Edmund Spenser's *The Faerie Queen* is published.
◆ **1595-6** Sir Walter Raleigh makes his first expedition to South America.
◆ **1601** Earl of Essex is executed for leading a revolt against Elizabeth's government.
◆ **1601** A Poor Law is passed introducing a poor relief rate on property owners.
◆ **1601** Shakespeare's *Hamlet* is performed on stage.
◆ **1603** Elizabeth I dies at Richmond Palace, Surrey.

THE BARBER JEWEL
Tradition has it that this jewel was made for William Barber to mark his delivery from the stake in 1558. He was saved when Mary died and Elizabeth became Queen.

ELIZABETH I

THE LATER YEARS

THE ARMADA

Personally, politically and on matters of religion, Elizabeth I was not on good terms with Philip II of Spain, her former brother-in-law. As an upholder of the Protestant faith, she had no wish to submit to Philip's demands that England return to Catholicism. Their uneasy relationship worsened after Elizabeth sent aid in 1585 to the Dutch Protestants who were fighting for independence from Spanish rule, and Philip retaliated by encouraging plots against the Queen, notably by Mary, Queen of Scots. Mary's subsequent execution, ordered by Elizabeth, proved the final straw, and in September 1587 the outraged Spanish king issued detailed orders for the preparation of a great Armada of ships to invade England.

RALLYING THE TROOPS
Fearing that an invasion was imminent Elizabeth visited her army gathered at Tilbury (right). In a famous speech, which began "I know I have but the body of a weak and feeble woman, but I have the heart and stomach of a king", she exhorted them to ward off the impending assault.

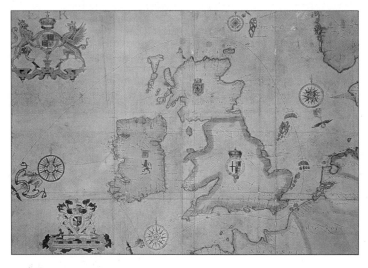

THE LONG VOYAGE
The contemporary map above shows the route the Armada took in its anti-clockwise circumnavigation of the British Isles. It is not known exactly how many ships were wrecked on the stormy voyage home, but at least 11,000 men – one-third of the total number of crew and soldiers on board – were lost at sea. The remnants of the Armada struggled into Spanish ports during autumn 1588.

THE SPANISH ARMADA

In July 1588, 130 Spanish ships set sail from Lisbon carrying a crew of 10,000 and an army of 20,000 soldiers for the invasion. The Armada was first sighted near the Lizard on 29 July 1588. A running battle followed as English ships attacked the vastly superior Spanish force as it sailed up the Channel and anchored off Calais. The English then sent in fireships to break up the Spanish fleet, forcing them out of formation and back into the Channel off Gravelines, where the decisive action was fought on 9 August. Battered by English guns, the Spanish eventually retreated up the east coast and around the north of Scotland, where severe Atlantic gales and the rocky coastline wrecked the majority of the surviving ships.

ROYAL FAVOURITES

Elizabeth spent her life surrounded by suitors yet she never married. A shrewd observer commented: "The Queen would like everyone to be in love with her, but I doubt whether she will ever be in love with anyone enough to marry him."

THE EARL OF LEICESTER

Robert Dudley, 1st Earl of Leicester (above), was a strong candidate for the Queen's hand after 1560. She refused him, although he continued to enjoy her favours until his death in 1588.

THE EARL OF ESSEX

Step-son of Robert Dudley, Robert Devereux, 2nd Earl of Essex (right), was Elizabeth I's favourite during the 1590s. He was executed for treason in 1601 after he rebelled against the government.

IN RETROSPECT

On 30 November 1601 Elizabeth addressed her final Parliament with these words: "Though God hath raised me high, yet this I account the glory of any crown, that I have reigned with your loves. ... Of myself I must say this. I was never any greedy, scraping grasper, nor a strict fast-holding prince, nor yet a waster. It is not my desire to live or reign longer than my life and reign shall be for your good. You never had, nor shall have any that will love you better." Sixteen months later she was dead.

END OF AN ERA

Elizabeth died at Richmond Palace on 24 March 1603 at the age of 69. Her body was taken down river to Whitehall for her funeral in Westminster Abbey on 28 April. Her funeral cortège is shown above.

CHAPTER SEVEN

THE
KINGS & QUEENS
OF SCOTLAND
843 – 1603

Scotland, like Wales, has a much longer history than England. After some 1,200 years of pagan Celtic civilization, into which the Romans made inroads in the first and second centuries, Christianity reached the country at the end of the fourth century. By the time St Columba founded his great monastery at Iona in the 560s, Scotland was divided into four kingdoms: Dalriada in the west, peopled by Scots from Ireland; the Pictish kingdom in the north; Strathclyde in the south-west; and Bernicia, or Lothian, in the east.

The First King

In the 840s Kenneth MacAlpin, King of Dalriada, overcame the Picts and created a united country in the north of Scotland. This was the beginning of Scotland as a nation, and Kenneth is rightly regarded as its first king. Kenneth's descendant, Malcolm II, conquered Lothian in 1018; Strathclyde joined his kingdom a year later. Malcolm was thus king of a nation whose territory was much the same as it is today. For good or ill, Malcolm also began the process of

SCOTLAND
When Scotland was an independent nation, its kings ruled their country from Edinburgh Castle (left). One of those kings, James II, who reigned from 1437-60, is shown above.

introducing English ways into Scotland, a process pursued more vigorously by his great-grandson, Malcolm III, whose reign from 1057-93 marked the beginning of centuries of conflict between Scotland and England. Time and again English kings cast their greedy eyes upon their northern neighbour, determined one way or another to take it over.

War with England

The story of Scotland from the 11th to the 16th century is in large measure one of valiant struggle by the Scots to preserve their fragile independence, convinced as they were of their destiny as a separate people with a major contribution to make to European civilization. This struggle was often waged by the kings, notably Robert Bruce and the first four Jameses, the latter in the face of bitter opposition from their lords, who had less feeling for Scotland than for their own self-aggrandisement. Yet the union of the two countries came in the end not by war but through the peaceful succession of a Scottish king to the English throne in 1603.

SCOTLAND UNITED

843–1034

DURING THE PERIOD when the English kingdoms of the Heptarchy were struggling with one another for supremacy, there was a similar struggle in Scotland between the Picts, Scots and Angles. The Angles were crushed by the Picts in 685, who were in turn defeated by the Scots under Kenneth MacAlpin in 843. Kenneth then became the first King of Scotland, from whom all kings of Scotland were descended. Kenneth's immediate successors had to deal with continuous Viking raids, as well as aggravation from England. But in 1018 Malcolm II routed a huge Viking and English army, allowing him to bring Lothian and then Strathclyde into the kingdom and complete the unification of Scotland.

ABERLEMNO

The Pictish stone at Aberlemno, near Forfar in Angus, shows on one side a clash between rival armies using cavalry and infantry. There is evidence to show that the Picts were skilled horseriders, and Kenneth MacAlpin must doubtless have valued access to such cavalry resources once he had united the Picts with the Scots in 843.

CELTIC ART

As in Ireland, Celtic art and craft skills were of a high order in Scotland. Jewellers were adept at setting precious stones in silver, and displayed almost fastidious care in simpler decorative items such as rings, necklaces, bracelets and brooches.

HUNTERSTON BROOCH

A typical example of eighth century Celtic art, the brooch above was found in 1826 by workers digging drains at Hunterston Castle in West Kilbride.

THE PICTS

The chroniclers of the eighth and ninth centuries regarded the Picts as shadowy people who originally came from Scythia to the north of the Black Sea. Yet the Picts left behind several fascinating monuments that tell us much about them. Among these are upright stones with carvings of animals, symbols, portraits, landscapes, even battle scenes.

THE VIKING RAIDS

In 843 Kenneth MacAlpin united the whole of Scotland north of the Forth. But his successors faced the problem of continuous assaults on the Scottish mainland and islands by the Vikings. At times the Scots were successful, defeating the Vikings and expelling them from their coastal settlements, but the war was one of attrition with little success on either side.

ABERNETHY

In order to defend themselves against Viking raids, some of the monasteries built tall, round towers which acted as refuges during raids. Inside the towers were several floors able to house a community of monks and keep them safe from attack. Three of these towers still survive, the best known of which is at Abernethy (left). The Vikings were not just savage raiders, however, for they produced fine jewellery and other items (below).

COMING OF CHRISTIANITY

Christianity first came to Scotland with St Ninian, a British-born scholar who founded a church at Whithorn in Galloway in the 390s. About 150 years later, Columba, an Irish scholar from Derry, left Ireland and set up a monastery on Iona, off the west coast of Scotland, sending out missionaries to convert the Picts and Scots. By the time of Columba's death in 597 Christianity had taken root in much of Scotland.

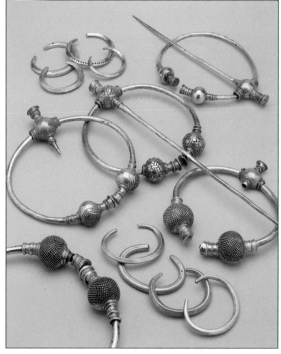

IONA

The monastery established by Columba on Iona (left) in the mid-sixth century became the most renowned seat of learning in the Celtic world throughout the next 300 years. At the end of the eighth century and the start of the ninth century, when Scotland began to endure Viking raids, there were several attacks on the monastery. These got so bad that the monks were forced to flee to Ireland for a few years.

SCOTLAND UNITED
843 – 1034

◆ **843** Kenneth MacAlpin, King of the Scots, defeats the Picts and unites Scotland north of the River Forth.
◆ **859** Death of Kenneth MacAlpin; he is succeeded by his brother Donald I.
◆ **863** Donald I dies and is succeeded by Kenneth's son, Constantine I.
◆ **877** Constantine I is defeated and killed in battle by the Danes and is succeeded by his brother Aedh.
◆ **878** Aedh is murdered and is succeeded by Eocha, grandson of Kenneth MacAlpin.
◆ **889** Death of Eocha; he is succeeded by Donald II, son of Constantine I.
◆ **900** Death of Donald II and succession of Aedh's son, Constantine II.
◆ **937** Constantine II, along with the Danes and others, is defeated at the Battle of Brunanburh by Acthelstan of England.
◆ **942** Constantine II abdicates and retires to a monastery; he is succeeded by Malcolm I, son of Donald II.
◆ **954** Malcolm I is killed and is succeeded by Indulphus, son of Constantine II.
◆ **962** Indulphus abdicates and is succeeded by Dubh (Duff), son of Malcolm I.
◆ **967** Dubh is murdered and is succeeded by Cuilean, son of Indulphus.
◆ **971** Cuilean dies and is succeeded by Kenneth II, Malcolm I's younger son.
◆ **995** Death of Kenneth II; he is succeeded by Constantine III, son of Cuilean.
◆ **997** Constantine III is murdered and succeeded by Kenneth III, son of Dubh.
◆ **1005** Kenneth III is killed in a civil war and is succeeded by Malcolm II, son of Kenneth II.
◆ **1018** Malcolm II wins the Battle of Carham against a huge army of English and Vikings, bringing Lothian, in the south-east of the country, into the kingdom. The independent Kingdom of Strathclyde, in the west of the country, joins Scotland shortly afterwards, uniting the whole of Scotland within roughly its present boundaries for the first time.
◆ **1031** Malcolm swears allegiance to Canute of England.
◆ **1034** Death of Malcolm II.

CONFLICT WITH ENGLAND

1034–1214

THE PERIOD BETWEEN the accession of Duncan I in 1034 and the death of William the Lyon in 1214 was marked by continual conflict with England. In 1040 Duncan I invaded England but was driven out and on his return was killed in a civil war. He was succeeded by his cousin Macbeth, not the king of Shakespeare's play but a ruler of stature who brought peace to his kingdom. His successor, Malcolm III, revived the war with England and invaded five times in an attempt to annex the northern counties. David I continued the attack, as did William the Lyon, who was captured by the English in 1174. He returned home only after accepting humiliating terms.

DURHAM CHARTER
At about the time of the brief reign of Duncan II, the practice of confirming grants of land by charter was introduced. The charter above was issued by Duncan to the monks of Durham.

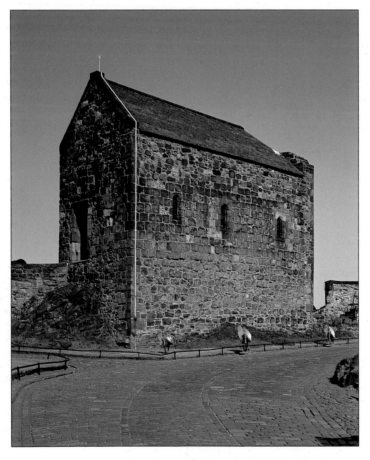

MALCOLM III
With the accession of Malcolm III in 1057, Scotland entered a new phase. Feudal institutions from Norman England were introduced into the country, and the first of many attempts was made to annex the three most northern counties of England. His second wife, Margaret, was a learned and devout woman who tried to reform the Scottish church.

MARGARET'S CHAPEL
The day before her death in 1093, Margaret heard mass in the chapel she had had built inside Edinburgh Castle (above).

FAMILY STRUGGLES
After the death of Malcolm III in 1093, there was a considerable period of confusion. His brother, Donald Bane, was his rightful successor but he was driven out in 1094 by Malcolm's son, Duncan, who died shortly after. Donald Bane was then restored for three years before once again losing the throne, this time to Duncan's half-brother Edgar, who ruled until 1107.

CASTLE BUILDING
During the reign of Malcolm III, the first castles were built in Scotland by the powerful barons. At first these constructions were simple motte-and-bailey castles, but by 1100 the first stone castle appeared by the side of Loch Sween in Argyll.

DAVID I

One of the greatest of Scotland's early kings was David I. The youngest of Malcolm III's sons, David continued the practice of introducing feudalism into Scotland. Several powerful Norman families settled in Scotland, including the de Brus (Bruce) family, the de Bailleuls (Balliol) from Picardy, and the FitzAlans from Brittany, whose senior representative became hereditary Steward of Scotland and took the name of Stewart.

DAVID I
A patron of the church, David founded several abbeys, notably Kelso, Dryburgh, Jedburgh and Melrose (right). A detail from the charter founding the abbey of Kelso is shown above, depicting its founder David I sitting next to his grandson Malcolm IV intertwined in the capital letter M.

CASTLE SWEEN
The first stone castle to be built in Scotland, Castle Sween (below) is on the shore of Loch Sween in Argyll.

TWO ALEXANDERS

1214–1306

THE 13TH CENTURY was a time of hope followed by despair for Scotland. Alexander II came to advantageous terms with Henry III which enabled him to direct his attentions to the Vikings, still dominant in the Western Isles. Alexander prepared an all-out assault, but died in 1249 before it was properly launched. His son, Alexander III, finally overcame the Vikings at the Battle of Largs in 1263, but within a generation, an English king was dictating to Scotland which king she should have, and with what powers. By 1296 Scotland was under direct English rule. This was resisted by William Wallace, who harassed the English until his death in 1305, when his role fell to Robert Bruce, defiantly crowned king in 1306.

ALEXANDER II

The son of William the Lyon, Alexander was made of stronger stuff than his mis-named father. He came to the throne in 1214 and determined to end the Viking occupation of the Western Isles and some areas of the mainland. In 1249 he assembled a huge fleet of ships to invade the Western Isles, but on his way to join the fleet, he died. The expedition was temporarily called off.

ALEXANDER III

Alexander became king in 1249 when he was only eight, and for a time Scotland was ruled by regents. In 1263, at the age of 22, he crushed an army of Vikings at Largs on the Firth of Clyde and finally expelled the Vikings from the Western Isles. Alexander then turned to domestic matters, showing great interest in the proper administration of justice and often sitting in judgement himself. He died suddenly in 1286 when he accidentally fell off his horse down a cliff, leaving the throne to his four-year-old granddaughter, Margaret.

A STRONG RULER
King of Scotland from 1214 to 1249, Alexander II married Joan, the sister of Henry III of England, and maintained good relations with his southern neighbour for most of his reign. A strong ruler, he asserted control over most of present-day Scotland. His seal is shown above.

BOTHWELL CASTLE
Alexander III repaired and improved a number of royal castles and started work on new ones, including Bothwell (right), one of the strongest castles in the kingdom.

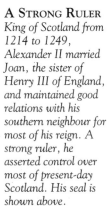

◆ **1214** Accession of Alexander II, son of William the Lyon.

◆ **1217** Peace treaty with England guarantees peace between the two countries for almost 20 years.

◆ **1222** Alexander conquers those parts of Argyll under Viking rule.

◆ **1237** Border between Scotland and England agreed by Treaty of York. The border runs along the River Tweed and the Cheviot Hills to the Solway Firth; Alexander renounces the Scottish claim to Northumberland and Westmoreland.

◆ **1249** Alexander launches an invasion of the Western Isles but dies before the expedition sets sail. He is succeeded by his son, Alexander III.

◆ **1263** Alexander III triumphs over a Viking army, led by Haakon IV of Norway, at the Battle of Largs.

◆ **1266** Western Isles acquired from Vikings.

◆ **1286** Alexander dies at Burntisland, Fife, after falling off his horse and down a cliff. His granddaughter Margaret, the Maid of Norway, aged only 4, succeeds him.

◆ **1290** Margaret dies on her way back to Scotland. The Scottish lords ask Edward I to select a successor.

◆ **1292** John Balliol, great-great-great-grandson of David I, is chosen to be king.

◆ **1295** Treaty between Scotland and France begins the "Auld Alliance".

◆ **1296** Edward I invades Scotland and deposes Balliol. As overlord of Scotland, he appoints officials to rule on his behalf.

◆ **1296** Edward seizes the Stone of Scone – on which the Scottish kings sit at their coronation – and takes it down to London (where it still is, under the Coronation Chair in Westminster Abbey).

◆ **1297** Rising of William Wallace, who defeats English army at Stirling Bridge.

◆ **1298** Wallace is defeated at Falkirk, and then conducts a lengthy guerrilla campaign against English rule.

◆ **1305** Wallace is captured by the English and taken to London, where he is tried for treason, and hanged, drawn and quartered.

◆ **1306** Robert Bruce assumes Wallace's role and is crowned at Scone as Robert I.

THE PATRIOT

In 1297 William Wallace, a patriotic Scot of Welsh descent, rose in revolt against English rule in Scotland. He defeated the English at Stirling Bridge but was himself defeated at Falkirk in 1298. For the next seven years he conducted a guerrilla campaign until he was betrayed in 1305 and sent to London, where he was executed for treason.

WILLIAM WALLACE

PAYING HOMAGE
When he became king in 1292, John Balliol had to pay homage to the English king, Edward I. His refusal to support Edward in 1296 led to an English invasion of Scotland.

CAERLAVEROCK
Much of the fighting between the English and the Scots after 1296 was centred on the possession of castles. Caerlaverock, on the Solway Firth, was besieged five times and changed hands often.

JOHN BALLIOL

In 1290 Alexander III's heir, the infant Margaret (who was known as the Maid of Norway because her father was King of Norway) died on her way home to Scotland. The Scottish lords could not agree about a successor, although there were several good candidates, and asked Edward I of England to chose. He picked the ineffectual John Balliol, a descendant of David I, who would do what Edward wanted. The English king frequently treated him with contempt, but in 1294 Balliol rejected a summons to join Edward on a campaign in France and instead made a treaty with France. In 1296 Edward retaliated by invading Scotland, massacring the garrison of Berwick and deposing Balliol. He then ruled Scotland directly.

ROBERT BRUCE

1306–1329

IN 1306 ROBERT BRUCE was crowned king at Scone, an event that enraged the dying Edward I of England, who set out once more to invade Scotland. Bruce had to flee, and for several years remained in hiding as he gathered his forces. After capturing several castles, he felt strong enough to attack Stirling Castle, one of the key fortresses occupied by the English. Edward II, the new English king, tried to relieve the siege in 1314 but his army was routed at the Battle of Bannockburn. This defeat did not, however, result in recognition of Scotland's independence: the Declaration of Arbroath, which demanded recognition of Scottish independence, made the Scots happy but achieved little south of the border. The fighting continued until 1328, when Edward III formally recognized Bruce as king of an independent Scotland.

ROBERT BRUCE

Bruce was of medium height, broad shouldered, with a fine head and penetrating eyes. He had considerable inventive powers, was extremely resilient, good natured, humane and courageous. For a time he had supported Edward I's activities in Scotland, partly because his family had had a number of privileges from the English kings, but he had joined Wallace's revolt when he was a young man, and in 1305, the capture and execution of Wallace confirmed his opposition to the rule of Edward I. Despite his involvement in the murder of his cousin, Sir John Comyn, in 1306, he was welcomed by his countrymen when he formally claimed the Scottish throne as Robert I.

THE NATURAL LEADER
When Edward I died in 1307 Bruce initiated a campaign to get the English out of Scotland, and quickly gathered widespread support largely through his personal magnetism. His victory at Bannockburn showed to the full his powers of leadership. The statue to the right, which stands at Bannockburn, commemorates his victory.

DEFIANCE
The threat to Scottish independence remained even after Bannockburn. Fighting continued until an invasion of England in 1327 persuaded the new king, Edward III, to recognize Scottish independence. The French chronicler, Froissart, reported the continuing Scottish defiance in his record of contemporary events, the Chronique. The scene he depicted above shows a message of defiance being delivered from Bruce to the young Edward III.

THE DECLARATION OF ARBROATH

After his victory at Bannockburn, Bruce expected England to leave the country alone. This did not happen and, in 1320 a number of Scottish lords and bishops met in Arbroath and wrote to Pope John XXII insisting that he recognize Scotland's independence. " For as long as one hundred of us shall remain alive we shall never in any wise consent to submit to the rule of the English, for it is not for glory we fight... but for freedom alone."

THE DECLARATION OF ARBROATH (above)

THE MONYMUSK RELIQUARY

A wooden casket in the shape of a Celtic chapel, the Monymusk Reliquary (below) is supposed to have been used by Kenneth MacAlpin to carry the relics of St Columba from Iona to Dunkeld, where they were reinterred. The casket was carried into battle at Bannockburn by the Abbot of Arbroath Abbey.

BANNOCKBURN

In June 1314 Robert Bruce besieged Stirling Castle. The English king sent a huge army to relieve the castle and it encamped at Bannockburn, about two miles to the south. On 24 June the two armies met. Bruce's Scottish army was one-third the size of the English army, but by forming schiltrons – rings of men with spears levelled at every point of assault – his soldiers managed to repel an attack and break the English lines. Amid scenes of chaos, the English ranks gave ground and then fled from the field, the defeated Edward II among them.

ROBERT BRUCE 1306 – 1329

◆ **1306** Robert Bruce is crowned as Robert I at Scone but is immediately driven into hiding by the English occupation army of Edward I.

◆ **1307** Edward I launches his final invasion of Scotland but dies on his way north. Bruce begins his campaign to drive the English out of Scotland.

◆ **1314** Bruce besieges Stirling Castle. An English army sent to break the siege is routed at the Battle of Bannockburn.

◆ **1315** Edward Bruce, Robert Bruce's brother, is offered and accepts the crown of Ireland by Irish lords.

◆ **1320** Declaration of Arbroath is signed by nearly all the lords and bishops in Scotland and is sent to the Pope.

◆ **1323** Truce between Robert Bruce and Edward II fails to prevent continuing warfare between the two countries.

◆ **1327** Edward II is deposed and is succeeded by Edward III.

◆ **1327** Bruce launches an invasion of England to force English recognition of Scotland's independence by England.

◆ **1328** English recognize Scotland's independence by the Treaty of Edinburgh; the treaty is ratified by the English in the Treaty of Northampton. Bruce is now formally recognized as King of Scotland.

◆ **1329** Death of Robert Bruce.

THE STATESMAN

Robert Bruce was a fine statesman, recognizing the desire of his kingdom for national sovereignty, and he devoted his life to achieving that end. The Declaration of Arbroath by so many lords and clergy was ample proof that they understood and appreciated what he was doing for his and their Scotland. The seal of Robert Bruce (above) shows the king mounted on horseback.

"DARK AND DRUBLIE DAYS"

1329–1406

THE REIGN OF DAVID II, son of Robert Bruce, was described by a contemporary as "dark and drublie days". David undid most of Bruce's good work and even offered to bequeath his kingdom to Edward III of England. His successor, Robert, became the first Stewart king of Scotland. Known as Old Blearie because of his bloodshot eyes, he was unable to give the country good government, and passed power over to his son, who eventually succeeded him as Robert III. But he was as ineffectual as his father, and died heartbroken in 1406 when his son James was captured at sea by pirates and taken to London, where Henry IV held him in confinement.

PRISONER OF THE ENGLISH

In 1332 Edward III of England engineered a bid for the Scottish throne by John Balliol's son, Edward, who drove David II into exile and had himself crowned. It was an uneasy usurpation, for it entailed the surrender of large parts of southern Scotland to English rule and in 1341 Balliol was expelled and David reclaimed his throne.

But in 1346 David invaded England in support of his hard-pressed French allies and was defeated at Neville's Cross. For the next 11 years he remained a prisoner in England until released in 1357 on payment of a huge ransom. By 1363 the financial situation in Scotland had got so bad that David returned to London to negotiate a cancellation of the ransom payments if he bequeathed his throne to Edward III. The Scottish Parliament repudiated the proposal, preferring to bankrupt the country rather than surrender its independence.

THE ALLIANCE IN ACTION
Both Scottish and French coats of arms are borne together in battle against the common enemy – the English (above).

EDWARD III AND DAVID II
For 11 years his prisoner, David II of Scotland offered Edward III of England the Scottish throne in return for his freedom (left).

THE AULD ALLIANCE

When, in 1294, John Balliol refused to join Edward I in a projected campaign in France, he entered into an alliance with France instead. It was the first in a long line of such arrangements between the two countries known as the "Auld Alliance". Over the next two centuries Scotland looked to France for help in its conflicts with England but it was not always forthcoming. The French were dismayed that the Scots preferred guerrilla warfare to open battle, and did not like the way they were expected to pay compensation for the damage their troops caused trampling over Scottish fields. Nevertheless the alliance held until the 1560s, when Scotland became Protestant and France remained Catholic.

ELGIN ABBEY
In 1390, in retaliation for criticism of his general conduct by the Bishop of Moray, Alexander Stewart collected a gang of "wyld, wykkyd Helandmen" and descended upon the Bishop's cathedral at Elgin and set fire to it. He then burned down the town as well. Because he was the King's brother, he was not called to account.

ROBERT III

The reign of Robert III (1390-1406) was characterized by violence and lawlessness. As one chronicler wrote in 1398, "there was no law in Scotland, but he who was stronger oppressed him who was weaker, and the whole realm was a den of thieves … justice… lay in exile outwith the bounds of the kingdom." Allowing for exaggeration, it was clearly a gloomy time. One of the chief villains was Alexander Stewart, the King's brother, a man with a horrendous reputation for violence and cruelty.

HERMITAGE CASTLE
One of the Scottish noble families emerging to great power in the late 14th century was the Douglas family, which owned huge tracts of land in the Lowlands and occupied many castles. One of these was Hermitage (left), which was begun in the late 13th century as simple rectangular tower-house. Extensively developed in the late 14th and 15th centuries, by 1560 it belonged to James Hepburn, Earl of Bothwell and lover of Mary, Queen of Scots.

EARLY STEWARTS

1406–1513

THE 15TH CENTURY in Scotland is sometimes written off as an age of lawlessness, dominated by endless conflict between the Stewart kings and the nobility, particularly a handful of great families which squabbled among themselves and almost ruined Scotland. It was also an age in which three out of the four kings were extremely powerful and dealt effectively with the dangers they faced. The Stewarts were immensely ambitious. They had come to greatness through marriage and held on to power with ruthlessness and skill. They also presided over a period of artistic advancement in which they played a leading role. All four kings succeeded to the throne as children, all four died violently. Yet they were on the whole good for Scotland.

RAVENSCRAIG

In the mid-15th century castles began to be built (and some older ones adapted) specifically for systematic defence by guns. One such castle was Ravenscraig in Fife, which was built by James II. James was enormously interested in artillery and pyrotechnics, an interest which led to his death in 1460, when he was killed by an exploding cannon.

THE POET KING
An accomplished poet and musician, James I encouraged an artistic revival in Scotland. This painting of his court (left) is by the Italian Pinturicchio.

FIREPOWER
The castle of Ravenscraig (above) was the first castle in Britain designed to be defended by artillery.

JAMES I

James I was only 12 when he became king in 1406, but as a prisoner of Henry IV he was to remain in captivity in England until 1424, Scotland being governed in his absence by the Duke of Albany. During the regency, some of the lords expanded their power enormously, and on his return, James determined to reform his country. His first parliament rectified abuses in taxation and in the dispensation of justice, and dealt severely with the factious Highland lords. These reforming policies made James many enemies, and he was assassinated in 1437.

JAMES IV

Described as "courageous, more than a king should be" and "of noble stature, and handsome", James IV was a popular king under whom Scotland reached its apogee as an independent nation.

JAMES IV (*above*)

JAMES III
(*left*)

JAMES II AND JAMES III

James II ruled from 1437 to 1460, successfully crushing the power of the great families. He helped Scotland's participation in the European Renaissance, founding Glasgow University in 1450. His son James III was only nine when he became king and so the country was governed by a Regency Council. In the 1470s James took matters into his own hands, but he was not of the same calibre as his father. Like his two predecessors, he patronized the arts and was a fine musician.

THE GREAT MICHAEL

One of James IV's many initiatives was a major expansion of the navy. The star of the new fleet was the Great Michael, *which, at 75 metres (240 feet) long and with 300 guns, was the biggest warship in the world at that time.*

LATER STEWARTS

1513–1603

THE LAST CENTURY of Scottish independence was probably the most disastrous. When James IV was killed at Flodden Field in 1513, it put Scotland at the mercy of the English. The new king, James V, was only 17 months old, and for 15 years Scotland was ruled by a Regency. In 1528 James took power himself and proved to be a competent and fair ruler. He died in 1542 a few days after his army had invaded England. His successor, Mary, had been born only the week before, and it perhaps would have been better for Scotland had she not been born at all, while her successor, James VI, who likewise succeeded as an infant in 1567, was in most respects to prove quite unworthy of the former greatness of the Stewarts.

THE CROWN JEWELS

Like most countries in Europe, Scotland has its royal regalia, (below), which are known as the "Honours of Scotland". The crown was restyled in about 1540 by James V, but it is not clear how much of it is older than that date, or how far back it goes. The sceptre was presented to James IV by Pope Alexander VI and was renovated by James V. The sword was made in Rome and was given to James IV by Pope Julius II in 1507.

JAMES V

James V grew up in an unsettled and often dangerous environment, pulled in all directions by family and associates divided between favouring closer links with England and stronger ties with France. When he took control in 1528, he displayed courage and ruthlessness. He had little time for the nobility which, in his view, had let Scotland down, and preferred to be a king of the commoners. A generous and enthusiastic patron of art and architecture, James initiated major works at the royal palaces at Falkland, Holyrood and Linlithgow.

JAMES V

THE SCOTTISH REFORMATION

The Reformation in Scotland was both religious and political in nature. It began in the 1540s and turned Scotland from a Catholic into a Protestant nation in less than 20 years, ended the Auld Alliance with France and brought Scotland so close to England that union became inevitable. Above all, it introduced to the character of the Scottish people a high morality that has never left them. The principal, though not only, architect of this transformation was the fiery priest John Knox.

JOHN KNOX (right)

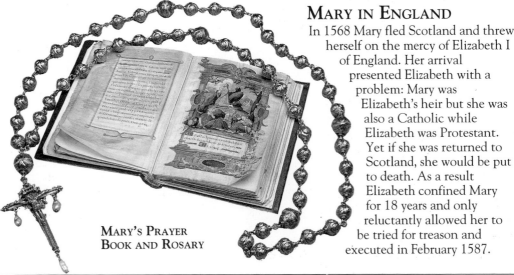

MARY'S PRAYER
BOOK AND ROSARY

MARY, QUEEN OF SCOTS

Endowed with considerable intellectual gifts, Mary was also hot-tempered and arrogant. Her childhood was spent in a country bitterly divided by religion, and at the age of 16 she was married to the French Dauphin, who briefly became king before his death in 1560. She then returned to Scotland and married her cousin Henry, Lord Darnley, but before long she fell in love with her secretary, who was killed by Darnley and his friends in front of her eyes. In 1567 Darnley was killed in an explosion and she married the Earl of Bothwell. All this was too much for her Protestant lords, who forced her to abdicate in 1567.

MARY, QUEEN OF SCOTS (left)

MARY IN ENGLAND

In 1568 Mary fled Scotland and threw herself on the mercy of Elizabeth I of England. Her arrival presented Elizabeth with a problem: Mary was Elizabeth's heir but she was also a Catholic while Elizabeth was Protestant. Yet if she was returned to Scotland, she would be put to death. As a result Elizabeth confined Mary for 18 years and only reluctantly allowed her to be tried for treason and executed in February 1587.

LATER STEWARTS
1513 – 1603

◆ **1513** The infant James V becomes king on the death of his father, James IV, at Flodden Field.
◆ **1528** James dispenses with the Regency and rules for himself.
◆ **1532** Foundation of the Court of Session, the central court for civil justice.
◆ **1538** James marries the French Mary of Guise.
◆ **1542** James invades England but is defeated at the Battle of Solway Moss and dies a few weeks later. His daughter, the one-week old Mary, succeeds.
◆ **1548** Mary is sent to France to be educated and cared for by her mother's family.
◆ **1554** Mary of Guise takes over as Regent.
◆ **1558** Mary marries the French Dauphin in Paris.
◆ **1559** The Protestant priest John Knox returns from exile much influenced by John Calvin of Geneva, and promotes the Scottish Reformation.
◆ **1559** Mary becomes Queen of France when her husband becomes François II.
◆ **1560** Reformation Parliament decides that Scotland is to be a Protestant nation.
◆ **1560** François II dies and Mary returns to Scotland in 1561.
◆ **1565** Mary marries her cousin, Henry, Lord Darnley.
◆ **1566** Mary's Italian secretary, David Rizzio, is murdered.
◆ **1567** Darnley is murdered in an explosion in a house in an Edinburgh suburb. Mary is implicated, but nothing is proved.
◆ **1567** Mary marries James Hepburn, Earl of Bothwell.
◆ **1567** The Scottish lords rebel and defeat Mary, who abdicates and then flees to England, where she is imprisoned by Elizabeth I. Mary's son becomes king as James VI and the Earl of Moray, her half-brother, becomes Regent.
◆ **1570** Moray is assassinated at Linlithgow.
◆ **1572** John Knox dies.
◆ **1582** Edinburgh University is founded.
◆ **1587** After being implicated in the Babington Conspiracy, Mary is tried and executed at Fotheringhay Castle.
◆ **1603** On the death of Elizabeth I of England, James VI of Scotland becomes James I of England, Scotland and Ireland and unites the two crowns. He moves south to live in London.

JAMES I *m* Anne
♛ 1603-1625   of Denmark

Henry
Prince
of Wales
(*d* 1612)

Elizabeth *m* Frederick V
Elector Palatine

CHARLES I *m* Henrietta Maria
♛ 1625-1649   of France
(*d* 1669)

and
others

Rupert   Sophia *m* Ernest Augustus
Elector
of Hanover

CHARLES II *m* Catherine
♛ 1660-1685   of Braganza

Mary *m* William II
of Orange

(1) Anne Hyde *m*
(*d* 1671)

JAMES II *m*
♛ 1685-1688
(*d* 1701)

(2) Mary of Modena
(*d* 1718)

and
others

WILLIAM III *m* MARY II
♛ 1688-1702   ♛ 1688-1694

ANNE *m* George
♛ 1702-1714   of Denmark

GEORGE I
♛ 1714-1727

James Francis Edward *m* Clementina
The Old Pretender
(*d* 1766)

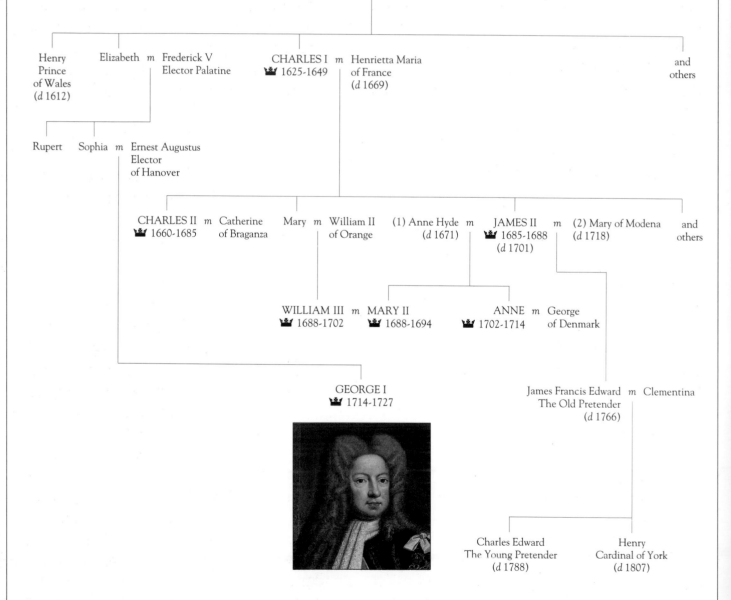

Charles Edward
The Young Pretender
(*d* 1788)

Henry
Cardinal of York
(*d* 1807)

CHAPTER EIGHT

THE
STUARTS
1603–1714

Elizabeth I's heir was James VI of Scotland, who was the great-grandson of Henry VIII's sister Margaret Tudor, wife of James IV. By 1603 James's family name of Stewart was being spelled the French way, Stuart, a practice which arose when James's grandfather took French nationality in 1537. James's accession in 1603 united the crowns of England and Scotland. He was a Protestant but was tolerant of Catholics and was quite prepared to allow his heir, Charles, to be engaged to a French Catholic princess.

Catholicism
The next two Stuart kings, Charles I and his son Charles II, though outwardly Protestant, tolerated Catholics, while James II was an open convert to Catholicism. This association of the monarchs with Catholicism continually alarmed the predominately Protestant population of England and Scotland and was a major factor underlying the long-running conflict between king and Parliament that dominated politics throughout the century. In the end, the 1701 Act of Settlement guaranteed that the country should never be ruled by a Catholic monarch. The other characteristic of the Stuart kings was their obsession with the doctrine of the Divine Right of Kings, by which kings were answerable not to man but to God. When faced with the obstinacy of Charles I in upholding this doctrine, it is no small wonder that Parliament decided that a republican government was preferable.

THE UNION FLAG
Following the union of the crowns of England and Scotland in 1603, designs were drawn up for a joint flag. None of the above were chosen; the union flag which emerged in 1606 combined the two flags one on top of the other.

Parliament
The all-too-short experiment of the Commonwealth and the Protectorate between 1649-60 was the single redeeming feature of a depressing period when the monarchy struggled with Parliament over where sovereignty ultimately lay. But what Cromwell was unable to achieve finally emerged from the Glorious Revolution of 1688, when William III and Mary II, as joint sovereigns, accepted the Bill of Rights, which defined exactly what monarchs could and could not do. Parliament at the end of the 17th century was not the same as today, but it was much more in command of the nation's destiny than it had been at the century's beginning.

JAMES I

1603–1625

THE COAT OF ARMS OF JAMES I
The Scottish lion was added to the coat of arms when James became King.

WHEN JAMES ASCENDED the English throne in 1603, he had already been King of Scotland for 36 years. In Scotland he had ruled by the Divine Right of Kings – the doctrine under which kings were appointed by God and so were not answerable to men. This style of government was unacceptable in England, and so James ruled for long periods without Parliament, relying on his favourites for advice. He thus squandered the legacy of strong government left to him by Elizabeth. Yet to his credit, James ordered a new translation of the Bible and, ahead of his time, wrote a *Counterblaste to Tobacco*, a well-argued attack on smoking.

JAMES I

◆ *Born* Edinburgh, 19 June 1566, son of Mary, Queen of Scots and Lord Darnley.
◆ *Acceded* 24 Mar 1603.
◆ *Married* Anne of Denmark, Oslo, 23 Nov 1589, 9 children.
◆ *Crowned* Westminster Abbey, 25 July 1603.
◆ *Died* Hertfordshire, 27 Mar 1625, aged 58.

PEACE WITH SPAIN

For over a generation, England had looked upon Spain as its natural enemy, with the Spanish Armada of 1588 merely one of the many acts of war between the two nations. Yet within months of his succession, James had started to make peace with Spain.

THE PEACE CONFERENCE
In 1604, a peace conference was held in London's Somerset House, left, with diplomats from Spain and England.

THE KING'S FAVOURITES

The two principal favourites of James I were, in succession, Robert Ker and George Villiers. Both were good-looking and high-spirited young men. Ker had been the King's page and was created Earl of Somerset in 1613, made a member of the Privy Council and entrusted with the King's most intimate business. He angered the nation by encouraging the King to make an alliance with Spain, and by helping him to raise dubious taxes.

By 1616 the King had taken to George Villiers, who quickly became Earl of Buckingham. Villiers dominated the King, to the extent that James put himself into the position of a humbled husband, writing to Villiers a letter that ended, "God Bless you, my sweet child and wife, and grant that ye may ever be a comfort to your dear dad and husband, James, R." When James died in 1625, Buckingham had already managed to transfer his affections and loyalty to the King's son, Charles, serving him until his untimely death in 1628.

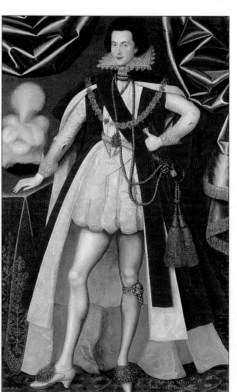

ELIZABETH OF BOHEMIA
The eldest daughter of James I, Elizabeth (above) married Frederick, the Elector Palatine, in 1613. It was his acceptance of the throne of Bohemia in 1618 that started the European cataclysm known as the Thirty Years' War. The 1701 Act of Settlement gave the throne of England to Elizabeth's grandson George, the Elector of Hanover.

GEORGE VILLIERS, EARL AND LATER DUKE OF BUCKINGHAM

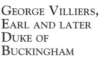

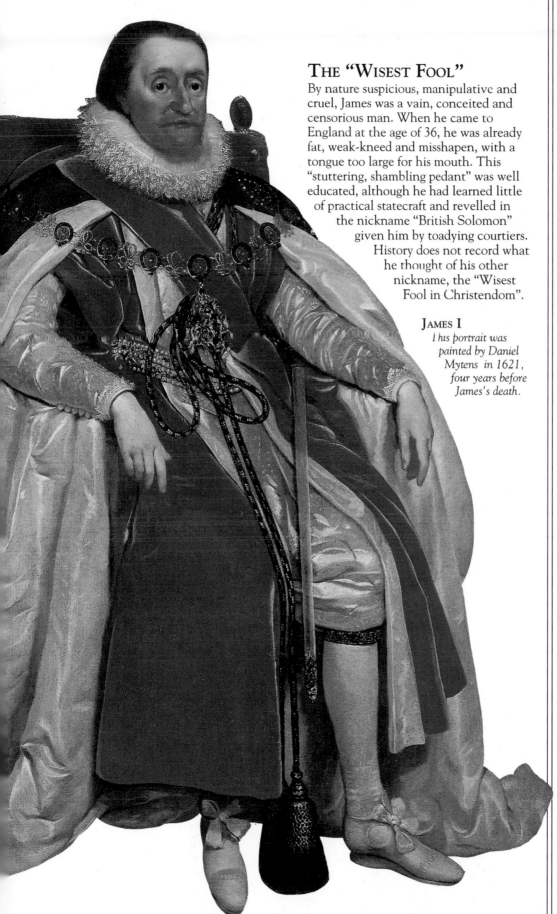

THE "WISEST FOOL"

By nature suspicious, manipulative and cruel, James was a vain, conceited and censorious man. When he came to England at the age of 36, he was already fat, weak-kneed and misshapen, with a tongue too large for his mouth. This "stuttering, shambling pedant" was well educated, although he had learned little of practical statecraft and revelled in the nickname "British Solomon" given him by toadying courtiers. History does not record what he thought of his other nickname, the "Wisest Fool in Christendom".

JAMES I
This portrait was painted by Daniel Mytens in 1621, four years before James's death.

THE GIFT WATCH
James had this gold and silver pocketwatch made in about 1615 for his first favourite, Robert Ker, Earl of Somerset.

THE GUNPOWDER PLOT

1605

IN HIS FIRST YEARS AS KING of England and Scotland, James I faced a number of conspiracies, the most serious of which was the Gunpowder Plot. It was also the most unreal, so unreal in fact that some historians believe that it was a fabrication by the authorities to provide an excuse to crack down on Roman Catholics in Britain. From the beginning of his reign, James had been under pressure to grant Catholics toleration. This he was unable to do, and after two attempts to depose him had failed in 1603, the Gunpowder Plot was hatched to assassinate him in the Houses of Parliament on 5 November 1605.

Parliament House

THE PLOT

The conspirators planned to blow up the King at the state opening of Parliament in November 1605. In May 1604 they rented a house next to Parliament and dug a tunnel through to the cellar underneath the House of Lords. They then rented a room above the cellar and filled it with gunpowder. At this stage, one of the conspirators became alarmed at the potential destruction and warned his brother-in-law, Lord Monteagle, who was a member of the House of Lords, to avoid the state opening. Monteagle alerted the Secretary of State, who informed the King on 4 November and so the plot was foiled.

THE CONSPIRATORS

The conspirators were recruited by Sir Robert Catesby, a Warwickshire Catholic disgruntled with the King's failure to grant toleration to Catholics. Among his recruits was Guy Fawkes, who had been born a Protestant but had then converted to Catholicism and served in the Spanish army.

WESTMINSTER

At the time of the Gunpowder Plot, the Houses of Parliament met in St Stephen's Chapel, which is labelled Parliament House on the left of the print above, engraved by Wenceslaus Hollar in 1647. Westminster Hall, the seat of the Law Courts until 1882, is in the centre and Westminster Abbey is on the right.

THE GUILTY MEN

Eight of the twelve conspirators are shown in this contemporary illustration, including Sir Robert Catesby, the originator of the plot (second from right), and Guido Fawkes, better known as Guy Fawkes (third from right).

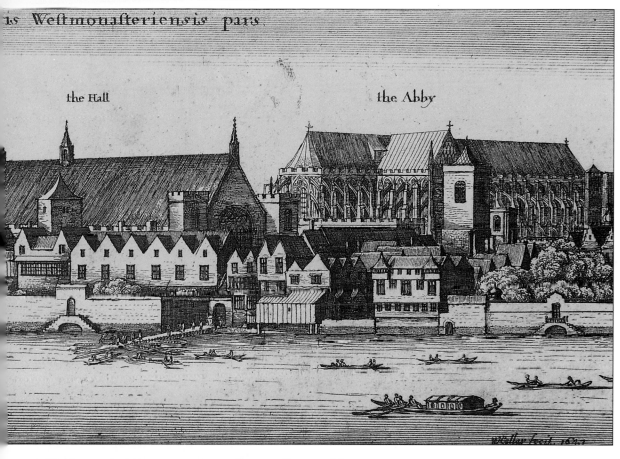

is Westmonasteriensis pars

the Hall

the Abby

TORTURE

After James signed the warrant (below), Guy Fawkes was tortured for some months. We do not know what cruelties were inflicted upon him, but the difference between his signatures before and after torture (the two signatures are shown beneath the warrant) gives us a good idea.

BONFIRE NIGHT

In commemoration of the Gunpowder Plot, bonfires are lit every year in Britain on the night of 5 November and an effigy of Guy Fawkes is burned on the top (left). Fireworks often accompany the burning of the "guy".

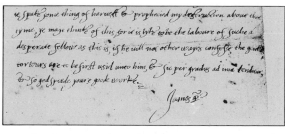

THE PUNISHMENT

As soon as the plot was revealed to the King, a search of the House of Lords was ordered. At midnight, Guy Fawkes was discovered with the gunpowder in the cellar. Other conspirators were quickly arrested and all were taken to the Tower of London.

Guy Fawkes was put in the vaults of the White Tower and tortured. James wrote the warrant permitting torture himself, allowing Fawkes to be tortured gently at first, and then *et sic per gradus ad ima tenditur* (and so on step by step to the limit). He was finally tried along with the others, and then hanged, drawn and quartered.

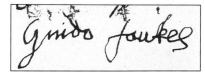

ROYAL PATRONAGE

THE ENCOURAGEMENT OF THE ARTS

ART AND ARCHITECTURE flourished in England during the early 17th century under the patronage of James I and his son Charles. James commissioned numerous family portraits from Flemish painters and patronized the architect and stage-designer Inigo Jones. Charles was a connoisseur of art and transformed the royal collection into one of the most important in Europe. In particular he patronized the work of Van Dyck, whose portraits of him and his family were to revolutionize English portrait painting. The trend among the wealthy to take a Grand Tour of Europe, coupled with the kings' patronage, encouraged others in England to build new residences, commission portraits and collect paintings and sculptures.

INFLUENCE OF VAN DYCK

The Flemish painter Paul Van Somer and the Dutch painters Daniel Mytens and Cornelius Johnson were the leading painters in the royal court, but from 1632, their place was taken by the Flemish painter, Anthony Van Dyck. Charles I was so taken with him that he awarded him a pension and knighthood as an inducement to stay in England. Van Dyck painted many portraits of the Royal Family and court in a flamboyant, elegant style that was to influence British portrait painting for more than 200 years.

CHARLES I
Carlo Maratti painted the triple portrait of Charles 1 (top) in the style of the Flemish painter Van Dyck.

WHITEHALL
Built in the classical style, the Banqueting House in Whitehall (above) was designed by Inigo Jones.

Inigo Jones

Born in London in 1573, Inigo Jones studied architecture in Italy and was strongly influenced by the buildings of Palladio. He worked on the Queen's House at Greenwich before designing his best-known work, the Banqueting House in Whitehall, in 1619. A leading designer of stage sets and the inventor of moveable stage scenery, he was employed by James I to produce the scenery for Ben Jonson's masques.

The Polymath
An architect as well as a scenery and costume designer, Inigo Jones was one of the many versatile artists in the courts of James I and Charles I.

The Banqueting House

In 1619 James I commissioned Inigo Jones to build a new banqueting house in Whitehall Palace to replace the old one which had recently burned down. Originally part of the Whitehall Palace, the Banqueting House was the only building to survive the fire which destroyed the Palace in 1698. It was designed in a classical style and was finished in 1622, although the interior remained incomplete until 1635, when the ceiling paintings by Rubens were installed.

Rubens's Ceiling
The dominating feature of the Banqueting House in Whitehall is the glorious ceiling (left) by Peter Paul Rubens, commissioned by Charles I in 1635. Rubens worked on the canvases in the Netherlands which were then transported to London and placed in position on the ceiling. Once the paintings were installed, Charles banned masques from taking place inside the building in order to prevent the paintings being damaged by smoke.

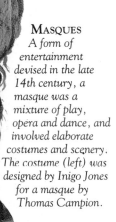

Masques
A form of entertainment devised in the late 14th century, a masque was a mixture of play, opera and dance, and involved elaborate costumes and scenery. The costume (left) was designed by Inigo Jones for a masque by Thomas Campion.

CHARLES I

1625–1649

THE COAT OF ARMS OF CHARLES I

THE SECOND SON OF JAMES I, Charles never expected to be king, only becoming heir to the throne after the death of his older brother Henry in 1612. Charles inherited his father's belief in the Divine Right of Kings and never wavered from that doctrine, even though it caused his own death. As a result, he was obstinate in his political dealings and constantly quarrelled with his parliaments, ruling without one for 11 years. Yet Charles was far from stupid; he was a learned man, and a connoisseur of art. To the end, however, he maintained that no one in England had the right to question what he did or his motives for doing it.

CHARLES I

- ***Born*** Dunfermline Palace, Fife, 19 Nov 1600, second son of James I and Anne of Denmark.
- ***Acceded*** 27 Mar 1625.
- ***Married*** Henrietta Maria of France, Canterbury Cathedral, 13 June 1625, 9 children.
- ***Crowned*** Westminster Abbey, 2 Feb 1626.
- ***Executed*** 30 Jan 1649, aged 48.

DINING IN PUBLIC

Charles was acutely conscious of his dignity as king, and insisted on being approached with respect. This formality was reflected in the proceedings of his Court: no one was allowed to sit in his presence save his wife and possibly one or other of his children, and formal dinners were often held in public. Yet despite this public display of eating, Charles was a light eater and drank very little, preferring music, dancing and masques to conspicuous consumption.

CHARLES'S QUEEN

When she was married to Charles at the beginning of his reign, Henrietta Maria was only 16 years old. The first few years were difficult for her, for she was not yet fond of her husband, who was totally under the influence of his favourite, George Villiers, Duke of Buckingham. When Buckingham was assassinated in 1628, Charles was at first distraught but was reconciled to his wife who, with great tact and understanding, comforted him over his loss. The two soon fell in love, and remained utterly devoted to each other until Charles's death in 1649.

HENRIETTA MARIA

The daughter of the French king Henry IV, who was assassinated when she was less than a year old, Henrietta Maria (right) was born in 1609 at the Louvre Palace in Paris. After her husband's death in 1649, she returned to her beloved France, where she died in 1669.

CHARLES I
Daniel Mytens painted this portrait of the King in 1631.

"SO BAD A KING"

"Men wondered that so good a man should be so bad a king", wrote the wife of one of the signatories of Charles's death warrant, a comment that highlights the extraordinary contrast between the private and public man. Shy and serious from his earliest days, and cursed with a speech impediment as well as almost diminutive stature, Charles was a strange mixture of great personal charm, modesty and politeness mixed with a lack of humour, a lot of nervous tension and no self-confidence.

KING'S STYLE
Charles took great pride in his appearance wearing fine clothes, such as these intricately designed gloves.

EVENTS OF THE REIGN 1625 – 1649

- **1625** Charles I succeeds his father James I.
- **1626** Parliament attempts to impeach Buckingham and is dissolved by Charles.
- **1627** England goes to war with France, but at La Rochelle the Duke of Buckingham fails to relieve the besieged Huguenots.
- **1628** The Duke of Buckingham is assassinated.
- **1628** The Petition of Right – a declaration of the "rights and liberties of the subject" – is presented to the King, who agrees to it under protest.
- **1629** Charles dissolves Parliament and rules by himself to 1640.
- **1632** Van Dyck settles in England as Court painter.
- **1637** Charles tries to force new prayer book on Scots, who resist by signing National Covenant.
- **1640** Charles summons Short Parliament, which lasts 3 weeks.
- **1640** Long Parliament summoned, which lasts until 1660.
- **1641** The Star Chamber and Court of High Commission are both abolished.
- **1642** Charles fails in his attempt to arrest five MPs.
- **1642-9** Civil War.
- **1649** Charles is tried and executed by Parliament.

The High Commission-Court and Starr-Chamber voted down, and pluralities & non residencies damned by Parliament.

ABSOLUTE RULE

For 11 years, Charles attempted to rule without Parliament, enforcing the royal prerogative through the Court of Star Chamber and the Court of High Commission. Charles gave these courts arbitrary powers to suppress political and religious opposition to his personal rule.

STAR CHAMBER
A court of law that was able to hear individual petitions to the king, the Star Chamber came to prominence under Henry VII and was used to enforce the law without corruption. Charles misused the court, which was abolished in 1641.

THE CIVIL WAR

1642–1649

THE CIVIL WAR was one of the greatest upheavals in British history. The war broke out during the reign of Charles I, but its origins reached back more than a century. The basic cause was the rivalry between Parliament and the monarchy. Over the years, Parliament had evolved into an indispensable organ of government, not least because it had the sole right to raise taxes. Its members were increasingly drawn from the professional classes, who disliked Charles's autocratic rule. Antagonism between the two sides grew throughout Charles's reign and reached a head in 1642 when the King attempted to arrest five Members of Parliament. The five had been forewarned and had fled Parliament, but the event was the signal for the outbreak of civil war.

PRINCE RUPERT
The German-born nephew of Charles I, Prince Rupert came to England in 1642 to support his uncle. He had a reputation as a dashing cavalry commander and in the first few years of the War proved to be an effective fighter, winning several battles against the Parliamentary forces. He met his match in Oliver Cromwell, who defeated him at Marston Moor and Naseby.

BATTLE OF NASEBY
The major battle of the Civil War took place outside the Northamptonshire town of Naseby on 14 June 1645. The 15,000-strong Parliamentary New Model Army, an untried force trained by Oliver Cromwell and led by Cromwell and Thomas Fairfax, faced a Royalist army half its size led by the King. The defeat of the Royalist army was decisive in giving victory to Parliament in the Civil War.

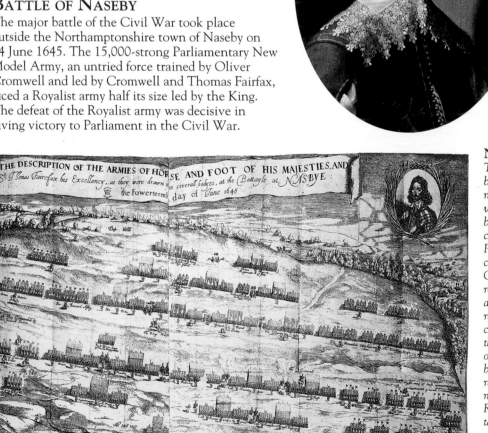

NASEBY
The Battle of Naseby began in the early morning of 14 June with a cavalry charge by Rupert, which chased some of the Parliamentary cavalry off the field. Cromwell then reformed his cavalry and attacked the remaining Royalist cavalry, scattering them before rounding on the infantry and breaking up their ranks. By nightfall, more than 5,000 Royalists had been taken prisoner.

THE ROYALIST COLLAPSE

The King's defeat at Naseby marked the end of the first stage of the Civil War. Charles fled to the supposed safety of his Scottish allies, but in 1646 the Scots handed him over to Parliament. Charles briefly escaped but was recaptured and imprisoned in Carisbrooke Castle on the Isle of Wight in November 1647. He negotiated with Parliament to secure his freedom, while arranging for a Scottish army to invade England. That army was routed by Cromwell at Preston in August 1648. Charles was now at the mercy of Parliament.

CARISBROOKE CASTLE
Charles remained a prisoner in this castle for a year, enjoying relative freedom within its fortified walls (left).

THE DEATH OF CHARLES

In early 1649 Parliament took the decision to try the King for waging war against his kingdom and against Parliament. The trial commenced on 20 January in Westminster Hall and was held in front of about 50 Members of Parliament. Throughout the trial the King stubbornly refused to recognize the legality of the court. On 27 January he was found guilty and sentenced to death by execution. The sentence was carried out on the morning of 30 January on a specially erected scaffold in front of the Banqueting House in Whitehall.

THE CIVIL WAR 1642 – 1649

◆ **1642** Charles attempts to arrest five MPs, leaves London and raises his standard at Nottingham.
◆ **1642** Royalists defeat Parliamentary army at Edgehill.
◆ **1643** Royalists defeat Parliamentary army at Chalgrove Field. Further battles result in stalemate.
◆ **1644** Royalists defeated at Marston Moor – the turning point in the Civil War.
◆ **1645** Parliament creates New Model Army, which crushes Royalist army at Naseby.
◆ **1646** Charles surrenders to the Scots, who hand him over to Parliament.
◆ **1646-8** Negotiations between King and Parliament. King conspires with Scots to invade England on his behalf.
◆ **1648** Scots defeated at Preston
◆ **1649** Execution of Charles.

THE DEATH WARRANT OF CHARLES I

THE EXECUTION
Before he was executed, Charles attempted to justify his role as king: "For the people truly I desire their liberty and freedom as much as anybody whatsoever; but I must tell you that their liberty and freedom consists in having government, those laws by which their lives and goods maybe most their own. It is not their having a share in the government; that is nothing appertaining to them; a subject and sovereign are clean different things…"

THE COMMONWEALTH

1649–1660

THE PERIOD BETWEEN THE EXECUTION of Charles I in 1649 and the restoration of his son Charles II in 1660 can be divided into two parts: the Commonwealth, or republic, which lasted from 1649-53, and the Protectorate, or monarchy in all but name, of Oliver Cromwell, and then his son Richard, from 1653-9. The first period was dominated by the attempts of Cromwell and others to work with the existing institutions of Parliament, the second by the efforts of Cromwell to fashion new institutions commanding popular consent. Throughout both periods, the dominant figure was Cromwell, one of the most brilliant commanders in English history.

OLIVER CROMWELL

The son of a Huntingdonshire squire, Oliver Cromwell was born in 1599 and first entered Parliament in 1628. When the Civil War broke out in 1642, Cromwell developed an effective cavalry force in East Anglia, becoming Parliament's leading general by 1645. After the execution of the King in 1649, he was the natural choice to become chairman of the new Council of State and dominated English politics until his death in 1658.

A man of intense religious devotion, Cromwell believed that everything he did was guided by God's will. This made him agonizingly hesitant, but once a decision was made, "the swift, daring hammer-stroke" followed. A man of masterful energy and with considerable personal charm, Cromwell was, for his time, amazingly tolerant of religious and political dissent.

CROMWELL
Nearly 2m (6ft) tall, with grey eyes and a large nose, Oliver Cromwell was not at all handsome, although he was once described (by an enemy) as "of majestic deportment and comely presence". Contrary to public perception he was not adverse to pleasure and enjoyed hunting, riding and music.

THE COMMONWEALTH

The execution of the King in 1649 unleashed a period of unprecedented radical and revolutionary activity across the country. As Chairman of the Council of State, Cromwell struggled to devise an acceptable system of republican government. He ruled at first through the Rump Parliament – the 53 Members of Parliament who had supported the army's call in 1649 for Charles I to be tried – but when it obstructed his reforms, it was abolished in 1653 and he became Lord Protector, ruling with a Council of 15 and a Parliament of 400.

THE PARLIAMENTARY LEADER

In 1657 the Protectorate Parliament offered Cromwell the title of king. He refused it, preferring always to govern with popular consent rather than by hereditary principle. This statue of Cromwell outside the Houses of Parliament (right) commemorates his democratic credentials.

THE ROYAL OAK

As Oliver Cromwell looks on, "The Royall Oake of Brittayne", the symbol of authority and stability, is felled. Beneath the tree, the common herd graze, oblivious of the situation (left).

DUNBAR

After the execution of Charles I in 1649, the Scots proclaimed his son Charles as king. Cromwell's defeat of the Scottish army at Dunbar (right) in September 1650 ended this threat to his rule.

THE PROTECTORATE

During Cromwell's five years as Lord Protector, English military prestige was lifted to new heights. Jamaica was taken from the Spanish, and the Dutch were routed at sea by the navy under the brilliant command of Robert Blake. Throughout Europe, England was regarded with admiration and awe.

THE FIRST DUTCH WAR

War broke out with Holland in 1652 after the Navigation Act of 1651 gave English ships a monopoly over foreign trade into and out of English ports.

THE COMMONWEALTH 1649 – 1660

◆ **1649** Following the execution of Charles I, a Council of State is appointed with Oliver Cromwell as Chairman.

◆ **1649** England is declared a republic.

◆ **1649** Irish royalists defeated by Cromwell at Wexford and at the Siege of Drogheda.

◆ **1650** Scots royalists defeated by Cromwell at Dunbar.

◆ **1651** Scots Royalists led by Charles II defeated at Worcester; Charles flees into exile.

◆ **1651** Navigation Act secures trade monopoly for English ships.

◆ **1652-4** First Dutch War.

◆ **1653** Cromwell expels the Rump Parliament.

◆ **1653** Cromwell becomes Lord Protector of England.

◆ **1654-5** First Protectorate Parliament sits.

◆ **1655** Cromwell dismisses Parliament and divides the country into 11 districts, each ruled by a Major-General.

◆ **1655** Jamaica is captured from the Spanish.

◆ **1656** Second Protectorate Parliament abolishes rule of Major-Generals.

◆ **1657** Cromwell refuses an offer of the throne.

◆ **1658** Cromwell dismisses Third Protectorate Parliament.

◆ **1658** Cromwell dies, aged 59.

◆ **1658-9** Oliver's son Richard rules as Lord Protector.

◆ **1659** The Rump is recalled and then dismissed by the army.

◆ **1660** A new Parliament is summoned and negotiates the restoration of the monarchy.

CHARLES II

1660–1685

THE COAT OF ARMS
OF CHARLES II

ALTHOUGH TECHNICALLY KING after the execution of his father Charles I in 1649, Charles did not ascend the throne until the restoration of the monarchy in 1660. As king, he divided his time between devious diplomatic activity centred on getting as much financial support as he could from the Catholic Louis XIV of France, and a full and often sensuous life devoted to his own pleasure. After the puritan zeal of the Commonwealth period, Charles's private life attracted controversy but also much popularity.

♛ CHARLES II

♦ *Born* St James's Palace, 29 May 1630, eldest son of Charles I and Henrietta Maria.
♦ *Acceded* 29 May 1660.
♦ *Crowned* Westminster Abbey, 23 April 1661.
♦ *Married* Catherine of Braganza, Portsmouth, 21 May 1662.
♦ *Died* Whitehall, 6 Feb 1685, aged 54.

PRIVATE LIFE
Although a married man, Charles kept a succession of mistresses, sometimes two at a time, throughout his life. The most famous were Barbara Villiers and the Duchess of Portsmouth, but his own favourite was Nell Gwynne, whom he met at the theatre in 1668. Nell had charm and wit, and was always devoted to Charles. On his death bed, Charles requested "Let not poor Nelly starve."

NELL GWYNNE
Charles's favourite mistress (right) was one of the leading actresses of the day and was adored by the general public for remaining "one of them".

CATHERINE OF BRAGANZA
The daughter of the King of Portugal, Catherine (far left) married Charles in 1662.

THE ROYAL YACHTS
Charles owned a number of yachts, including Mary, built by the shipbuilder Phineas Pett in 1677. Altogether, 26 yachts were built in England during the reign of Charles, establishing the sport of yachting in the country for the first time.

THE ROYAL SPORTSMAN
Throughout his life, Charles was a keen sportsman, enjoying horse racing, bowls and yachting. The latter was a new sport to England, introduced by Charles from Holland, where he had spent his years in exile sailing. In 1661 the world's first yacht race took place between Charles and his brother James, who raced each other down the Thames.

THE "MERRY MONARCH"

About two metres (six feet) tall, dark, with long, curly black hair, sparkling eyes and a sensuous mouth, Charles was attractive to women and exploited that fact liberally for almost 30 years. As a child he had a happy life until the 1640s, but his father's execution in 1649 had a profound effect on him, making him both cynical and sceptical. Yet he always remained open-minded, and took great interest in science and architecture, giving support to Christopher Wren and encouraging, through the Royal Society, such scientists as Newton and Boyle.

CHARLES II
Sir Godfrey Kneller painted this portrait of Charles in the early 1680s near the end of his reign.

THE POPISH PLOT

In 1678, an Anglican parson, Titus Oates, disclosed a Catholic plot to murder Charles and restore Catholicism to England. Although the plot was fabricated, the resulting furore led Parliament to attempt to exclude Charles's Catholic brother James from the throne.

TITUS OATES
Although Oates was given a state pension during Charles's reign, he was tried and whipped through the streets during the reign of James II.

THE GREAT FIRE

1666

IN JUNE 1665 the first of two major disasters hit the City of London. On 7 June the diarist Samuel Pepys noted that while walking down Drury Lane he had seen red crosses painted on three front doors, the tell-tale sign that the occupants had become sick with the bubonic plague. By September, more than 100,000 Londoners had died. Charles II, by nature indifferent to danger, stayed in the capital for several weeks, unlike many rich people, but by August he too had left, taking up temporary residence in Salisbury.

Six months after Charles's return to London in the spring of 1666, disaster struck again. On 2 September, a fire started in a bakery in Pudding Lane. The burning shop collapsed and the flames spread along the entire street, fanned by the strong easterly winds. Within hours, the warren of streets and lanes in the City was in flames. For four days and three nights the fire blazed out of control until, on 5 September, the wind abated and the fire burned itself out.

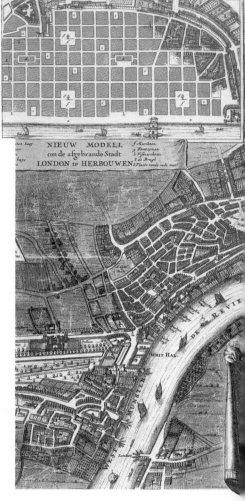

FIGHTING THE FIRE

In order to contain the fire, Londoners blew up or pulled down buildings in the path of the flames to create firebreaks. Charles and his brother James spent hours in the thick of the conflagration, leading gangs of men with picks and shovels in the demolition work. When the Tower of London was threatened, the King ordered that a row of buildings between its western gates and the City be blown up, thereby preventing the possibility of a far greater catastrophe had the repository of state-controlled gunpowder supplies exploded.

THE FIRE BY NIGHT
The fire raged for four days and three nights, destroying many famous buildings, including old St Paul's Cathedral and 88 other churches, as can be seen in this contemporary painting.

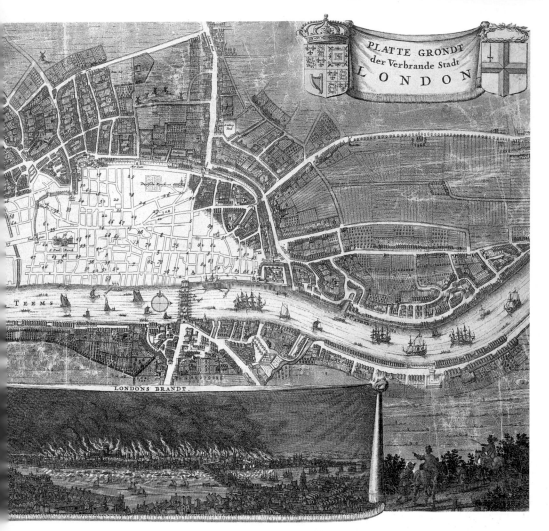

THE DAMAGE

Four-fifths of the City of London within the city walls was destroyed by the fire, an area of about 440 acres. Over 13,000 houses and public buildings – including the Royal Exchange, the Guildhall and the Customs House – were gutted, nearly all beyond repair. Miraculously, less than a dozen people lost their lives. The site of the fire's origin in Pudding Lane, next to London Bridge, is marked today with a column, known as The Monument, designed by Wren.

EXTENT OF THE FIRE
The devastation wrought by the fire in the heart of London can be clearly seen in this contemporary map (left).

CHRISTOPHER WREN

Within days of the fire ending, the architect Christopher Wren had submitted a simple but revolutionary plan to rebuild the city with straight, wide boulevards intersected by smaller streets. Sadly, his plan was not adopted, for there was not enough money and Londoners did not want to alter their capital, nor lose their precious plots of land.

MASTERPIECES
Christopher Wren (right) had begun his career as a scientist and did not turn to architecture until he was 30. After the fire, he was responsible for the rebuilding of more than 50 churches, including St Paul's Cathedral (below). In later years he designed the naval hospital at Greenwich (below right).

JAMES II

1685–1688

THE COAT OF ARMS
OF JAMES II

THE SECOND SON OF CHARLES I, James returned to England on Charles II's restoration in 1660. Because of his experience in naval matters, he was made Lord High Admiral and served in the war against the Dutch in 1665. James's conversion to Catholicism in the late 1660s led to his removal from high office and an attempt by Parliament to exclude him from the succession. The attempt failed, and on his brother's death in 1685, James ascended the throne. He made it clear that he intended to restore Catholicism, and his policies led to conflict with Church and Parliament. The birth of a son in 1688 was the excuse his opponents needed, and within six months, James had fled into exile.

♛ JAMES II

- **Born** St James's Palace, 24 Oct 1633, second son of Charles I and Henrietta Maria.
- **Married** Anne Hyde, London, 3 Sept 1660, 8 children; Mary of Modena, Dover, Kent, 21 Nov 1673, 11 children.
- **Acceded** 6 Feb 1685.
- **Crowned** Westminster Abbey, 23 April 1685.
- **Deposed** 23 Dec 1688.
- **Died** France, 16 Sept 1701, aged 77.

TWO WIVES

In 1660, James married Anne Hyde, daughter of the Earl of Clarendon, Charles II's chief adviser, who died in 1671. Two years later, James married again, this time to the Catholic Mary of Modena, an Italian princess. Ten of their children died in infancy, but the news that Mary was expecting another child in 1688 was greeted with dismay by Protestants, who feared that Mary would produce a Catholic son and heir for James. The birth of a son on 10 June confirmed their worst fears. Many Protestants, including James's two daughters, Mary and Anne, believed that the royal baby was in fact a foundling smuggled into the royal bedchamber.

THE FOUNDLING
It was alleged that the royal foundling was smuggled into this bed.

MARY OF MODENA
When James married Mary Beatrice d'Este de Modena (right) in 1673, she was 15 and about to enter a convent.

TRIAL OF THE SEVEN BISHOPS

In May 1688 James issued the Declaration of Indulgence, which suspended the penal laws against Roman Catholics and Protestant dissenters, and ordered the clergy to read the Declaration in their churches. Seven bishops, including the Archbishop of Canterbury, petitioned the King to be excused. James responded by treating their petition as an act of seditious libel and had them arrested and taken to the Tower of London. They arrived in the Tower in mid-June, where they were kept in one room. Their trial at Westminster Hall found them all not guilty.

NOT GUILTY
The release of the Seven Bishops from their imprisonment in the Tower for seditious libel was greeted with huge celebrations throughout Britain.

THE YOUNGER BROTHER

"Two yards high" was how the "Wanted" posters issued by Parliament in 1649 described James, for he was a tall man, and more good looking than his brother Charles. For over half a century James had played second fiddle to his brother, whom he loved, was loyal to but actually had little respect for. James was of a finer quality in many ways: gentler, more honest, nicer mannered, and undoubtedly more courageous.

JAMES II
This portrait of James before he became king was completed in 1685 by Sir Godfrey Kneller.

MONMOUTH'S REBELLION

Four months after he became king, James faced a rebellion by the Duke of Monmouth, illegitimate son of Charles II. The revolt was put down, and, after a series of trials known as the Bloody Assizes, 320 were executed and 800 transported to America as slaves.

BATTLE OF SEDGMOOR
The battle that took place in Somerset on 6 July 1685, at which Monmouth's rebellion was put down, was the last battle to be fought on English soil.

THE GLORIOUS REVOLUTION

1688

AT THE END OF JUNE 1688, seven leading statesmen invited William of Orange, the effective ruler of Holland, to come to Britain with an army "to rescue the nation and the religion" from the Catholic rule of James II. What finally goaded the statesmen to commit high treason was the recent birth of James's son and heir, whom they feared would be reared as a Catholic. William was chosen to save the nation because he was a Protestant and was married to James's eldest daughter Mary. He readily accepted the invitation for, as champion of the Protestants in Europe and principal opponent of Louis XIV of France, he was keen to add England's wealth to his own resources.

THE LANDING
The invasion fleet of more than 200 transport ships and 50 warships anchored in Torbay, allowing William and his followers to disembark in Brixham on 5 November 1688.

THE INVASION

On 1 November 1688 William left the Netherlands and sailed down the English Channel, landing at Brixham on 5 November. His reception was cool, although not hostile, but as he marched towards London, his ranks grew and support for James melted away. Before the end of the year, William was in London and James was in exile in France.

THE BILL OF RIGHTS

After the Revolution, Parliament agreed to settle the throne jointly on William and Mary and grant executive power to William. The two monarchs also accepted the Declaration of Rights, which was embodied later in the Bill of Rights. The principal terms of this keystone of the British Constitution were that no Catholic could become king or queen; taxes were not to be raised without the consent of Parliament; and no laws were to be dispensed with without Parliamentary approval.

THE BILL OF RIGHTS

...nol. Hoheit Prjntz von Or...
...elanget jn Engelandt, Año. 1689.
Ñ.5.Februarÿ.

WILLIAM & MARY

1689–1702

THE COAT OF ARMS OF WILLIAM III
The lion of Nassau, in Holland, was added to the royal coat of arms by William to emphasize his Dutch upbringing.

WHEN WILLIAM OF ORANGE – his name comes from the Dutch royal house – was invited over to Britain to replace James II, it was arranged that he should rule jointly with his wife Mary, daughter of James. This unique arrangement lasted until the death of Mary in 1694, after which date William ruled by himself until his death in 1702. William's main aim throughout his life was to contain French expansion in Europe. To this end, he was happy to accept the British throne, not because he was bothered about the liberties he pledged to restore, but because he saw the crown as the best way to obtain British support against France. As a result, William never enjoyed great popularity, although Mary was much loved.

♛ WILLIAM III

- ◆ **Born** The Hague, Holland, 14 Nov 1650, son of William of Nassau and Mary Stuart.
- ◆ **Married** Mary, London, 4 Nov 1677.
- ◆ **Acceded** Jointly with Mary, 13 Feb 1689.
- ◆ **Crowned** Jointly with Mary, Westminster Abbey, 11 April 1689.
- ◆ **Died** Kensington Palace, 8 March 1702, aged 51.

GLENCOE
The Macdonalds of Glencoe, a valley in Scotland (right), were slow in taking the oath of allegiance to William. In February 1692, 38 of them were massacred by the rival Campbell clan on William's orders.

A ROYAL VASE
This Delft-ware tulip vase is decorated with the intertwined initials of the two monarchs.

DUTCH STYLE

Dutch influence on English art and architecture was marked during William's reign. Rounded, Dutch-style gables on the ends of buildings and blue-and-white Delft ware both became very popular.

KENSINGTON PALACE
William and Mary purchased Kensington House from the Earl of Nottingham and commissioned Christopher Wren to draw up plans to enlarge it. Both Mary and William died in the palace, which has been a royal residence ever since.

👑 MARY II

◆ **Born** St James's Palace, 30 April 1662, daughter of James II and Anne Hyde.
◆ **Died** Kensington Palace, 28 Dec 1694, aged 32.

THE FAULTLESS QUEEN

When Mary died of smallpox at the end of 1694, William said that during the course of their marriage he had never known a single fault in her. History has said much the same. She was a sweet-natured, loving woman who was devoted to her husband.

WILLIAM III

This portrait (left) of William by an unknown artist was painted sometime in the 1690s.

THE DUTCH KING

Small, thin and with a slight stoop, William was nevertheless a vigorous man who enjoyed horse riding and hunting. Always calm and controlled, his shyness made him disliked, though many admired his military and political abilities.

THE BANK OF ENGLAND

Established in 1694 to provide finance for wars against the French, the Bank of England laid the foundations of a secure system of government credit. For the first 40 years, the Bank of England resided in the Grocers' Hall, Poultry Street (above), before moving to its present site in Threadneedle Street.

EVENTS OF THE REIGN 1689 – 1702

◆ **1689** Parliament draws up the Declaration of Right detailing the unconstitutional acts of James II. Upon acceptance of this declaration, William and Mary become joint sovereigns, a unique constitutional agreement.
◆ **1689** Toleration Act guarantees freedom of worship for all Protestant dissenters.
◆ **1689** First Mutiny Bill passed, making a standing army illegal without parliamentary consent.
◆ **1689** Scottish rebellion against William put down.
◆ **1689** Bill of Rights embodies main constitutional provisions of the Declaration and determines the succession to the throne.

MARY II
This portrait of Mary was painted by William Wissing during the 1680s.

◆ **1689** Catholic Forces loyal to James II land in Ireland from France and lay siege to Londonderry.
◆ **1690** William defeats James at the Battle of the Boyne.
◆ **1691** Treaty of Limerick allows Catholics in Ireland to exercise their religion freely, but severe penal laws against them follow soon afterwards.
◆ **1691** Outbreak of French war.
◆ **1692** Lloyds insurance office opens in London.
◆ **1692** Glencoe Massacre.
◆ **1693** National Debt set up.
◆ **1694** Foundation of the Bank of England.
◆ **1694** Death of Mary; William now rules alone.
◆ **1697** Peace of Ryswick ends war with France.
◆ **1701** Act of Settlement provides for the succession to pass to the Electress Sophia of Hanover or her heirs.
◆ **1701** James II dies in exile in France. Louis XIV of France immediately recognises his son James Edward as James III.
◆ **1701** William forms grand alliance between England, Holland and Austria to prevent the union of the French and Spanish crowns.
◆ **1701** War of Spanish Succession breaks out in Europe over the vacant Spanish throne.
◆ **1702** William dies after falling from his horse. He is succeeded by his sister-in-law Anne.

THE SETTLEMENT OF IRELAND

THE ESTABLISHMENT OF PROTESTANT RULE

ALTHOUGH THE KING OF ENGLAND had been nominal Lord of Ireland since 1171, English rule in Ireland was confined to districts around Dublin which were known as The Pale. Henry VIII declared himself King of Ireland in 1541 and both Elizabeth I and James I extended English authority by "planting" Protestant English settlers mainly in the province of Ulster. The Catholic Irish objected but were unable to prevent increasing Protestant domination of their island. When, in 1688, James II was deposed by William of Orange, the Irish Catholics sided with him; the Protestants of Ulster sided with William. After overcoming Irish resistance to his rule by 1691, William tried to grant favourable terms to Catholics, but the Irish Parliament, dominated by Protestants, introduced a series of harsh Penal Laws that made the Catholic majority second-class citizens, thereby creating the Protestant Ascendancy.

THE SIEGE OF LONDONDERRY

When the Irish Catholics rose in support of James II in 1689, many thousands of Irish Protestants took refuge in Londonderry. Besieged by James's forces, the city held out for 105 days until an English fleet relieved the starving population.

BEHIND THE WALLS
More than 30,000 people sheltered within the city walls of Londonderry during the siege of 1689.

BATTLE OF THE BOYNE

After their failure to capture Londonderry, James's army moved south and took up positions by the side of the River Boyne near Drogheda, 40 km (25 miles) north of Dublin. There it faced a slightly larger army led by William III. Battle was joined on 1 July 1690, but James's forces were soon overwhelmed by the superior artillery of William's army. James did not expect to win the battle, nor did William wish to capture his father-in-law, and so James was allowed to slip away into exile in France.

THE BATTLE
William III's army consisted of troops drawn from Ulster, England, Denmark and his native Holland. James's smaller army was almost exclusively Irish; a French force sent by Louis XIV to help James gave him no assistance.

ANNE

1702–1714

THE COAT OF ARMS OF ANNE

THE LAST STUART MONARCH, Queen Anne succeeded her brother-in-law, William of Orange, in 1702. Her inheritance from William included a turbulent political relationship with France, notably a dispute that began in 1700 over the French claim to the vacant Spanish throne and broke into open war two months after Anne's accession. Known as the War of the Spanish Succession, this conflict gave the British, under the generalship of John Churchill, Duke of Marlborough, four great victories in battle and established Britain as a major European power. At home, there were upheavals in domestic politics as rivalry between Whig and Tory factions in parliament and the country grew stronger. Throughout these momentous years, Anne was a virtual invalid, worn out by frequent pregnancies. She died without an heir in 1714.

 ANNE

- **Born** St James's Palace, 6 Feb 1665, second daughter of James II and Anne Hyde.
- **Married** George, Prince of Denmark, St James's Palace, 28 July 1683, 18 children.
- **Acceded** 8 Mar 1702.
- **Crowned** Westminster Abbey, 23 April 1702.
- **Died** Kensington Palace, 1 Aug 1714, aged 49.

SARAH CHURCHILL

Sarah Jennings first met Anne when the latter was 5 and Sarah 10. Sarah grew up to be one of the great beauties of her age, and in 1677 married a young army officer, John Churchill, later the Duke of Marlborough. Their joint advancement was inextricably bound up with their close relationship with Anne. Sarah dominated Anne to the extent that in 1691 Anne suggested that she and Sarah should correspond with each other as Mrs Morley (Anne) and Mrs Freeman (Sarah) to demonstrate the equality of their relationship.

SARAH CHURCHILL (above)

FINE FURNITURE
This Queen Anne walnut card table (below) features the elegant cabriole legs characteristic of the period.

QUEEN ANNE STYLE

The distinctive taste in decorative arts that came to full flower in Anne's reign was characterized by simple ornament and well-proportioned, elegant lines. Furniture was decorated in veneers – notably walnut – and inlay, rather than the elaborate wood-carving previously popular. New designs were adopted from overseas: chairs and tables, for example, featured the curved cabriole leg, a design that had been brought into Europe from China.

THE ACT OF UNION
Under the Act of Union with England in 1707, Scotland lost its own parliament but was represented in the new parliament of Great Britain by 45 members and 16 peers. Scotland also gained free trade with England. A copy of the Act is shown below.

UNITING THE KINGDOMS

Although the crowns of England and Scotland were formally united in 1603, when James VI of Scotland became James I of England, Scotland retained a separate parliament. Parliamentary union between the two countries was achieved in 1707 when the parliament in Scotland was abolished, although Scotland has retained its own religious, legal and educational systems to the present day.

ANNE
*This portrait of Anne
(left), attributed to Sir
Godfrey Kneller, was
painted about 1690,
when Anne was 25.*

PRINCE GEORGE OF DENMARK
*Although thoughtful and polite, George had
few accomplishments. Charles II, no mean
judge of men, stated that "I have tried him
drunk and I have tried him sober, and there is
nothing in him". Anne, however, was devoted
to her husband and in 1708 personally nursed
him day and night as he lay on his death bed.*

THE LAST STUART

In her youth Queen Anne was not
unattractive, although her short
sightedness gave her a disconcerting
squint. But when she came to the
throne she was plump and subject to
severe attacks of gout. Following her
marriage to George, Prince of
Denmark, she became pregnant 18
times, suffering 13 still-births. She
failed to produce an heir as all
her five surviving children
died young. A devout
Protestant, Anne favoured the
Tories, whom she saw as the
Church party, and this led to
conflict with her favourite, Sarah
Churchill, who devoted herself to the
Whigs. Anne was tenacious in her
opinions when she thought she was
right, and the quarrel between the two
women was never settled.

EVENTS OF THE REIGN 1702 – 1714

- **1702** Anne succeeds her brother-in-law, William III.
- **1702** England declares war on France in the War of the Spanish Succession.
- **1702** *The Daily Courant*, the first daily newspaper in London, is published.
- **1702** *The History of the Great Rebellion*, by Edward Hyde, the Earl of Clarendon and Anne's grandfather, is published.
- **1704** English, Bavarian and Austrian troops under Marlborough defeat the French at the Battle of Blenheim and save Austria from invasion.
- **1704** Sir George Rooke captures Gibraltar from Spain.
- **1705** The Earl of Peterborough captures Barcelona.
- **1706** Marlborough defeats the French at the Battle of Ramillies and expels the French from the Netherlands.
- **1707** The Act of Union unites the kingdoms of England and Scotland and transfers the seat of Scottish government from Edinburgh to London.
- **1708** Marlborough defeats the French at the Battle of Oudenarde, the French incurring heavy losses.
- **1708** Anne vetoes a parliamentary bill to reorganize the Scottish militia, the last time a bill is vetoed by the sovereign.
- **1708** Prince George dies at Kensington Palace.
- **1708** Minorca is captured.
- **1709** Marlborough defeats the French at the Battle of Malplaquet, but the English army incurs heavy losses.
- **1710** The Whig government falls and a Tory ministry is formed.
- **1711** Marlborough is accused of sequestering military funds for his own use and is removed from command of the army.
- **1711** Queen Anne establishes horse racing at Ascot.
- **1712** The last execution for witchcraft in England occurs.
- **1713** The Treaty of Utrecht is signed by Britain and France, bringing to an end the War of the Spanish Succession.
- **1714** The Electress Sophia of Hanover dies, and her son George becomes heir to the English throne.
- **1714** Queen Anne dies at Kensington Palace, London, at the age of 49.

THE DUKE OF MARLBOROUGH

THE SUPREME COMMANDER

JOHN CHURCHILL WAS BORN IN 1650, the son of a poor Devonshire knight, and entered the army in 1667. He quickly distinguished himself in the wars against the Dutch, and as second-in-command of the royal army crushed the Duke of Monmouth's rebellion against James II in 1685. Three years later, however, Churchill deserted James in favour of William of Orange, and was rewarded with the Earldom of Marlborough in 1689 (he became a duke in 1702). As supreme commander of the allied forces against the armies of Louis XIV of France, Marlborough won a series of stunning victories between 1704 and 1709.

THE MIGHTY DUKE
This portrait by Sir Godfrey Kneller of the Duke of Marlborough (left) was painted at the height of his success against the French forces in 1706. Marlborough was an outstanding military genius, a gifted statesman, a skilful diplomatist and a generous enemy. But he was also untrustworthy, avaricious and inordinately ambitious.

BLENHEIM PALACE
In gratitude for his victory at Blenheim against the French in 1704, Queen Anne gave to Marlborough the royal estate of Woodstock, near Oxford, and promised to build for him and his wife a house at her expense. Blenheim Palace, named after his famous victory in Bavaria, was largely erected between 1705 and 1722. About £240,000 of its cost was contributed by the Queen and Parliament, although the actual cost was much higher, and the building was not finished when the Duke of Marlborough died in 1722.

THE GREAT PALACE
The architect of Blenheim Palace (right) was John Vanburgh, the acclaimed designer of Castle Howard in Yorkshire. Among the great craftworkers of the early 18th century who worked with him were the carver Grinling Gibbons and the architects William Chambers and Nicholas Hawksmoor.

THE HANOVERIANS

1714–1910

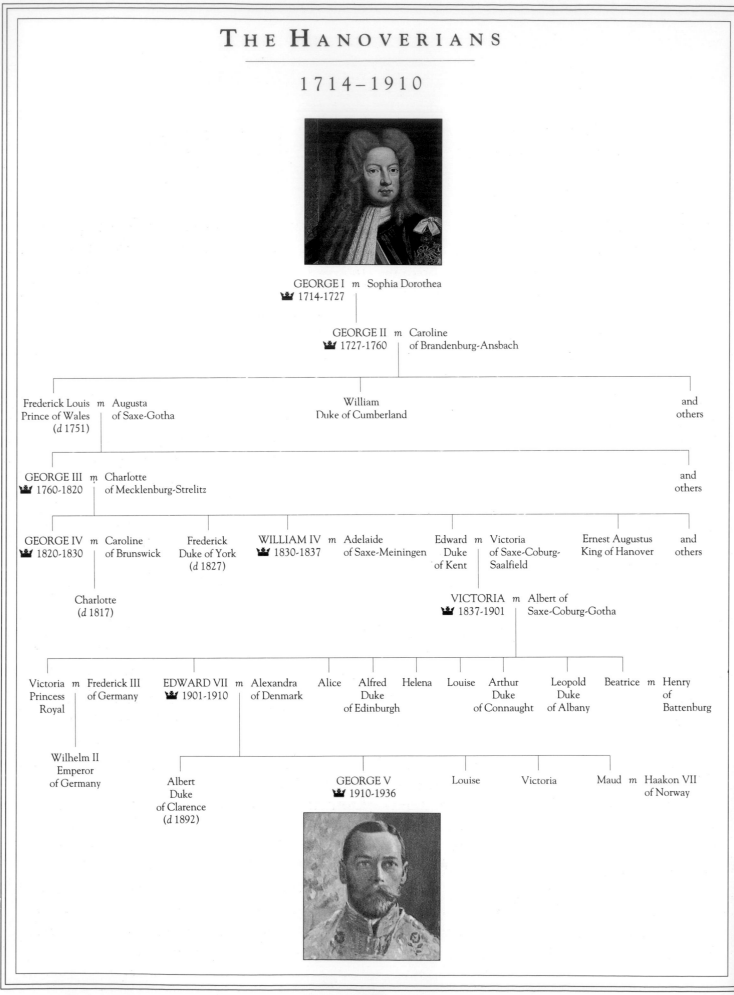

GEORGE I *m* Sophia Dorothea
♛ 1714-1727

GEORGE II *m* Caroline
♛ 1727-1760 of Brandenburg-Ansbach

Frederick Louis *m* Augusta
Prince of Wales of Saxe-Gotha
(*d* 1751)

William
Duke of Cumberland

and
others

GEORGE III *m* Charlotte
♛ 1760-1820 of Mecklenburg-Strelitz

and
others

GEORGE IV *m* Caroline
♛ 1820-1830 of Brunswick

Frederick
Duke of York
(*d* 1827)

WILLIAM IV *m* Adelaide
♛ 1830-1837 of Saxe-Meiningen

Edward *m* Victoria
Duke of Saxe-Coburg-
of Kent Saalfield

Ernest Augustus
King of Hanover

and
others

Charlotte
(*d* 1817)

VICTORIA *m* Albert of
♛ 1837-1901 Saxe-Coburg-Gotha

Victoria *m* Frederick III
Princess of Germany
Royal

EDWARD VII *m* Alexandra
♛ 1901-1910 of Denmark

Alice

Alfred
Duke
of Edinburgh

Helena

Louise

Arthur
Duke
of Connaught

Leopold
Duke
of Albany

Beatrice *m* Henry
of
Battenburg

Wilhelm II
Emperor
of Germany

Albert
Duke
of Clarence
(*d* 1892)

GEORGE V
♛ 1910-1936

Louise

Victoria

Maud *m* Haakon VII
of Norway

CHAPTER NINE

THE
HANOVERIANS
1714–1910

The 1701 Act of Settlement ensured once and for all that Britain would never be ruled by a Catholic monarch. The succession was settled upon the Protestant Electress of Hanover, Sophia, who was the granddaughter of James I. When she died in 1714, the succession passed to her son, George, who later in the same year became the first Hanoverian king on the death of Queen Anne.

The New Kings

To begin with, the Hanoverian kings had little going for them in Britain. Their electorate in Germany did not have representative government as Britain knew it, and was landlocked, and so they knew little about the sea, merchant shipping or the navy. George himself could speak no English and few statesmen in England could understand German. Although the majority of the English population was Protestant and approved of the Act of Settlement, understandably they wished Anne's successor could have been someone more congenial. The minority who still preferred the Jacobite cause were vociferous, influential and trouble-making, and made difficulties for the new dynasty for more than 30 years.

Popular Monarchy

Despite these problems, the Hanoverians worked hard to make themselves adaptable and to learn British ways. George III, who was born and brought up in England, once said that "I glory in the name of Briton", and while it was some time before he fully understood the complexities of the relationship between monarchy and Parliament, he was probably one of the most popular monarchs Britain had ever had. In 1837 the accession of Victoria was widely welcomed, but her marriage to a German prince, Albert, was criticized and Albert was resented until the enormous success of the 1851 Great Exhibition earned him widespread public approval. By the end of Victoria's long reign, the monarchy had surrendered most of its actual power but it retained very considerable influence and enjoyed even more popularity.

RULE BRITANNIA
The Hanoverian period saw a considerable expansion of British power overseas. The picture above shows the Royal Navy defeating the Dutch at the Battle of Camperdown in 1797.

GEORGE I

1714–1727

GEORGE I ARRIVED IN ENGLAND from Hanover at the age of 54, unable to speak English and with only a limited knowledge of his new kingdom. It was a difficult inheritance, for many people wanted the Stuart dynasty to continue and within a year of his accession he had to face a Jacobite rising in Scotland. More than most monarchs, George needed to be able to trust his advisers and ministers, but most British politicians, while men of considerable ability, were almost devoid of integrity. George therefore relied on his Hanoverian associates, and it was only after 1721 that firm government was established when Robert Walpole became, in effect, Britain's first Prime Minister.

THE COAT OF ARMS OF GEORGE I
On the accession of George I, the royal coat of arms was changed to include the arms of his German possessions.

♛ GEORGE I

- *Born* Osnabruck, Hanover, 7 June 1660, son of George, Duke of Brunswick-Luneberg and Sophia of Bohemia.
- *Married* Sophia Dorothea, Germany, 21 Nov 1682, 2 children.
- *Acceded* 1 Aug 1714.
- *Crowned* Westminster Abbey, 20 Oct 1714.
- *Died* Hanover, 11 June 1727, aged 67.

THE OLD PRETENDER

THE 1715 RISING
Soon after the accession of George in 1714, a rebellion began in Scotland to place the "Old Pretender" – James Edward Stuart, heir to James II – on the throne. The rising in 1715 was easily crushed.

THE HORSE OF HANOVER
Two views of the Horse of Hanover are shown above: left, as a symbol of unity on the coronation medal of George I, and right, as a symbol of tyranny on a Jacobite medal of 1721.

THE ROYAL COUPLE
George and Sophia are shown on the stoneware teapot below.

SOPHIA DOROTHEA
George married Sophia Dorothea, the pretty but headstrong 16-year-old daughter of the Duke of Celle, in 1682. They disliked each other from the start, and after having two children, soon drifted apart. George took a number of mistresses, while his wife fell for Count Philip von Konigsmarck, a Swedish diplomat. Their affair soon created a scandal and in 1694 George had Konigsmarck killed and banished his wife to Ahlden Castle until her death in 1726.

SOUTH SEA BUBBLE
In 1711, a company was set up to trade with the South Seas. Thousands of people invested savings in the company, but in 1720 the speculative bubble burst. Most investors lost their money and the government was engulfed in scandal. Confidence in the financial system was only restored on the appointment of Sir Robert Walpole as First Lord of the Treasury.

THE GERMAN KING

Other than his patronage of Handel, George had little taste for the arts, could only speak German, seldom read anything of merit, and was phlegmatic, lazy and dull-witted. Yet George did have redeeming features, notably loyalty to his friends.

GEORGE I
This portrait of the King, from the studio of Sir Godfrey Kneller, was painted in 1714.

EVENTS OF THE REIGN 1714 – 1727

◆ **1714** George I succeeds his distant cousin Anne.
◆ **1714** A new Parliament is elected with a strong Whig majority, led by Charles Townshend and Robert Walpole.
◆ **1715** Jacobite Rising in Scotland is easily defeated.
◆ **1716** The Septennial Act allows for General Elections to be held every seven years.
◆ **1717** Townshend is dismissed from the government by George, causing Walpole to resign.
◆ **1719** Daniel Defoe publishes *Robinson Crusoe*.
◆ **1720** South Sea Bubble bursts, leaving many investors ruined.
◆ **1721** Sir Robert Walpole returns to government as First Lord of the Treasury until 1742; he is effectively the first Prime Minister.
◆ **1722** Death of the Duke of Marlborough.
◆ **1726** First circulating library in Britain opened in Edinburgh.
◆ **1726** Jonathan Swift publishes *Gulliver's Travels*
◆ **1726** Death of Sophia Dorothea, wife of George I.
◆ **1727** Death of the scientist, Isaac Newton.
◆ **1727** Death of George I in Hanover.

THE DEVIL'S WORK
William Hogarth's cartoon satirizes the effects of the South Sea Bubble on London, many of whose inhabitants were ruined by speculation in the company. On the left the Devil can be seen admiring his handiwork, while in the foreground, his victims – religion, honesty and honour – are sacrificed.

THE FIRST PRIME MINISTER

1721–1742

DURING THE REIGN OF CHARLES II, the practice arose for the King to consult a few important ministers about affairs of state in his private apartment or cabinet. By the time of William and Mary, this "cabinet" of ministers – the term Cabinet was not in regular use until the reign of Anne – was in charge of the government and held weekly meetings usually presided over by the sovereign. Cabinet members were drawn from the political party having the largest number of Members of Parliament in the House of Commons and they chose one of the number to be their nominal head. The accession of George I presented a problem in that the new king spoke no English and could not therefore preside at Cabinet meetings. As First Lord of the Treasury from 1721-42, Robert Walpole fulfilled that role, becoming prime or first minister of the king.

THE FIRST LORD
As First Lord of the Treasury, Walpole worked from an office in Downing Street. Among the items he used is this silver writing box, engraved with his crest and motto.

ROBERT WALPOLE

The son of a West Norfolk landowner, Robert Walpole was born in 1676 and entered Parliament in 1701 for the Whig party. He proved to be an effective debater and rose rapidly in the Whig hierarchy, becoming First Lord of the Treasury and Chancellor of the Exchequer in 1715.

Walpole left the government in 1717 but returned in 1720 to help restore order in public affairs following the South Sea Bubble crisis. In 1721 he was appointed First Lord of the Treasury once again – in effect Prime Minister – and remained in office until his resignation in 1742. Created First Earl of Orford, Walpole died in 1745.

THE COUNTRY SQUIRE
A good natured, cheerful and tolerant man, Walpole remained at heart a quintessentially English country squire throughout his lengthy and often turbulent political career. He possessed great political skill and an unflappable nature, remarking once that: "I throw off my cares when I throw off my clothes."

No 10
The most famous front door in Britain (above), guarded round the clock by a police officer, today looks out across Downing Street to the Victorian splendour of the Foreign Office. In Walpole's time, however, Downing Street was a cul-de-sac of late 17th-century and early 18th-century town houses (left).

DOWNING STREET
Named after Sir George Downing, a 17th-century secretary to the Treasury, Downing Street has become synonymous with British government. No 10 Downing Street has been the official residence of all Prime Ministers since George II gave it to the government as an office and town house for the First Lord of the Treasury, Robert Walpole. The house was built in the late 17th century and was then renovated for Walpole's use in the 1730s by William Kent, who had designed the interior of Walpole's country home at Houghton in West Norfolk.

THE CABINET ROOM
At the heart of No 10 is the Cabinet Room, where the Prime Minister and members of the government hold their Cabinet meetings. The Cabinet members sit at a baize-covered table, boat-shaped to ensure that everybody sitting down can be seen and heard by everyone else.

GEORGE II

1727–1760

THE COAT OF ARMS OF GEORGE II

FOR THE FIRST 12 YEARS of his reign, George was well served by the peaceful policies of the Prime Minister Robert Walpole, who kept Britain out of all major foreign entanglements. But after 1739 Britain was involved in almost continuous conflict in Europe, first with Spain, then with France during the eight-year War of the Austrian Succession, and then again with France during the Seven Years' War. This period also saw a substantial extension to the British Empire in North America and India. By the time of George's death in 1760, Britain was on its way to becoming a truly world power.

👑 GEORGE II

- **Born** Hanover, 9 Nov 1683, son of George I and Sophia Dorothea.
- **Married** Caroline of Brandenburg-Ansbach, Hanover, 2 Sept 1705, 10 children.
- **Acceded** 11 June 1727.
- **Crowned** Westminster Abbey, 11 Oct 1727.
- **Died** Kensington Palace, 25 Oct 1760, aged 76.

ROYAL PATRONAGE

The Hanoverians have earned a false reputation for philistinism; in fact, they were keenly interest in the arts, notably music. George I gave money to the first Royal Academy of Music in 1719 (which failed a few years later), while George II patronized Handel. His son Frederick, Prince of Wales, was an enthusiastic cellist, while George III confessed to Fanny Burney, a novelist and diarist, that it was as strange for him to meet people who had no ear for music as it was to meet people who were dumb.

ROYAL FIREWORKS

The signing in 1748 of the peace treaty of Aix-la-Chapelle at the end of the War of the Austrian Succession was celebrated in London the following year by a fireworks display in Hyde Park, for which Handel wrote the now-famous Music for the Royal Fireworks. *One week later the Duke of Richmond staged his own display on the Thames (right).*

BLIND EYE

Throughout their long marriage, Caroline (left) was well aware of George's propensity for love affairs and took a tolerant line towards his mistresses. On her deathbed in 1737, she suggested that George should marry again, but he swore he would only have mistresses. After her death, he said he had known many women but not one of them was fit to buckle Caroline's shoe.

QUEEN CAROLINE

The daughter of the Margrave of Brandenburg-Ansbach, Caroline married George in 1705, when she was 22. A large, blonde-haired, sensual woman, she had great charm and greater intelligence. When the couple came to live in London in 1714 on George I's accession to the throne, Caroline gathered a circle of literary and artistic friends around her. She also became deeply involved in politics and supported Robert Walpole. Caroline's strong and beneficial influence over her husband was powerful enough to prevent him dismissing Walpole when George became king in 1727.

"THE BEST MASTER"

Tall, with bulging blue eyes and a large nose, George had few intellectual interests beyond a passing fondness for history and military memorabilia. He was strongly criticized by contemporaries, who saw him as arrogant, vain, ungracious, obstinate, selfish, even ridiculous. Yet he was also brave, as shown by his leadership at Dettingen, and was held in awe by some of his ministers: the Duke of Newcastle, his final Prime Minister, said on George's death that he had "lost the best ... master and the best friend that subject ever had".

GEORGE II
This portrait of George was painted in the studio of Charles Jervas in 1727, the year in which George became king.

DETTINGEN
In 1743 George took command of an army sent to drive the French out of Germany. His involvement in the Battle of Dettingen (above), when he led troops into action, was the last time a British king led an army into battle.

EVENTS OF THE REIGN
1727 – 1760

◆ 1727 George succeeds his father George I.
◆ 1732 A royal charter is granted for the founding of Georgia.
◆ 1736 Witchcraft is finally abolished as a crime.
◆ 1737 Death of Queen Caroline.
◆ 1738 John and Charles Wesley start the Methodist movement.
◆ 1739 Britain goes to war with Spain over Captain Jenkins's ear, claimed to have been cut off in a skirmish at sea.
◆ 1740-48 War of Austrian Succession breaks out in Europe.
◆ 1742 First performance of Handel's *Messiah* in Dublin.
◆ 1742 Walpole resigns as Prime Minister and is created Earl of Orford; he dies in 1745.
◆ 1743 George leads troops into battle at Dettingen in Bavaria.
◆ 1745 Jacobite Rising in Scotland: Scottish victory at Prestonpans.
◆ 1746 Scots crushed at the Battle of Culloden.
◆ 1751 Death of Frederick, Prince of Wales; his son George becomes heir to the throne.
◆ 1753 Foundation of the British Museum, opened 1759.
◆ 1756-63 Seven Years' War.
◆ 1757 Robert Clive wins Battle of Plassey and secures the Indian province of Bengal for Britain.
◆ 1757 William Pitt becomes Prime Minister.
◆ 1759 James Wolfe captures Quebec and expels the French from Canada.
◆ 1760 George II dies.

THE PRINCE OF WALES
Frederick was loathed by his parents. Caroline was comforted on her death in 1737 that she would "never see that monster again".

JACOBITE RISING

1745

THE JACOBITES – their name was derived from the Latin *Jacobus*, meaning James – were the supporters of James II and his heirs' claim to the English throne. For almost 60 years after James had fled into exile in 1688, his supporters kept alive the hope of a Jacobite restoration, and with it the return of Catholicism to Britain. A rising in 1715 against George I by James Edward Stuart, the Old Pretender and son of James II, had been a disastrous failure, but in 1745, the Jacobites tried again. The Young Pretender, Charles Edward Stuart – son of the Old Pretender – returned to Scotland from exile in France. He raised an army among the Highland clans and marched into England claiming the throne for his father. Like the previous attempt, it ended in failure.

THE MILITARY CAMPAIGN

Charles Edward Stuart landed in Scotland with a handful of officers in July 1745. Six weeks later, he was at the head of an army of nearly 3,000 men drawn up outside Edinburgh. After the city surrendered, Charles proclaimed his father king, routing an English force under Sir John Cope at Prestonpans, 10 miles east of the city. Inexplicably, Charles dallied for weeks in Edinburgh and did not cross the English border until November. The delay doomed the enterprise. The English assembled a force of nearly 10,000 men under William, Duke of Cumberland, son of George II. Charles retreated to the Scottish Highlands and met defeat in April 1746 at the Battle of Culloden.

THE YOUNG PRETENDER
This portrait of Charles Edward Stuart was painted in Antonio David's studio, c.1732, when the Prince was only 12.

BONNIE PRINCE CHARLIE

Charles Edward Stuart was born in France in 1720. He believed that he had a legitimate claim to the English throne and that the Hanoverian kings had deprived him and his father of their birthright. Affectionately known as Bonnie Prince Charlie, he inspired great loyalty among his followers and commanded his forces to great effect during the early stages of the rising. However, he was somewhat naive in his belief that large numbers of Englishmen would rally to his cause, and he was unable to stave off final defeat.

THE BATTLE OF CULLODEN
On 15 April 1746, on Culloden Moor, the tired and hungry Jacobite army was heavily defeated by a superior English force. After the Duke of Cumberland (seen on the white horse), ordered that "no quarter" be given, the Jacobites were pursued and cut down without mercy.

ESCAPE FROM SCOTLAND

After Charles escaped from Culloden, the English government put a price on his head. A manhunt ensued and Charles spent months hiding in the Scottish Highlands and islands. One refuge was the island of South Uist, from which he was rescued by Flora MacDonald, a local woman. She smuggled him, dressed in woman's clothing, "over the seas to Skye" under the pseudonym of Betty Burke. Later, Charles fled Skye for the mainland, where he hid in a cave occupied by robbers (who did not turn him in, despite the huge reward) before finally boarding a frigate destined for France. His hopes dashed, he took to drink and died in relative poverty in Rome in 1788, aged 68.

THE LOST CAUSE
After the defeat in 1746, the lost cause of the Jacobites was kept alive in numerous ways. This Staffordshire china teapot depicting Bonnie Prince Charlie was produced in the late 1750s.

THE AFTERMATH

Following the slaughter at Culloden, the English determined to destroy Jacobite support forever. Jacobite prisoners were either shot, neglected to the point of starvation, or sold as slaves to American plantations. Clan chiefs were stripped of their authority, and the wearing of tartans and kilts, the playing of pipes and the owning of weapons were all forbidden on pain of death. These and other measures finally snuffed out the Jacobite cause.

EXECUTION OF THE REBEL PEERS
Many of the Jacobite leaders were executed on Tower Hill (below) The 80-year-old Lord Lovat was the last person to be beheaded in public in England.

FAREWELL TO FLORA
In this 19th-century painting by George W. Joy (left), Charles is seen bidding farewell to Flora MacDonald after she had helped him to escape to the island of Skye. Flora was subsequently imprisoned by the English as an accomplice but was later released.

GEORGE III

1760–1820

THE FIRST HANOVERIAN MONARCH to be born and bred in England, George III was a conscientious ruler who believed in personal rule, albeit through constitutional means. Although sometimes accused of interfering in politics, George had a successful working relationship with most of his prime ministers. He was in need of good advisers, for his reign spanned a period of great change. From 1788, George suffered from porphyria, a disease that made him appear deranged. By 1811 his health was so bad that his son was created Prince Regent until his father died in 1820.

GEORGE III

- *Born* Norfolk House, London, 4 June 1738, son of Frederick, Prince of Wales, and Augusta of Saxe-Gotha.
- *Acceded* 25 Oct 1760.
- *Married* Charlotte of Mecklenburg-Strelitz, St James's Palace, 8 Sept 1761, 15 children.
- *Crowned* Westminster Abbey, 21 Sept 1761.
- *Died* Windsor Castle, 29 Jan 1820, aged 81.

THE COAT OF ARMS OF GEORGE III
In 1801 the royal coat of arms was changed to remove the royal arms of France (top). In 1816 the arms were changed again when the Electorate of Hanover became a kingdom, the crown replacing the Electoral bonnet.

FARMER GEORGE
Early in his reign George III became interested in the study of agriculture, which he put to practical use on his farms at Windsor and Richmond, multiplying profits ten-fold under his personal supervision. In 1788-9, during a period of convalescence, George toured farms in the south and west of the country. Numerous conversations about farming with country folk earned him the nickname of Farmer George.

EARLY POLITICS
George III came to the throne well-trained for his constitutional role, and was clearly determined to rule by constitutional means. Yet the early years were difficult. George's first Prime Minister, Bute, was so unpopular that he had to be protected by a bodyguard and was soon forced to resign. He was followed by a succession of ministers who failed to please either the King or Parliament. In 1770 George chose Lord North, a man who did what George requested and managed to square it with Parliament. Though North is usually remembered for the loss of the American colonies, the fact remains that he and the King worked well together.

THE EARL OF BUTE
Lord Bute was tutor to George III before his accession, Prime Minister from 1762-3, and rumoured to be George's mother's lover.

WATERLOO
Wellington's victory over Napoleon at the Battle of Waterloo, fought outside Brussels on 18 June 1815, marked the end of 22 years of almost continuous warfare in Europe.

THE FRENCH WARS

The revolution and the establishment of a republic in France after 1789 provoked considerable consternation in Britain. Republican sentiment posed a threat to the government, causing Prime Minister William Pitt the Younger to introduce repressive measures to maintain control. George's second son, Frederick, Duke of York, became Commander-in-Chief of the army for part of the lengthy war, although the heir to the throne, George, was not allowed to fight.

GEORGE III
This portrait of the King was painted in the studio of Allan Ramsay in 1767, when George was 29 (left).

HORATIO NELSON
Britain's greatest naval commander, Admiral Lord Nelson, was much mourned after his death in action at Trafalgar in 1805 (above).

A RESPECTED MONARCH

A tall, dignified man, George III was a hard-working monarch who took his royal role seriously. Although obstinate he believed that "no one should be above confessing when they have been mistaken". Deeply religious, he remained faithful to his wife, Queen Charlotte, throughout their marriage, and his sense of duty, both public and private, and his ability to speak to ordinary people, earned him popularity and respect.

EVENTS OF THE REIGN 1760 – 1820

- ◆ **1760** George becomes king on the death of his grandfather George II.
- ◆ **1762** Earl of Bute is appointed Prime Minister.
- ◆ **1763** Peace of Paris ends Seven Years' War.
- ◆ **1765** Stamp Act raises taxes in American colonies.
- ◆ **1769-70** James Cook's first voyage round the world.
- ◆ **1770-82** Lord North serves as Prime Minister.
- ◆ **1771** *Encyclopedia Britannica* is first published.
- ◆ **1773** Boston Tea Party.
- ◆ **1773** The world's first cast-iron bridge is constructed over the River Severn at Coalbrookdale.
- ◆ **1775-83** American War of Independence.
- ◆ **1775** James Watt develops the steam engine.
- ◆ **1782** Ireland obtains a short-lived parliament.
- ◆ **1783** Britain recognizes US independence.
- ◆ **1783-1801** William Pitt the Younger serves as Prime Minister.
- ◆ **1788** George suffers his first attack of porphyria.
- ◆ **1789** Outbreak of the French Revolution.
- ◆ **1791** Publication of James Boswell's *Life of Johnson* and Thomas Paine's *Rights of Man*.
- ◆ **1793-1802** War between Britain and France.
- ◆ **1800** Act of Union with Ireland.
- ◆ **1803-15** Napoleonic Wars.
- ◆ **1805** Nelson destroys combined French and Spanish fleet off Trafalgar but is killed during the battle.
- ◆ **1808-14** Peninsular War to drive French out of Spain.
- ◆ **1810** Final illness of George III leads to his son becoming Regent in 1811.
- ◆ **1812** Prime Minister Spencer Perceval is assassinated in the House of Commons by a disgruntled bankrupt.
- ◆ **1813** Publication of *Pride and Prejudice* by Jane Austen.
- ◆ **1815** Defeat of Napoleon at Waterloo marks end of Napoleonic Wars.
- ◆ **1815** Corn Laws passed to protect British agriculture from cheap imports.
- ◆ **1818** Queen Charlotte dies.
- ◆ **1819** Peterloo Massacre of political reform campaigners in Manchester.
- ◆ **1820** Death of George III.

GEORGE III

THE FAMILY MAN

FATHER AND SON

One characteristic of the Hanoverian monarchs was their inability to get on with their sons and heirs. George III became hostile to his eldest son George when the latter was still a boy, and from his mid-teens Prince George did what he could to annoy his father. Attempts at reconciliation were made, and most failed, although the two came to terms with each other when Prince George was appointed Regent on his father's final illness in 1811.

A RECONCILIATION

The reconciliation between George and the Prince of Wales in 1804 is lampooned in this cartoon (left). One of the things they quarrelled about was the question of political rights for Catholics, which the King strongly opposed.

THE YOUNG FAMILY

Johann Zoffany's portrait of George, Charlotte and the first six of their fifteen children (below) captures well the formality and regality of the young King.

KING LEAR

A contemporary picture (above) cruelly depicts George III as the mad King Lear from William Shakespeare's play.

UNFIT TO RULE

In 1788, 1801 and 1804 George III suffered a series of incapacitating fits that had all the appearance of progressively worsening mental illness. Although he recovered from these early attacks, in 1810-11 he had a relapse and descended into permanent derangement and blindness for the last nine years of his life. Medical science has since discovered that George was suffering from an hereditary physical illness known as porphyria, in which the victim displays symptoms of delirium and delusions, and gives an impression of madness.

CHARLOTTE'S COTTAGE

In 1770 Charlotte had constructed a pavilion in the grounds of the Botanical Gardens at Kew from which guests could observe her menagerie of exotic animals, including, at a later date, kangaroos from Botany Bay, which lived in a three-acre paddock.

QUEEN CHARLOTTE

During the early years of her marriage, Queen Charlotte displayed simple tastes that coincided with the king's own regimen of plenty of fresh air and exercise and a light, near-vegetarian diet and austere living. However, after 1804 as George's illness worsened she drifted away from her husband and her personality changed. Once gracious and cultivated, she became fat and unpleasant, and indulged in huge meals. During George's illness she supported the doctors who were making his life a misery. Although she visited her husband regularly, he did not recognize her. She died in 1818.

CHARLOTTE

Although gracious, cultivated and pretty in her youth, Charlotte became fat and unpleasant after 1804. It is possible that she became depressed by her husband's illness.

THE QUEEN'S WEDDING RING

During her married life, Queen Charlotte wore a ring bearing a portrait of George III.

THE ROYAL FAMILY

Princess Charlotte of Mecklenburg-Strelitz married George III in 1761, at the age of 18. The two met for the first time at about 3 o'clock on 8 September in St James's Palace, and six hours later walked across the road to be wed in the Chapel Royal. The marriage was successful, and they had 15 children. As someone observed: "they did not fall in love and marry; they married and fell in love".

AMERICAN WAR OF INDEPENDENCE
1775–1783

THE LAST KING to rule the American colonies was George III, for it was during his reign that the 13 British colonies in North America fought for and won their independence. The colonies had enjoyed only limited self-government from Britain, which continually interfered in their affairs. But when the British Government began to increase taxation in 1765, the colonists resisted, arguing for "No taxation without representation" in the British Parliament. The argument eventually led to war in 1775. It was the first revolt in the British Empire. Eight years later, in 1783, the United States of America was free.

GEORGE WASHINGTON
Born in Virginia in 1732, George Washington was the great-grandson of an English squire from Northamptonshire. He had fought with British colonial forces against American Indians and the French and was therefore well qualified to lead the colonists as their commander-in-chief.

THE BOSTON TEA PARTY
On 16 December 1773, 50 colonists, disguised as Indians, boarded ships in Boston Harbor and emptied 300 chests of tea into the water (left).

THE COURSE OF THE WAR

In 1770 the Boston Massacre took place after British troops fired on a crowd of unarmed civilians, killing five people. The situation worsened after the Boston Tea Party in 1773 and the despatch of more troops to quell the numerous disturbances. Following the establishment of a colonial army under George Washington in early 1775, the first military skirmishes took place at Lexington and Concord in April.

After the colonies' Declaration of Independence on 4 July 1776, General Howe landed his British troops on Long Island and inflicted a defeat on Washington's army at White Plains. However, the tide turned in 1777 when the British suffered a decisive defeat at Saratoga. When the French recognized the new nation and sent it military aid, a colonial victory was assured. Although the British continued to do well in the south of the country, a defeat at Yorktown in 1781 settled the matter.

SURRENDER AT YORKTOWN
On 19 October 1781 the British troops under General Cornwallis were surrounded in their base at Yorktown, Virginia, trapped by a combined American and French force and cut off from the sea by French ships. Cornwallis had no choice but to surrender. This defeat finally convinced the British that the war was unwinnable.

INDEPENDENCE

The Continental Congress of the 13 states issued the Declaration of Independence on 4 July 1776. Drawn up by the lawyer, and future President of the United States, Thomas Jefferson, in consultation with the diplomat and scientist Benjamin Franklin, the Declaration stated that "all men are created equal", that they "are endowed by their creator with certain inalienable rights", that among these are the right to "life, liberty and the pursuit of happiness", and that to secure these rights "governments are instituted among men, deriving their powers from the consent of the governed". In other words, to be ruled and taxed by the British without any form of political representation in Parliament was in breach of their inalienable rights.

THE DECLARATION OF INDEPENDENCE

A delegation (above), led by Thomas Jefferson and Benjamin Franklin, presented the draft of the Declaration of Independence to the Continental Congress for debate in July 1776. The Declaration (left) claims that "..these united colonies are, and ought to be, Free and Independent States", that is, free from rule by the British government and crown.

BUCKINGHAM PALACE

THE HOME OF BRITISH ROYALTY

FOR SO LONG IDENTIFIED with the British monarchy, Buckingham Palace began life not as a royal palace but as a London town house. Buckingham House, as it was then known, was built in 1703 for the Duke of Buckingham. It was described at the time as a "graceful palace not to be contemned by the greatest monarch." In 1762 George III, looking for a London residence to replace the "dust-trap" of St James's Palace, bought the house for £28,000 from the son of the last Duke of Buckingham. It was well situated, for at that time it was outside the centre of the city and was surrounded by fields. Ever since that year, Buckingham Palace has served as the official London residence of every British sovereign, a place where public ceremonial and private lives combine in one building.

BUCKINGHAM HOUSE
The original building was designed by William Winde in 1702. The picture above shows the house as it was in 1754 before it was purchased by George III.

THE ROYAL COLLECTION

Over the years, the Royal Family has accumulated a wealth of treasures from around the world. Paintings, sculptures, fine porcelain, gold and silver work, and collections of jade and other items, many of which have been given to the Royal Family as presents, are on display in the Palace. In 1961, the Queen's Gallery was built to house some of the many fine works of art from the royal collection.

CHELSEA TIME
Among the many fine pieces of china on display in Buckingham Palace is this Chelsea porcelain clock, one of a pair dating from c.1760.

THE EAST FRONT
After the addition of the East Front between 1847-53, Buckingham Palace looked much as it does today, as can be seen above from this watercolour dating from the 1850s.

REBUILDING THE PALACE

Over the years, Buckingham Palace has undergone numerous alterations. In 1820, George IV commissioned the architect John Nash to design a new palace on the site, using what was required of the old house. Nash planned a building situated around three sides of a courtyard, but, although the work was begun during George's reign, it remained unfinished until 1837.

STATE BANQUET
The places are laid for a banquet to entertain a visiting head of state, a regular occurrence in the Palace (right).

AFFAIRS OF STATE

As the official home of the sovereign in London, Buckingham Palace plays host to numerous ceremonial occasions. Investitures of people honoured by the monarch or state, official receptions for visiting heads of state, weekly meetings with the Prime Minister, and informal summer garden parties all take place within its walls.

THE VICTORIAN PALACE

Although Victoria became disenchanted with the formality of Buckingham Palace and preferred to stay at Balmoral or Windsor, extensive alterations to the Palace were made to accommodate her growing family. An East Front was added between 1847-53 to enclose the courtyard, and a suite of state apartments was built in 1854. More changes were made during the reign of George V, when Sir Aston Webb remodelled the East Front in Portland stone in 1913.

THE PALACE TODAY
The East Front of the Palace the public sees today was remodelled as recently as 1913 (right). Much of the interior of the Palace is, however, of 18th- or 19th-century origin.

GEORGE IV

1820–1830

THE COAT OF ARMS OF GEORGE IV

GEORGE IV ACCEDED to the throne in 1820, having spent the previous nine years as Prince Regent for his blind and deranged father, George III. Although his reign was notable for the granting of political rights to Catholics, George IV is best remembered for his years as Prince of Wales. During that time he was a great patron of the arts, but led an immoral life. His marriage to Caroline of Brunswick proved troubled, and the couple parted amid accusations of infidelity. When George refused to allow Caroline to attend his coronation, he lost much of his popularity.

GEORGE IV

- **Born** St James's Palace, 12 Aug 1762, eldest son of George III and Queen Charlotte.
- **Married** Maria FitzHerbert, 15 Sept 1785; Caroline of Brunswick, 8 April 1795, 1 daughter.
- **Acceded** 29 Jan 1820.
- **Crowned** Westminster Abbey, 19 July 1821.
- **Died** Windsor, 26 June 1830, aged 67.

ROYAL ROMANCES

Throughout his life George enjoyed a succession of mistresses. They included the actress Mary Robinson (nicknamed Perdita), the Countess of Jersey, the Marchioness of Hertford, Lady Melbourne and the Marchioness of Conyngham. George also contracted a secret marriage to Maria FitzHerbert in 1785 and then 10 years later reluctantly agreed to marry his somewhat plain and overweight cousin, Caroline of Brunswick.

CONTEMPLATING MATRIMONY
Forced to choose an official wife (right), George was less than enamoured by the women he saw.

QUEEN CAROLINE'S TRIAL

A SECRET WIFE

In 1785 George secretly married a 28-year-old widow, Maria FitzHerbert when, as a virtuous Catholic, she refused to be his mistress. Her religion prevented an open marriage as the 1701 Act of Settlement prohibited the succession of a Catholic to the throne.

MRS FITZHERBERT

AN UNHAPPY MARRIAGE

In 1795 George was forced into marrying Caroline of Brunswick in order to get Parliament to pay off his huge debts. Within months, the couple parted and rumours spread of Caroline's infidelities. When George acceded to the throne in 1820, Caroline arrived from Italy to claim her rights as Queen. George wanted a divorce to deprive Caroline of her rank, and he accused her of adultery at a public trial. He failed and the following year Caroline was excluded from George's coronation; she died a few weeks later.

◆ **1820** George IV accedes to the throne after the death of his father George III.

◆ **1820** Failure of the Cato Street Conspiracy, a radical plot to murder the Cabinet.

◆ **1820** Trial of Queen Caroline in which George IV attempts to divorce her for adultery.

◆ **1821** Queen Caroline excluded from George IV's coronation.

◆ **1823** Construction begins of the British Museum, the first public museum in the world.

◆ **1824** The National Gallery is established in London.

◆ **1825** The Stockton and Darlington Railway is opened, the world's first railway service.

◆ **1825** Trade unions legalized.

◆ **1828** Wellington becomes British Prime Minister.

◆ **1829** The Metropolitan Police Force is set up by Robert Peel.

◆ **1829** The Catholic Relief Act is passed, permitting Catholics to become Members of Parliament.

◆ **1830** George IV dies at Windsor.

CONTROVERSY IN PARLIAMENT
A cartoon of 1827, entitled "A British Battering Ram preparing the way for a Popish Bull", depicts the forceful agitation for Catholic participation in the political process.

CATHOLIC EMANCIPATION
In 1828, the voters of County Clare in Ireland elected a Roman Catholic to represent them as their Member of Parliament. However, by law, Catholics were forbidden to sit in Parliament. After many demonstrations the law was changed in 1829.

GEORGE IV
This portrait was painted in 1815 by Thomas Lawrence.

THE DISSOLUTE PRINCE
When he was Prince of Wales, George was a handsome and popular young man with extravagant tastes in food and drink, women, and the arts. He commissioned the Royal Pavilion in Brighton, Sussex, which began the fashion for seaside resorts. As a result of years of dissolute behaviour, his health suffered and he became grossly overweight, spending the last years of his reign as a virtual recluse at Windsor .

THE DUKE OF WELLINGTON
Arthur Wellesley, First Duke of Wellington (1769-1852), defeated Napoleon at the battle of Waterloo in 1815. Commander-in-Chief of the British Army, he entered British politics as a Tory and became Prime Minister in 1828. Although he soon relinquished his army post, the Duke was the only man since Cromwell to be head of government and head of the army at the same time.

BRIGHTON PAVILION

A ROYAL EXTRAVAGANCE

THE ROYAL PAVILION at Brighton is a monument to the flamboyant Prince Regent, later George IV. It began life as a simple farmhouse and was bought by the Prince in 1786 to house his secret bride, Mrs FitzHerbert. It was then extensively rebuilt and redesigned into an exotic palace. Work on the building took a total of 35 years, during which time the Prince and his friends turned the tiny port of Brighthelmstone, as Brighton was then known, into a fashionable seaside resort. The Prince's imagination was checked only by his lack of funds: redesigns cost over half a million pounds, a huge sum at the time, and several contractors were ruined when he ran out of money. In 1820 George became king and abandoned the building; it was sold to the town council of Brighton in 1848.

ROYAL LUXURY
The opulence of the King's Apartments (above) is in fact a restrained example of the fantastical interiors of the Royal Pavilion. The French cartel clock (left) is one of the many objects on display.

WORLD VIEWS
The domes, spires and pagodas of the Pavilion (right) reflect details from almost every major culture around the world.

A ROYAL THEME PARK

Brighton Pavilion went through several reincarnations during its ownership by the Prince Regent. Its original architect, Henry Holland, designed the building as a neo-classical villa. Later, William Porden furnished it in oriental style and built an Indian-style dome into the roof of the stables. The Prince then asked for this design to be incorporated into the rest of the building, which was done by John Nash, who added the onion-shaped domes and miniature pagodas to complete the present bizarre mixture of styles.

WILLIAM IV

1830–1837

THE COAT OF ARMS OF WILLIAM IV

AS GEORGE III'S THIRD SON, William IV did not expect to accede to the throne. He only became heir to his eldest brother, George IV, at the age of 61, when George III's second son, the Duke of York, died in 1827. William finally came to the throne in 1830 at the age of 64. There was considerable concern that he would not be fit for the task. However, he acquitted himself well, showing enough sense to accept advice from his ministers during a period of great political and constitutional reform.

☙ WILLIAM IV

- **Born** Buckingham Palace, 21 Aug 1765, third son of George III and Queen Charlotte.
- **Married** Adelaide of Saxe-Meiningen, Kew Palace, 13 July 1818.
- **Acceded** 26 June 1830.
- **Crowned** Westminster Abbey, 8 Sept 1831.
- **Died** Windsor Castle, 20 June 1837, aged 71.

EARLY LIFE

William entered the navy as a midshipman at the age of 13 and rose through the ranks to take command of his own ship in 1786. In 1790 William retired from active service and settled down at Bushey Park, where he lived in bliss with his mistress, the actress Dorothea Jordan, who bore him 10 illegitimate children. In 1811 financial difficulties drove William to leave her and begin the search for a wife. He finally married Princess Adelaide of Saxe-Meiningen in 1818.

THE ROYAL MISTRESS
Dorothea Jordan was William's mistress for 22 years prior to his marriage to Princess Adelaide.

THE SAILOR KING
William takes the helm of the ship of state.

LONDON BRIDGE
By the beginning of the 19th century, the old London Bridge – built in the 13th century and covered with houses and shops – was no longer adequate for the needs of a growing metropolis. The bridge was pulled down and a replacement built, designed by John Rennie the Elder. Amid great pomp and ceremony, the new bridge was opened on 1 August 1831 by William IV and Queen Adelaide, who both attended a banquet held in a marquee erected on the bridge.

"SILLY BILLY"

William's early life in the navy shaped his character. A man of strong language and forthright opinions, he was affable, at times excitable and often lacking in tact, characteristics which earned him the nickname "Silly Billy". However, his blunt speech, friendly manner and lack of extravagance – he insisted on a coronation that was one-tenth the cost of his brother's – endeared him to the public.

WILLIAM IV
This portrait of William was painted c.1800 by Sir Martin Archer Shee.

POLITICAL REFORM

The general election of 1831 brought to power a Whig Government, led by Lord Grey, determined to extend the franchise. However, attempts to pass a Reform Bill through Parliament were blocked by the House of Lords which, feeling threatened by this extension of democracy to the middle classes, voted against it. After considerable constitutional upheaval, the Reform Bill became law in 1832.

EVENTS OF THE REIGN 1830 – 1837

◆ **1830** William IV succeeds his brother George IV.
◆ **1830** Liverpool-Manchester railway line opened.
◆ **1831** The new London Bridge is opened over the River Thames.
◆ **1832** The First Reform Act is passed, extending the vote to a further 500,000 people and redistributing Parliamentary seats on a more equitable basis.
◆ **1833** Slavery abolished throughout the British Empire.
◆ **1833** Factory Act passed, prohibiting children under the age of nine working in factories and reducing the working hours of women and older children.
◆ **1834** Poor Law Act passed, creating workhouses for the poor.
◆ **1834** The Tolpuddle Martyrs sentenced to transportation to Australia for attempting to form a trade union.
◆ **1834** The Houses of Parliament destroyed by fire.
◆ **1835** The Municipal Reform Act passed, requiring members of town councils to be elected by ratepayers and councils to publish their financial accounts.
◆ **1836** Births, marriages and deaths must be registered by law.
◆ **1837** Charles Dickens publishes *Oliver Twist*, a novel that draws attention to the plight of the poor in Britain.
◆ **1837** William IV dies at Windsor Castle.

REFORM BILL
William ponders the writing on the wall, wondering whether the message is addressed to him.

VICTORIA

1837–1901

THE COAT OF ARMS OF VICTORIA
As a woman, Victoria could not accede to the crown of Hanover, and so the Hanoverian throne passed to the Duke of Cumberland. The arms of Hanover were removed from the coat of arms, which has not altered to the present day.

QUEEN VICTORIA SUCCEEDED to the throne at the age of 18 on the death of her uncle, William IV, in 1837. Happy to escape an over-protective upbringing by her mother and Sir John Conroy, controller of her mother's household (Victoria's father, Edward, Duke of Kent, had died when she was eight months old), Victoria took on her responsibilities with enthusiasm. Guided initially by Lord Melbourne – the first of many able Prime Ministers – she received support and advice from her husband Prince Albert, whom she married in 1840. When Albert died in 1861, Victoria was prostrated with grief, withdrew from public life and remained in mourning so long there were calls for the ending of the monarchy. But coaxed back to her public role, she became a much-loved and respected monarch who presided over the industrial and social transformation of Britain and a massive expansion of the Empire.

VICTORIA
- ◆ *Born* Kensington Palace, 24 May 1819, daughter of Edward, Duke of Kent and Victoria of Saxe-Coburg-Saalfield.
- ◆ *Acceded* 20 June 1837.
- ◆ *Crowned* Westminster Abbey, 28 June 1838.
- ◆ *Married* Prince Albert of Saxe-Coburg-Gotha, St James's Palace, 10 Feb 1840, 9 children.
- ◆ *Died* Osborne House, Isle of Wight, 22 Jan 1901, aged 81.

CHILDHOOD DOLLS
In a childhood, which she described as "a melancholy one", Victoria played with many elaborate dolls (above).

THE PRIVY COUNCIL
Victoria held her first Privy Council in 1837 (below right), a few hours after her accession. Those present included the Prime Minister, Lord Melbourne (above right), who advised the queen on her duties.

THE BEDCHAMBER CRISIS

During the first two years of Victoria's reign Lord Melbourne, the Whig Prime Minister, advised her on the intricacies of politics. In 1839 Melbourne was defeated by Sir Robert Peel, a cold, intellectual Tory, whom Victoria instantly disliked. When he demanded that Victoria replace her Whig ladies of the bedchamber with Tories, she refused. As a result, Peel declined to form a government and Melbourne returned as Prime Minister.

MARRIAGE
A lustre-ware jug commemorates the wedding of Victoria and Albert on 10 February 1840.

VICTORIA
Sir George Hayer painted this portrait of Victoria in her coronation robes in 1838.

THE YOUNG QUEEN
When Victoria came to the throne she was known for her honesty and belief in her own judgement, a determination to have her own way and a streak of obstinacy in her make-up. At the same time, she seemed to need advice and support of an almost paternal nature.

EVENTS OF THE REIGN
1837 – 1901

◆ 1837 Victoria succeeds her uncle William IV.
◆ 1838 People's Charter issued by Chartists campaigning for political reform.
◆ 1840 Victoria marries Albert of Saxe-Coburg-Gotha.
◆ 1840 Penny Post introduced.
◆ 1841-6 Sir Robert Peel is Prime Minister.
◆ 1845-8 Potato Famine in Ireland kills more than 1 million.
◆ 1846 Repeal of the Corn Laws.
◆ 1848 Major Chartist demonstration in London.
◆ 1851 Great Exhibition takes place in Hyde Park.
◆ 1852 Death of the Duke of Wellington.
◆ 1853 Vaccination against smallpox made compulsory.
◆ 1854-6 Crimean War fought by Britain and France against Russia.
◆ 1856 Victoria Cross instituted for military bravery.
◆ 1857-8 Indian Mutiny against British rule in India.
◆ 1859 Charles Darwin writes *The Origin of the Species.*
◆ 1861 Death of Prince Albert.
◆ 1863 Edward, Prince of Wales, marries Alexandra of Denmark.
◆ 1863 Salvation Army founded.
◆ 1867 Second Reform Bill doubles the franchise to 2 million.
◆ 1867 Canada becomes first independent dominion in Empire.
◆ 1868-74 Gladstone becomes Prime Minister for first time.
◆ 1869 The Irish Church is disestablished.
◆ 1870 Education Act makes primary education compulsory.
◆ 1871 Trade Unions legalized.
◆ 1872 Secret voting introduced for elections.
◆ 1874-80 Disraeli becomes Prime Minister for second time.
◆ 1875 Suez Canal shares purchased for Britain.
◆ 1876 Victoria becomes Empress of India.
◆ 1884 Third Reform Act further extends franchise.
◆ 1886 First Irish Home Rule Bill fails to pass House of Commons.
◆ 1887 Victoria celebrates her Golden Jubilee.
◆ 1887 Independent Labour Party founded.
◆ 1893 Second Irish Home Rule Bill fails to pass House of Lords.
◆ 1897 Victoria celebrates her Diamond Jubilee.
◆ 1899-1902 Boer War in South Africa.
◆ 1901 Death of Queen Victoria.

VICTORIA

1837–1901

PRIVATE GRIEF

In November 1861 Victoria's husband, Prince Albert, died of typhoid. His premature death at the age of 42 devastated the Queen, who loved Albert deeply and had come to rely on his advice regarding matters of state. For the next 13 years Victoria went into mourning, refusing to appear in public or attend Privy Council meetings, seeing all state papers in private and living in virtual seclusion in the royal residences of Osborne, Balmoral and Windsor.

During her withdrawal, Victoria drew comfort from her family and friends, notably her Scottish servant John Brown. But the public became disenchanted with such an excessive period of mourning, and there were calls for her abdication in favour of the Prince of Wales. Adverse comments about her behaviour started to appear in the press, and some politicians even went as far as to suggest the abolition of the monarchy and the creation of a republic in Britain.

THE QUEEN IN MOURNING
Victoria was devoted to her husband, Prince Albert, and after his premature death in 1861 she wore funeral black for the rest of her life, in respect for his memory (below).

DIAMOND JUBILEE
On 22 June 1897, Victoria celebrated her Diamond Jubilee by driving in an open landau from Buckingham Palace through cheering crowds to a service of thanksgiving at St Paul's Cathedral. Representatives from every part of the empire were present to pay their respects to the aged Queen.

RETURN TO PUBLIC LIFE

Encouraged by her family, friends and the newly-elected Prime Minister, Disraeli, Victoria finally emerged from mourning in 1874. Disraeli knew how to deal with the Queen, believing that "when it comes to royalty, you should lay it [flattery] on with a trowel". This approach worked wonders. Victoria became less reticent about public life and happily accepted the title Empress of India in 1876. Her diaries reveal a renewed zest for activity: she attended state balls, made appearances around the country, and even appeared in an open carriage.

By the time of her Golden Jubilee in 1887 Victoria had won back the respect and affection of her people, and her 50 years on the throne were marked by celebrations and church services throughout the Empire. When she died 14 years later, in 1901, the nation went into deep mourning at the loss of a venerated and much-loved monarch.

POLITICAL LIFE

Political events during the second half of Victoria's reign were dominated by two men: Benjamin Disraeli and William Gladstone. The Queen liked Disraeli, created him Earl of Beaconsfield, and fully supported his imperialist policies, notably the take-over of the Suez Canal, an important trade route to India. Gladstone opposed Disraeli's policies, considering them jingoistic and morally wrong. His greater concern was to extend the franchise, improve education and introduce home rule to Ireland. For this, and his somewhat patronizing attitude to the Queen, Gladstone incurred Victoria's intense displeasure throughout his lengthy career.

GLADSTONE AND DISRAELI
A decorative plate and a Staffordshire figure commemorate the Tory Benjamin Disraeli (left) and the Liberal William Gladstone (above), the two great political leaders of the late 19th century.

OSBORNE AND BALMORAL

ALWAYS ANXIOUS TO GET AWAY FROM THE PUBLIC PRESSURES OF LIFE in London, Victoria retreated to Osborne House on the Isle of Wight and Balmoral in the Highlands of Scotland to enjoy the pleasures of family life and outdoor pursuits.

OSBORNE HOUSE
Albert designed Osborne in a fashionable Italian style (above).

BALMORAL
Victoria's favourite home (right) was rebuilt to Albert's plans in the 1850s.

THE GREAT EXHIBITION

1851

THE GREAT EXHIBITION OF 1851 was the world's first international exhibition. Conceived by Prince Albert to celebrate the Industrial Revolution, the venture proved a triumphant success. From the time it was opened by Victoria on 1 May to its closure on 15 October, more than six million people visited the exhibition.

THE CRYSTAL PALACE
Consisting of over 300,000 panes of glass supported by a cast-iron framework, this huge exhibition hall was designed by Joseph Paxton to house the Great Exhibition of 1851 in London's Hyde Park.

PRINCE ALBERT
Albert was the Prince Consort of Queen Victoria.

THE ROYAL PATRON

Prince Albert had always taken an interest in the development of British industry and visited many factories and engineering works. In 1850 believing that the promotion of industry would help to alleviate poverty, he suggested that an international exhibition of industrial products be held in London. Despite a lack of interest and financial support from the government, he won popular support for his scheme through the press and raised sufficient finance to start the project. It is doubtful that the exhibition would have taken place without Albert's deep commitment to the idea.

A CELEBRATION OF INGENUITY
The vast interior of the Crystal Palace provided space for some 13,000 exhibitors from all around the world, over half of whom were British. With more than 100,000 industrial products on display, the Great Exhibition was both a gigantic display cabinet for manufacturing goods and a celebration of the Industrial Revolution and ingenuity of mankind. Prince Albert envisaged that it should "..combine engineering, utility and beauty in one staggering whole".

In the six months it was open, over six million people visited the Crystal Palace. Given that the population of Britain was less than 20 million at the time, this was a huge number. People of all classes attended. Workers clubbed together to afford the special excursion trains from industrial towns, while many Londoners visited the palace several times.

A MONUMENT TO ENTERPRISE

Joseph Paxton, estate manager to the Duke of Devonshire, based his design for the exhibition hall in Hyde Park on a huge glazed conservatory he had built at the Duke's stately home of Chatsworth, Derbyshire. Nicknamed the Crystal Palace by the satirical magazine *Punch*, the new building was 549 metres (600 yards) long, and provided over 9,300 square metres (1 million square feet) of floor space for exhibitors. When the exhibition finished, the palace was dismantled and rebuilt at Sydenham, in south London, in 1854. It remained standing until 1936, when it was accidently burned down.

THE ALBERT MEMORIAL

After Prince Albert died prematurely of typhoid in 1861, Queen Victoria was determined to perpetuate his memory. Buildings, stones, obelisks, busts and statues were erected all over the country. The greatest of these were the Albert Hall (opened by Victoria in 1871) and the nearby Albert Memorial. Both are sited on the edge of Hyde Park in London next to the cluster of museums and institutes, including the Victoria and Albert, Science, and Natural History museums, which were founded in Albert's lifetime with finance from the profits of the Great Exhibition.

THE EMPIRE

RULING THE GLOBE

WHAT USED TO BE CALLED the British Empire and is today known as the Commonwealth began over four centuries ago with the activities of Elizabethan mariners, who combined seamanship with business enterprise to make the first attempts at colonization in North America. Over the next 300 years, British colonies were established all over the globe so that by the end of the 19th century, Victoria ruled over "the greatest empire the world had ever seen." Today this vast empire is no more, its constituent nations all having received their independence. Yet in its heyday, one quarter of the world's land surface was ruled from the imperial capital of London and flew the Union Jack.

THE WORLD PAINTED PINK
By the time this map was produced in 1886, the British Empire was reaching the height of its power. Its greatest extent came in 1920, when the former German colonies in Africa and the Far East came under British control.

IMPERIAL POWER
The image of Victoria the "Comforter of the Afflicted" (as depicted on the mug to the right) ran counter to the reality of British military power being used to crush Boer resistance, as the contemporary German cartoon above observes.

THE BOER WAR

One of the most vicious of imperial wars was fought in South Africa against the Boer republics of the Transvaal and the Orange Free State. The Boers, descendants of the original Dutch settlers of South Africa, resented British intrusion on to their lands, after the discovery of gold in the Transvaal during the 1880s. War broke out in 1899 and after initial Boer successes, Britain took over both states by 1902.

THE JEWEL IN THE CROWN

In 1757 Robert Clive won a victory at Plassey near Calcutta over the Nabob of Bengal. It marked the start of British rule in India which by the end of the 19th century extended over most of the sub-continent, including what is now Pakistan, Bangladesh, Burma and Sri Lanka. At first, British possessions were ruled by the East India Company, a trading company set up in 1600 to develop trading links with Asia, but after an army mutiny in 1857-8, India was ruled from London. In 1876 Victoria was proclaimed Empress of India; all future monarchs were Emperors of India until the country gained its independence in 1947.

"NEW CROWNS FOR OLD ONES!"
In this contemporary cartoon (above) which was printed in Punch *magazine, Victoria is seen wondering whether or not to accept from the British Prime Minister Benjamin Disraeli the imperial diadem of India in return for the traditional crown of England.*

RAISING THE FLAG
The establishment of British sovereignty was always marked by the raising of the Union Jack, as is happening below at Port Moresby at the commencement of British rule over New Guinea in 1884.

THE EMPIRE

At the start of her reign in 1837, Victoria ruled a growing but still small overseas empire. Canada was then a collection of colonies, Australia was only partly settled, India was still run by the East India Company and the Cape Colony was the only colony in South Africa. By the end of her reign in 1901, Canada and Australia were independent dominions, New Zealand was on its way to independence, the whole of India was under British rule, South Africa was soon to be united as an independent nation, and large parts of Africa, the Far East and Oceania were under British control.

VICTORIA'S FAMILY
THE FIRST FAMILY OF EUROPE

BETWEEN 1840 AND 1857, QUEEN VICTORIA gave birth to nine children. By all accounts, the family was a happy one, with both Victoria and Albert agreeing that it was better to set a good example to their children than to chastise them, although Victoria was always highly critical of her eldest son Edward, Prince of Wales. After Prince Albert's death in 1861, Victoria was burdened with the fact that she alone bore the responsibility for the moral development of their children.

DEAREST MAMA, DEAREST VICKY

FOR OVER 40 YEARS QUEEN Victoria maintained an almost daily correspondence with her eldest daughter Victoria (Vicky), the Princess Royal. The correspondence began in 1858 after Vicky left England following her marriage to Frederick, Crown Prince of Prussia and German Emperor for a short time before his death in 1888, and ended in 1901 on the death of the Queen, shortly before that of her daughter. The correspondence ranges from family matters to political events abroad.

PRINCESS VICKY
Born in 1840, Princess Vicky was always her mother's favourite child.

ELDEST CHILDREN
Winterhalter's portrait of 1846 shows, from left to right, Alfred, Edward, Alice, Helena and Vicky.

GRANDMOTHER OF EUROPE

The royal families of Europe were an exclusive society, intermarrying and exchanging personal visits frequently. Both Victoria and Albert were related to just about every one of the European ruling houses, either through their own relations or the marriages of their children. The Queen relished this because, as she was once heard to remark, she could relax with any European royal since they were all equals. In later life she enjoyed the role of "Grandmother" of the European royal families.

ROYAL LINKS
Through the marriages of her children and grandchildren, Victoria was related to the royal houses of Germany, Norway, Russia, Greece, Sweden, Romania and Spain, as well as numerous German princedoms and duchies. In this photograph taken in   7, Edward VII of England (seated on the left) is joined by Kaiser Wilhelm II of Germany (standing behind Edward), his son George V (standing seventh from the left) and other relations.

THE ROYAL FAMILY

Of Victoria's nine children, three died before their mother: Alice in 1878, Leopold in 1884 and Alfred in 1900. Her eldest daughter Vicky only just outlived her, dying six months after her mother in July 1901. The last surviving child of Victoria, Beatrice, died in 1944.

THE FAMILY
Photographed in 1859, Victoria and Albert are surrounded by their complete family of nine children (above).

THE FIRST BORN
Victoria nursed her first child, Victoria, in this swing cot after her birth in November 1840.

FOUR GENERATIONS

Victoria's longevity – she died in 1901 aged 81 – meant that her son and heir Edward had been a grandfather since 1894. As Victoria wrote to her daughter Vicky, it was the first time in English history that "there should be three direct Heirs as well as the Sovereign alive", a record of which the Queen was justly proud.

THE ROYAL LINE
In this photograph taken shortly before her death in 1901, Victoria is sitting with her son, the future Edward VII (top right), his son and her grandson, the future George V (left), and his son and her great-grandson, the future Edward VIII (far right).

EDWARD VII

1901–1910

THE COAT OF ARMS OF EDWARD VII

EDWARD VII DID NOT ACCEDE to the throne until the relatively late age of 59. As Prince of Wales, he undertook many duties for his mother Queen Victoria, making frequent goodwill visits at home and abroad. But his mother refused to involve him in domestic political duties, feeling that she could not trust his discretion in such matters. Excluded from Victoria's circle of advisers, Edward spent much of his time enjoying himself at society events. This only helped further to tarnish his reputation in the eyes of his mother. Yet throughout his nine-year reign, he was a popular and respected king. His love of foreign travel and public ceremonial pioneered an ambassadorial style of monarchy that was to replace its earlier political role.

♛ EDWARD VII

- **Born** St James's Palace, 9 Nov 1841, eldest son of Queen Victoria and Prince Albert.
- **Married** Alexandra of Schleswig-Holstein-Sanderberg-Glucksburg 1863, 6 children.
- **Acceded** 22 Jan 1901.
- **Crowned** Westminster Abbey 9 Aug 1902.
- **Died** Buckingham Palace, 6 May 1910, aged 68.

EDWARD AND VICTORIA

For most of his life Edward had a strained relationship with his mother, Queen Victoria. Throughout most of her reign Victoria prevented Edward from seeing copies of diplomatic correspondence, state papers and cabinet reports.

"THE LAST VISIT TO WINDSOR"

This cartoon (left) by Sir Max Beerbohm depicts the strained relationship between Queen Victoria and her heir, Edward, Prince of Wales.

STATE OPENING

The King and Queen open Parliament on 14 February 1901, from a painting by S. Begey (above right).

OPENING OF PARLIAMENT

Queen Victoria had not always attended the state opening of Parliament. Edward, who adored public ceremonial, established the tradition of the monarch opening Parliament on a regular basis.

THE CORONATION

This German cigar label of 1902 celebrates the coronation of Edward VII and Queen Alexandra. Throughout his life, Edward was a keen cigar smoker.

EDWARD AND ALEXANDRA

Edward married Princess Alexandra, elder daughter of King Christian IX of Denmark, on 10 March 1863 at St George's Chapel, Windsor. Alexandra was both elegant and beautiful, and their relationship has been described as "affectionate". Despite this, Edward indulged in many affairs with actresses and society beauties throughout his marriage. However, Alexandra showed amazing tolerance of his behaviour, remarking that "he always loved me the best".

A POPULAR KING

Short in stature and possessing a weak chin, Edward VII's appearance improved considerably with age and the addition of a beard. As a youth he had been selfish and inconsiderate, but this phase passed and he became an affectionate father and a loyal friend. An immense amount of goodwill surrounded him at his accession and his death nine years later was felt by many as a personal loss.

EDWARD VII
Edward VII in his state robes, painted in 1902 by Sir Luke Fildes.

EVENTS OF THE REIGN 1901 – 1910

◆ **1901** Edward VII becomes king on the death of his mother, Queen Victoria.
◆ **1901** Australia granted dominion status.
◆ **1902** Edward VII institutes the Order of Merit.
◆ **1903** Wilbur and Orville Wright make the first flight.
◆ **1903** The Women's Social and Political Union, demanding votes for women, founded by Mrs Emmeline Pankhurst.
◆ **1904** Britain and France sign the *Entente Cordiale*, settling outstanding territorial disputes.
◆ **1907** New Zealand granted dominion status.
◆ **1908** The 4th Olympic Games are held in London.
◆ **1908** Herbert Henry Asquith becomes Liberal Prime Minister.
◆ **1908** The Triple Entente is signed between Russia, France and Britain.
◆ **1909** Chancellor of the Exchequer Lloyd George introduces the People's Budget, increasing taxes on the rich to pay for social reforms; a major constitutional crisis breaks out.
◆ **1910** Parliament Bill introduced to curb the power of the House of Lords.
◆ **1910** Edward dies at Buckingham Palace.

THE ENTENTE CORDIALE
Edward VII visited Paris in 1903, and is seen below with Georges Clemenceau, the future Prime Minister. His visit paved the way for an Entente Cordiale *between Britain and France.*

EDWARD VII

A LIFE OF LEISURE

A SPORTING LIFE

Edward VII spent many years as King-in-waiting, only ascending the throne when he was 59 years old. As a result, much of his life was devoted to enjoyment rather than work, and he was renowned as a good-humoured seeker of pleasure. As Prince of Wales, Edward often travelled abroad, particularly to his beloved France. He was a sociable person who preferred human company to books, especially if the company was female.

Edward's sporting interests included yachting, shooting, hunting and horseracing, and he owned many horses, including one Grand National and three Derby winners. He was also fascinated by mechanical horsepower and took up the newly fashionable pursuit of motoring. Edward's preoccupation with pleasure made him extremely popular among all classes, and both the theatrical world and the racing fraternity had much to be grateful for in the shape of his patronage and his participation.

AT EASE
A French cartoon (above) makes fun of Edward's easy-going relationship with France and its people.

COUNTRY PURSUITS
Edward VII enjoyed the excellent sport on his Sandringham estate. The picture on the left shows Edward hunting with stag hounds.

EDWARD'S LOVE OF FRANCE

Edward VII's passion for France began at the age of 13, after his first visit to Paris in 1854. When the Franco-Prussian War broke out in 1870, Edward spoke out in France's favour, to the annoyance of his mother, Queen Victoria, who favoured Prussia. After France lost the war, Edward witnessed the resurgence of French republicanism on a visit to Paris in 1878. He acknowledged cries of "Vive la République" and made speeches stressing his love of France.

By the end of the 19th century, territorial disputes had led to a deterioration in Anglo-French relations. In 1903 Edward met the French President, Emile Loubet, in an effort to improve public relations between the two countries. The visit was a prelude to negotiations that culminated in the *Entente Cordiale* of 1904, which settled the disputes.

THE HORSELESS CARRIAGE

The first automobile took to the road in 1885, and the new recreation of motoring soon became fashionable among the rich. Edward developed a keen interest in motor cars and first drove a car during a stay at Warwick Castle in 1898. Shortly after his coronation in 1902, Edward bought several cars. Among his purchases were a Renault and a Mercedes. Like his horse-drawn carriages, these were painted in the royal livery and displayed the royal coat of arms on each of the door panels.

EDWARD AT THE WHEEL
Edward about to drive off in a new 12hp Daimler belonging to Lord Montagu of Beaulieu.

THE SANDRINGHAM ESTATE

IN 1862, WHILE HE WAS STILL PRINCE OF WALES, Edward VII bought the Sandringham Estate near King's Lynn in Norfolk. It cost him £220,000 and consisted of a neglected house, a series of farms and about 7,000 acres of land. Over the years he enlarged the house considerably, landscaped the gardens, improved the farms and bought another 4,000 acres to extend the estate. Edward took his bride Alexandra to Sandringham after their honeymoon in 1863, and the Royal Family have used Sandringham as a country retreat ever since.

SANDRINGHAM TODAY
The Sandringham estate (right) is a favoured venue for royal Christmas celebrations. The photograph above shows Elizabeth II and her family in front of Sandringham Church on Christmas Day.

THE HOUSE OF WINDSOR

1910–

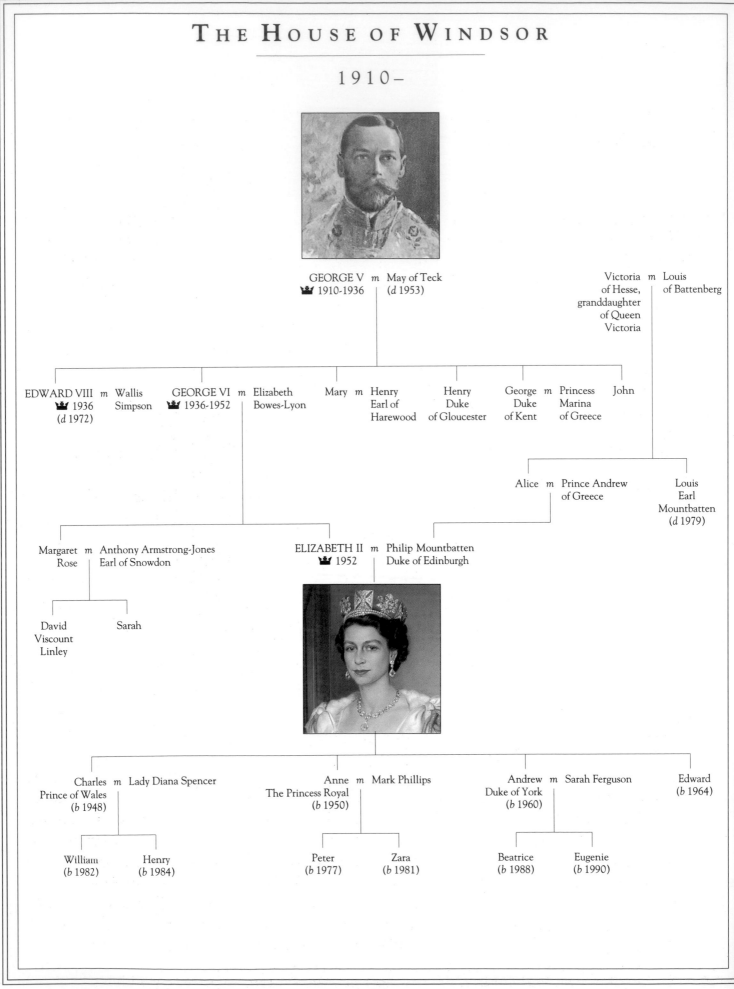

GEORGE V *m* May of Teck
👑 1910-1936 (*d* 1953)

Victoria *m* Louis
of Hesse, of Battenberg
granddaughter
of Queen
Victoria

EDWARD VIII *m* Wallis
👑 1936 Simpson
(*d* 1972)

GEORGE VI *m* Elizabeth
👑 1936-1952 Bowes-Lyon

Mary *m* Henry
Earl of
Harewood

Henry
Duke
of Gloucester

George *m* Princess
Duke Marina
of Kent of Greece

John

Alice *m* Prince Andrew
of Greece

Louis
Earl
Mountbatten
(*d* 1979)

Margaret *m* Anthony Armstrong-Jones
Rose Earl of Snowdon

ELIZABETH II *m* Philip Mountbatten
👑 1952 Duke of Edinburgh

David
Viscount
Linley

Sarah

Charles *m* Lady Diana Spencer
Prince of Wales
(*b* 1948)

Anne *m* Mark Phillips
The Princess Royal
(*b* 1950)

Andrew *m* Sarah Ferguson
Duke of York
(*b* 1960)

Edward
(*b* 1964)

William
(*b* 1982)

Henry
(*b* 1984)

Peter
(*b* 1977)

Zara
(*b* 1981)

Beatrice
(*b* 1988)

Eugenie
(*b* 1990)

CHAPTER TEN

THE HOUSE OF WINDSOR

1910–

When George V became king in 1910, his family name was Saxe-Coburg-Gotha, which was the family name of his father, Edward VII, and his grandfather, Prince Albert. For the first seven years of his reign, he kept this German surname, but in 1917, in recognition of the vociferous anti-German feelings of the British people during the First World War, George changed his surname to Windsor and his family followed suit. It was a symbolic and popular gesture by a King who took his role seriously and who worked hard to instil a sense of duty in his children.

Controversy

George V adhered strictly to the constitution and knew both his rights and his responsibilities. When he succeeded he was immediately plunged into a major constitutional crisis over the powers of the House of Lords. The Prime Minister asked the King to create enough new peers to vote through a bill to reform the Lords, but George objected to the manner in which his position was abused: "If it was the monarch's duty to keep out of party politics, it was equally the duty of politicians to avoid dragging him in." Further controversy erupted in 1936 when his son, Edward VIII, decided to abdicate rather than give up the woman he loved. His brother, George VI, restored the honour of the royal family and made it extremely popular through sharing the worst dangers of the Second World War with his beleaguered subjects.

WINDSOR
In 1917 George V changed the Royal Family's surname to Windsor, which is where the British monarchy's main residence out of London is situated. The Round Tower of Windsor Castle is shown above.

Elizabeth II

Perhaps the most experienced head of state in the world, Elizabeth II has reigned with eight different prime ministers. As a strict constitutionalist she has demonstrated her profound knowledge of the role the sovereign is expected to play in domestic and foreign affairs. Her children have been groomed to uphold the dignity and honour of the monarchy in a disrespectful age, and Prince Charles has had opportunity and encouragement to develop those particular traits that he will need, when the time comes, to keep the institution of monarchy safe from encroachment.

GEORGE V

1910–1936

THE COAT OF ARMS
OF GEORGE V

THE SECOND SON OF EDWARD VII, George became his father's heir when his elder brother Eddy unexpectedly died in 1892. He came to the throne in 1910 in the middle of a constitutional crisis caused by the House of Commons' attempt to limit the powers of the Lords, and within four years was leading a country fighting for its survival during the First World War. The post-war years were equally turbulent, with war in Ireland, a general strike, world depression and the formation of a national government, all requiring steady leadership from the King. Throughout these difficult years, George maintained the dignity of the monarchy, and saw its popularity rise when he celebrated his Silver Jubilee in 1935.

♛ GEORGE V

◆ **Born** 3 June 1865, second son of Edward VII and Alexandra.
◆ **Married** May of Teck, St James's Palace, 6 July 1893, 6 children.
◆ **Acceded** 6 May 1910.
◆ **Crowned** Westminster Abbey, 22 June 1911.
◆ **Died** 20 Jan 1936, aged 70.

KING AND KAISER

Although George was a cousin of the Kaiser, he did not approve of the militarist gestures Wilhelm so liked to display and it irked him to be photographed with the Kaiser. When Wilhelm abdicated in 1918, George noted in his diary that "he has ruined his country and himself. I look upon him as the greatest criminal known for having plunged the world into this ghastly war."

THE FIRST WORLD WAR

Although George and his family had German blood and were related to the German Kaiser, Wilhelm II, George had no compunction at all about fully supporting his government's decision to go to war with Germany over the latter's invasion of Belgium in August 1914. In the four years of the war, George visited his troops more than 450 times and awarded more than 50,000 medals for gallantry.

THE CENOTAPH

In 1920 George unveiled the Cenotaph (a word which means empty tomb) in Whitehall, London, erected to commemorate those who died in the First World War (above). Each year since then, on or near 11 November, the day the Armistice was signed in 1918, a service of remembrance is held at the Cenotaph to remember those who have died in the two world wars.

VISITING THE TROOPS

George V regularly visited troops in France during the war. Here he can be seen (centre) with his son, the Prince of Wales (left), examining an unexploded gas bomb.

RADIO BROADCASTS
On Christmas Day 1932 George broadcast a personal message to the nation, establishing a tradition that has been maintained every year since then. The script for the broadcast was written by the author Rudyard Kipling.

THE PHILATELIST
Of short stature with blue eyes and a clear, ringing voice, George had a happy childhood and in adult life enjoyed a successful marriage and a rewarding family life. George was not an intellectual – his favourite hobby was philately – and he had the simplest of tastes, attributes which endeared him to many of his subjects.

GEORGE V
This portrait of George in his state robes was painted shortly after his coronation in 1911.

◆ **1910** George V becomes king and Emperor of India on the death of his father Edward VII.
◆ **1911** Parliament Act ensures the sovereignty of the House of Commons.
◆ **1911** National Insurance Act provides sickness and unemployment benefits.
◆ **1912** SS *Titanic* sinks on her maiden voyage, drowning more than 1,500 passengers.
◆ **1914** Anglican Church in Wales is disestablished.
◆ **1914-18** First World War.
◆ **1914** Battles of Mons, the Marne and Ypres.
◆ **1915** Second Battle of Ypres; Gallipoli expedition fails to remove Turkey from war.
◆ **1916** Battle of the Somme; naval battle off Jutland between British and German fleets results in stalemate.
◆ **1916** Easter Rising in Dublin in support of Irish independence.
◆ **1916** David Lloyd George becomes Prime Minister.
◆ **1917** Battle of Passchendaele.
◆ **1917** Russian Revolution leads to the abdication of the Tsar.
◆ **1918** Reform Act gives votes to women over 30.
◆ **1918** General Election produces landslide for Sinn Fein MPs in Ireland who refuse to take their seats in Westminster and form their own parliament (the Dail) in Dublin.
◆ **1919** Lady Astor becomes the first woman MP to sit in the House of Commons.
◆ **1920-21** Ireland partitioned into the Free State and the province of Northern Ireland.
◆ **1924** First Labour government formed by Ramsay MacDonald.
◆ **1926** General Strike in support of the coalminers fails to reverse wage cuts and imposition of longer hours.
◆ **1928** All women over 21 get the vote.
◆ **1931** Statute of Westminster recognizes the independence of the dominions.
◆ **1931** Great Depression leads to the formation of a national government of all three political parties under the leadership of Ramsay MacDonald.
◆ **1932** George makes first annual Christmas broadcast.
◆ **1935** George celebrates his Silver Jubilee on the throne.
◆ **1936** George V dies at Sandringham.

GEORGE V

HIS FAMILY LIFE

QUEEN MARY IN 1914

MAY OF TECK

Princess May was engaged to Prince Albert Victor ("Eddy"), the first son of the future King Edward VII. On Eddy's sudden death in 1892, she married his brother, the future King George V, in the following year and reigned with him as Queen Mary from 1910. She died in 1953.

FAMILY PORTRAIT
The Royal Family were photographed at Abergeldie, Scotland, in 1906. Front row, left to right: Mary, Henry, George, Edward (the future Edward VIII) and Albert (the future George VI). Back row: George V and Queen Mary, holding John.

THE SAILOR KING
Having trained in the navy as a young man, George loved sailing and was widely known as the "Sailor King". He raced the cutter Britannia (left), acquired from his father upon his death in 1910.

THE ROYAL FAMILY

George V enjoyed a happy marriage with his wife, May of Teck, whom he married in 1893. However, he found it difficult to get on with his six children and was very critical of them. Not surprisingly, they, for the most part, feared him. Fortunately, his relationship with his children improved markedly when they married, and he proved popular with his daughters-in-law and was adored by his many grandchildren .

QUEEN MARY'S DOLLS' HOUSE

THIS MINIATURE VERSION OF A CONTEMPORARY royal home was designed for Queen Mary in 1920 by Sir Edwin Lutyens, the famous British architect. It is made to a scale of one-twelfth life size, standing 2.34 metres (7 feet 8 inches) high. Built in the Georgian style, using only the finest materials, the house is furnished with faithful replicas of Chippendale and Queen Anne pieces. Miniature watercolours and drawings by well-known artists hang on the walls. Attention to detail extends to sash windows that open, doors with locks that actually work, and real marble and parquet on the floors. The diminutive palace is on display at Windsor Castle.

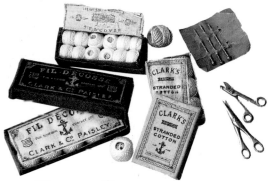

MINIATURE COLLECTION
Cotton reels, pins and scissors from Queen Mary's Dolls' House.

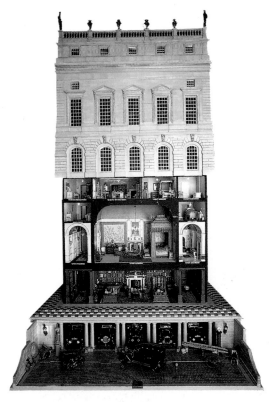

A PALACE IN MINIATURE

ILLNESS AND CONVALESCENCE

On 21 November 1928 George V was taken seriously ill during an audience at Buckingham Palace, London. Septicaemia, or blood poisoning, of the lung was diagnosed. Over the next few weeks George's condition deteriorated. His eldest son, Edward, Prince of Wales, returned immediately from a visit to East Africa. On 12 December 1928 the King's doctor, Lord Dawson of Penn, performed an operation to drain the infected fluid from the lung. For the next few days the King's condition was grave.

By the end of 1928 the worst was over. In February 1929 the King was driven by ambulance to Craigwell House, a convalescent home in Bognor, on the south coast of England. However, George did not like the house at all and was delighted when he was well enough to travel to Windsor Castle in May 1929. Despite two relapses that year, he refused to return to Bognor for further convalescence ("Bugger Bognor!" he exclaimed when it was suggested) and consequently did not regain his former vigour until the autumn of 1929.

ROYAL RECOVERY
In 1928 Queen Mary accompanied her sick husband, George V, down to Craigwell House near the English seaside resort of Bognor Regis, where he spent three months convalescing from a serious illness.

EDWARD VIII

JANUARY–DECEMBER 1936

THE COAT OF ARMS OF EDWARD VIII

EDWARD VIII'S FATHER, George V, once remarked to his Prime Minister, Stanley Baldwin: "After I am dead the boy will ruin himself in 12 months." These were prophetic words. Although a popular Prince of Wales, Edward's private life met with his father's disapproval. When Edward succeeded George in January 1936, he determined to marry Mrs Wallis Simpson, a twice-divorced American. This provoked a constitutional crisis. Baldwin informed Edward that the country would not accept her as queen. After much deliberation, Edward abdicated in December 1936.

♛ EDWARD VIII

- **Born** Richmond, Surrey, 23 June 1894, eldest son of George V and May of Teck.
- **Acceded** 20 Jan 1936.
- **Abdicated** 11 Dec 1936.
- **Married** Wallis Simpson, Tours, France, 3 June 1937.
- **Died** France, 28 May 1972, aged 77.

THE KING PROTESTS

In Britain, the Depression of the early 1930s led to high unemployment. South Wales was badly affected, with thousands of families reduced to poverty. On a visit there in the summer of 1936, Edward was sufficiently moved by what he saw to exclaim: "Something must be done to find these people work." This outspoken remark earned widespread public approval, but some Government ministers accused Edward of political interference.

EDWARD VISITS SOUTH WALES
In 1936 the King visited South Wales (right); the unemployed lined the towns' roads to greet him.

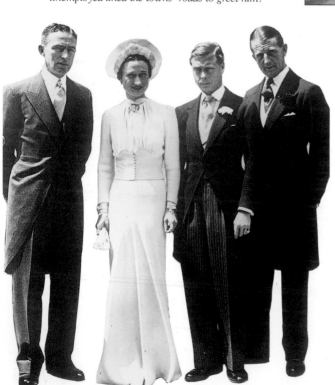

MARRIAGE TO WALLIS SIMPSON

Edward, created Duke of Windsor soon after his abdication, waited until his brother George's coronation in May 1937 before marrying Mrs Wallis Simpson. The simple civil ceremony took place on 3 June 1937 at the Château de Condé, near Tours in France. The photographer, Cecil Beaton, observed: "His [Edward's] expression though intent was essentially sad. Tragic eyes belied by impertinent tilt of the nose ... are bleary in spite of their brightness."

THE ROYAL WEDDING
The two witnesses at the wedding of the Duke of Windsor to Mrs Wallis Simpson were Major Edward "Fruity" Metcalfe (right), a long-standing friend of the ex-King, and Herman Rogers (left), an American friend of Wallis Simpson. Cecil Beaton took the photograph.

TOKEN OF AFFECTION
During the early years of their relationship, Edward gave Wallis Simpson a number of valuable jewels. This diamond leopard brooch was made by Cartier, the world famous jewellers.

EDWARD VIII
Photographed in 1936.

EXILE IN FRANCE
Apart from during the Second World War, when Edward was Governor of the Bahamas, the Duke and Duchess of Windsor lived for the most part in France (above). They made occasional visits to England, and Edward remained on friendly terms with his royal relatives, although Wallis was not accepted.

THE SOCIETY PRINCE

Educated at Dartmouth Naval College and Magdalen College, Oxford, Edward excelled at tennis and golf, but found academic work "a dreary chore". When older, he developed a similar attitude to ceremonies of state, and was scarcely able to conceal his boredom during them. Increasingly, he was disinclined to keep his appointments and only appeared content in the company of society friends.

THE ABDICATION

On 10 December 1936 Edward VIII signed the Instrument of Abdication. Witnessed by all his brothers, it was a simple declaration of intent to renounce the throne for himself and his descendants. The succession passed to his brother Prince Albert, who became George VI.

EVENTS OF THE REIGN 1936

◆ Edward VIII succeeds his father, George V, as King in January.
◆ Outbreak of Spanish Civil War.
◆ Germany, under Hitler, reoccupies the demilitarized left bank of the Rhine.
◆ Britain begins to re-arm as political tension increases in Europe and the prospect of military conflict arises.
◆ The Crystal Palace, once the home of the Great Exhibition in Hyde Park and later removed to Sydenham in south London, is destroyed by fire.
◆ J.M. Keynes publishes his book *General Theory of Employment, Interest and Money*, an internationally influential study of modern economics.
◆ Maiden voyage of luxury ocean liner, the *Queen Mary*.
◆ BBC inaugurates the world's first television service in London.
◆ Edward abdicates in December and is subsequently created Duke of Windsor.

INSTRUMENT OF ABDICATION

I, Edward the Eighth, of Great Britain, Ireland, and the British Dominions beyond the Seas, King, Emperor of India, do hereby declare My irrevocable determination to renounce the Throne for Myself and for My descendants, and My desire that effect should be given to this Instrument of Abdication immediately.

In token whereof I have hereunto set My hand this tenth day of December, nineteen hundred and thirty six, in the presence of the witnesses whose signatures are subscribed.

SIGNED AT
FORT BELVEDERE
IN THE PRESENCE
OF

INSTRUMENT OF ABDICATION

GEORGE VI

1936–1952

THE COAT OF ARMS OF GEORGE VI

AS THE SECOND SON OF George V, Prince Albert (as George was then known) had not expected to be King. Upon the death of his father he became heir to his unmarried elder brother, Edward VIII, but Edward's unprecedented abdication meant that Albert became King as George VI without any preparation for the role. Yet he became a popular figurehead for the nation during the dark days of the Second World War, led Britain into the post-war era and, with the help of his wife, restored the reputation of the monarchy after Edward's abdication.

GEORGE V1

♦ **Born** London, 14 Dec 1895, second son of George V and May of Teck.
♦ **Married** Lady Elizabeth Bowes-Lyon, Westminster Abbey, 26 April 1923, 2 daughters.
♦ **Acceded** 11 Dec 1936.
♦ **Crowned** Westminster Abbey, 12 May 1937.
♦ **Died** Sandringham House, Norfolk, 6 Feb 1952, aged 56.

THE FESTIVAL OF BRITAIN

In 1951 the Government organized a Festival of Britain to celebrate British arts and design and to stimulate trade after the economic dislocation of the Second World War. The Festival was held in the centenary year of the Great Exhibition of 1851. George VI was involved in the Festival right from the start, recognizing the need for Britain to move on from the austerity of the war years to a bright new future.

THE FESTIVAL OPENS
The Royal Family drive along the Strand in London, on their way to St Paul's Cathedral for the dedication service on 3 May 1951 to open the Festival of Britain.

THE KING AND FAMILY

After the birth of their two daughters, Elizabeth in 1926 and Margaret Rose in 1930, the Duke of York and his wife Elizabeth moved into the Royal Lodge in the grounds of Windsor Castle. There they settled down to a quiet family life. As king, George and his family fell under the glare of intense publicity. They coped particularly well with this dramatic change in lifestyle, fulfilling their demanding new role in public life with great success.

AN INFORMAL PORTRAIT
The Duke of York and his family relax in the grounds of the Royal Lodge, Windsor. When this picture was taken in June 1936, George VI was still Duke of York.

GEORGE VI
The state portrait of George VI was painted by Sir Gerald Kelly between 1938 and 1945.

THE SPORTING PRINCE
Although George was to suffer poor health in later life, he was a fit young prince and a keen sportsman. He played tennis to a high standard.

EVENTS OF THE REIGN 1936 – 1952

◆ **1936** George VI accedes to the throne upon the abdication of his brother, Edward VIII.

◆ **1938** Prime Minister Neville Chamberlain signs agreement with Hitler at Munich in attempt to stop outbreak of war in Europe.

◆ **1939** Outbreak of Second World War.

◆ **1940** Retreating British troops evacuated from beaches of Dunkirk as Germans advance.

◆ **1940** Winston Churchill becomes Prime Minister.

◆ **1940** Battle of Britain fought in the skies over England between RAF and German Luftwaffe.

◆ **1940** Heavy aerial bombing raids on British cities, which continue for much of the War.

◆ **1941** USA enters War after Japanese surprise air raid on US fleet stationed at Pearl Harbor.

◆ **1942** Decisive British victory over Germans in North Africa at El Alamein.

◆ **1944** D-Day landings in Normandy as the Allies begin to push the German forces back across Europe.

◆ **1945** Defeat of Germany marks end of the War in Europe.

◆ **1945** Japan surrenders, after US drops atomic bombs.

QUEEN ELIZABETH

◆ **1945** United Nations formed.

◆ **1945** Labour Government elected in Britain.

◆ **1947** India and Pakistan granted independence.

◆ **1948** National Health Service establishes free medical treatment for all in Britain.

◆ **1951** Festival of Britain.

◆ **1951** Winston Churchill becomes Prime Minister again.

◆ **1952** George VI dies.

"BERTIE"

George VI, or "Bertie" to his family and friends, was a good athlete as a young man at Dartmouth Naval College and later on at Cambridge University. Nevertheless, there was a somewhat diffident and anxious side to his character, which exhibited itself in an acute stammer. He did not lack bravery: he fought at the Battle of Jutland and become the first member of the Royal Family to learn to fly. When kingship was thrust upon him, he showed his determination and inner resolve by mastering his speech impediment. He knew how important it was to do so if he were to convey a sense of authority when performing his public duties, and even more so when the country was at war.

THE FAMILY AT WAR

1939–1945

DURING THE Second World War George VI was advised by the Prime Minister, Winston Churchill, not to go to the front line with his troops in case he was killed or captured by the Germans. Throughout the War, therefore, the King's role was to act as a figurehead, keeping up the morale of his armies and people. The Royal Family shared the hardships faced by the British people, visiting civilians injured in the bombing, as well as confining their diet to wartime rations.

SECOND LIEUTENANT ELIZABETH WINDSOR
On her 18th birthday, Elizabeth signed up with the Auxiliary Transport Service. She became an able driver.

THE TWO PRINCESSES

In 1939, at the outbreak of war, the young princesses Elizabeth and Margaret were despatched from Buckingham Palace to Windsor Castle, away from London and the threat of bombing. When it was suggested to their mother, Queen Elizabeth, that they might be safer abroad, she replied: "The children won't leave without me; I won't leave without the king; and the king will never leave."

THE GEORGE CROSS

During the War the George Cross (right) was awarded many times for acts of civilian gallantry. The most famous recipient of the decoration was the island of Malta. In 1942 the King awarded the island the Cross for holding out through persistent and heavy German bombing. The island was then known as Malta GC.

BRAVERY AWARDS

The heavy air raids on British cities during the war provoked a magnificent response from the civilian population. Men and women from all walks of life performed acts of courage under dangerous conditions. George VI witnessed many of these acts at close quarters and decided to create two new decorations for acts of civilian gallantry: the George Cross and George Medal. Both were ranked just below the Victoria Cross, which is only awarded to members of the forces.

THE PALACE IS BOMBED

On 12 September 1940 two bombs fell on Buckingham Palace (left). Windows were blown out and a private chapel was destroyed. A little later on Queen Elizabeth wrote of the incident: "I am glad we've been bombed. It makes me feel we can look the East End in the face."

VISITING THE TROOPS

During the war, George VI made several morale-boosting visits to his troops abroad. The King wanted to accompany the invasion forces on D-Day, 6 June 1944. However, Winston Churchill advised him against it, saying he should not risk his life. He reluctantly agreed.

GEORGE VI IN NORTH AFRICA

George VI flew to North Africa in June 1943 to congratulate the men of the 8th Army who had, under General Montgomery, overcome the combined might of the German and Italian forces under General Rommel.

THE CORONATION
THE CROWNING GLORY

THE CORONATION of a new monarch is one of royalty's most glittering pageants. Set in the splendour of Westminster Abbey, and watched by the eyes of the whole world, the ceremony takes place soon after the new king or queen has ascended the throne. Over the centuries, the coronation has become an increasingly ritualized occasion, combining ancient biblical traditions, such as the anointing of the sovereign with oil, and more recent European rites, such as the placing of the crown on the sovereign's head in front of an assembly of leading citizens and peers of the realm. As a time-honoured ritual it serves to emphasize the solemnity, continuity and majesty of the British monarchy.

THE LIBER REGALIS
The Liber Regalis or Royal Book (above) was written for the coronation in 1382 of Richard II's queen. The book contains a religious ceremony supposedly used at all coronations between 1399 and 1558.

THE CORONATION OF GEORGE VI

WESTMINSTER ABBEY
All kings and reigning queens of England have been crowned at Westminster Abbey ever since the coronation of Harold II took place in January 1066. The two exceptions have been Edward V, who was deposed in 1483 before he could be crowned, and Edward VIII, who abdicated in 1936 before his coronation, planned for the following year.

THE GOLD STATE COACH
Elizabeth II rides in state through the streets of London after her coronation in 1953.

THE SCEPTRE
During the coronation ceremony, the sovereign holds the Royal Sceptre (right) in his or her right hand. The sceptre is the symbol of kingly power and justice, and has at its head a huge heart-shaped diamond known as the Star of Africa. This is one of the largest diamonds in the world, weighing 530 carats.

AMPULLA AND SPOON
The holy oil is poured through the beak of the Ampulla, a vessel in the form of an eagle, into the Anointing Spoon. The sovereign is then anointed with the oil.

THE CHAIR
The names carved on the wooden back of the chair (right) belong to 18th-century Westminster schoolboys.

THE ORB
The Sovereign's Orb, below, is the most sacred ornament of all the coronation regalia. It symbolizes the dominion of the Christian religion.

THE CROWN
The crown used for the coronation of the sovereign is the St Edward's crown. The original, which dated back to, and was named after, Edward the Confessor, was destroyed in 1649. A new St Edward's Crown was made in 1660 and has been in use ever since. Made of gold, it contains some 440 precious and semi-precious stones, and weighs nearly five pounds.

THE CROWN JEWELS
Nearly all of the original crown jewels, some of which dated back to the time of Edward the Confessor (1042-66), were seized by Parliament after the execution of Charles I in 1649. Some of the pieces were sold and some were melted down. Two pieces that have survived are the Ampulla and the Anointing Spoon. The body of the eagle-shaped gold Ampulla was made in the 14th century, but the wings and base were added in about 1661. The silver gilt Anointing Spoon is thought to have been in use as far back as the coronation of King John in 1199.

THE CORONATION CHAIR
Edward I ordered the Coronation Chair to be made in 1301, five years after he had captured the Stone of Scone from the Scots. The Stone was the coronation seat of many early Scottish kings. The chair has been used for the coronation of every sovereign, but two, since 1308.

ELIZABETH II

1952–

THE REIGN OF ELIZABETH II is the longest-running this century and one of the longest in British history. Aged only 25 when she became Queen, Elizabeth began her reign as Britain was coming out of a period of post-war austerity and had begun to relinquish its empire. Forty years on, Britain's role in the world has changed irrevocably, while the country itself has undergone a fundamental transformation. In recognition of this, Elizabeth has modernized the monarchy without weakening its authority, adding to the prestige and popularity of the Royal Family.

THE COAT OF ARMS OF ELIZABETH II

♚ ELIZABETH II

- ◆ **Born** London, 21 April 1926, eldest daughter of George VI and Lady Elizabeth Bowes-Lyon.
- ◆ **Married** Philip Mountbatten, 20 Nov 1947, 4 children.
- ◆ **Acceded** 6 Feb 1952.
- ◆ **Crowned** Westminster Abbey, 2 June 1953.

PRINCE PHILIP
Created Duke of Edinburgh on his marriage in 1947, Prince Philip has been a solid, supportive and often outspoken partner of the Queen for over 40 years, shouldering his share of the burdens of state.

VISITING WINSTON
While Prime Ministers have weekly audiences with the Queen at Buckingham Palace, her visit to Winston Churchill at 10 Downing Street in 1955 on the occasion of his retirement as Prime Minister remains a unique event.

FORMAL ROLE

As the head of one of the few constitutional monarchies in the world, the Queen's role is largely formal. Regal ceremonies have remained virtually unchanged over the centuries, as have her responsibilities to Parliament, the armed forces, church and state. Yet as head of state she also has to respond to events and changes whenever they occur around the world, dealing with matters of diplomacy as well as national state events. She has worked alongside eight prime ministers and has had diplomatic discussions with all the major world leaders, notably those of the Commonwealth, bringing to those discussions a wealth of experience.

OPEN DAY
The Queen officially opens another session of Parliament.

HIGH COMMAND
As commander of the entire British armed forces, it is one of the Queen's duties to inspect the annual Trooping of the Colour.

THE PROFESSIONAL

Observers say that even as a child, Elizabeth was grave, reserved and wise beyond her years. Forty years as reigning monarch have made her utterly professional, ever mindful of the seriousness of her role, and rather shy. Off-duty, however, she is transformed into a mother, friend and relative, passionate about sports and the countryside and, from the countless photographs, not averse to spirited laughter.

ELIZABETH II
This state portrait was commissioned from Sir James Gunn in 1953.

EVENTS OF THE REIGN
1952 –

◆ **1952** Elizabeth accedes to the throne on the death of her father George VI.

◆ **1953** Edmund Hillary and Tenzing Norgay climb Everest just before Coronation Day.

◆ **1955** Winston Churchill resigns as Prime Minister and is succeeded by Anthony Eden.

◆ **1956** Anglo-French forces invade Egypt after the nationalization of the Suez Canal.

◆ **1956** John Osborne's *Look Back In Anger* is first performed in London.

◆ **1957** Harold Macmillan succeeds Eden as Prime Minister.

◆ **1957** The Gold Coast becomes independent as Ghana, the first British colony in Africa to receive its independence.

◆ **1958** Life Peerages are introduced in the House of Lords.

◆ **1959** Oil is discovered in the North Sea.

◆ **1960** Harold Macmillan makes his "wind of change" speech in South Africa.

◆ **1960** Nigeria and Cyprus become independent.

◆ **1963** The Beatles release their first LP.

◆ **1963** Scandal in high places weakens the government of Macmillan.

◆ **1964** Labour government of Harold Wilson takes office.

◆ **1965** Rhodesia unilaterally declares itself independent.

◆ **1969** Charles invested as Prince of Wales.

◆ **1969** Troubles break out in the north of Ireland.

◆ **1970** Edward Heath becomes Conservative Prime Minister.

◆ **1971** Decimal currency is introduced.

◆ **1973** Britain joins the European Community.

◆ **1974** Harold Wilson returns as Prime Minister.

◆ **1979** Margaret Thatcher becomes Britain's first woman Prime Minister.

◆ **1980** Rhodesia receives its independence as Zimbabwe.

◆ **1981** Prince Charles marries Lady Diana Spencer.

◆ **1982** Unemployment tops three million.

◆ **1982** Britain goes to war with Argentina over control of the Falkland (Las Malvinas) islands.

◆ **1987** Thatcher wins third term as Prime Minister.

◆ **1989-90** Poll tax introduced amid widespread protest.

ELIZABETH II

A VERY PRIVATE PERSON

HORSE LOVER

The Queen's passion for horses and the country life can be traced back to her childhood, when the young Elizabeth declared that she would marry a farmer when she grew up. She rode to hounds as a young girl, but soon developed a passion for horse racing, and horse breeding. Her first racehorse was Monaveen, which she raced in the National Hunt, but when Monaveen broke its leg in 1950, the Queen moved from the National Hunt to flat racing. Over the years her horses have collected innumerable prizes, both in Britain and abroad. The Queen was named top British horse breeder of the year in 1977, her Jubilee year.

ROYAL WINNERS
Both the Queen and Princess Anne are passionate equestrians. Here they share a particularly jubilant moment at the 1988 Derby (left).

PRIVATE LIFE

In 1969 the Queen instigated a new era of openness when she allowed the BBC to film *Royal Family*, a documentary about the private lives of the Windsors. Not so long before that, television and even radio were banned from some royal events, as it was feared that the populace would be watching or listening in unsuitable clothing, or in unsuitable places like pubs.

Nowadays that attitude would be unthinkable. The Royal Family is followed around the world, often to their chagrin, by a large and increasingly aggressive press pack, dozens strong, and press interest in the Royal Family has steadily increased over the years, culminating in the pursuit of Princess Diana in the 1980s. In 1981 the Queen stepped in and issued a statement, asking for the Princess to be allowed to lead her own life unharassed by the media. The chase has relented a little recently, but the Windsors remain one of the most photographed and written about families of the 20th century.

THE PRESS CORPS
The Queen, Prince Philip and a delegation from the Indian government face the international press at Delhi airport.

BIRTHDAY GREETINGS
On her 60th birthday, 21 April 1986, the Queen met a procession of schoolchildren in the Mall. Hundreds of children marched down the Mall to congratulate her, each of them carrying daffodils and singing a song specially composed for the birthday.

ON WALKABOUT

Although medieval monarchs mixed freely with their subjects, the royal walkabout is a fairly recent phenomenon and has become a feature of modern royalty. The Queen has consciously decided to build these impromptu chats into state visits, both in Britain and abroad, recognizing that contact with the public is also a necessary duty of the monarch.

THE COMMONWEALTH

THE QUEEN CLEARLY RELISHES HER ROLE AS head of the Commonwealth, an organization of 49 nations which has evolved out of the British Empire. The Commonwealth represents over a billion people on every continent – a quarter of the world's entire population – and holds regular meetings, usually every two years, where matters of common concern and interest are discussed.

ON TOUR
The Queen is borne aloft during a tour of the South Pacific (above left).

EMPIRE TO COMMONWEALTH
In 1962 the Commonwealth consisted of 16 countries, whose leaders met in London (left). Over the years, as new nations have joined, the Union Jack has been replaced, as in Zimbabwe (above).

"THE FAMILY FIRM"

THE ROYAL WORKERS

THE ROYAL FAMILY TODAY is the most public, and most popular, ever. The notion of a royal "family", as opposed to a single monarch and their partner, is a fairly modern one, promoted most notably by George VI, who called them "The Family Firm". His firm numbered a total of four: himself, Queen Elizabeth and the two princesses, Elizabeth and Margaret. Today, the firm fills the balcony at Buckingham Palace with four generations of Windsors and their spouses and offspring. Most if not all of them, with the obvious exception of the children, have public roles, duties and special interests in causes and charities.

QUEEN MOTHER

As old as the century, Queen Elizabeth the Queen Mother is a major link with an earlier era and style of monarchy. Yet she has adapted well over the years to the monarchy's changing role, and is today a much loved and respected matriarch to the entire Royal Family.

BIRTHDAY DRESS

Each year, crowds gather outside Clarence House to celebrate the birthday of the Queen Mother. Wearing a typically flamboyant costume, the Queen Mother (right) is accepting bouquets and other gifts on the occasion of her 89th birthday. The annual event is a measure of her abiding popularity.

CHILD WATCH

As President of the Save the Children Fund, Princess Anne has travelled around the world on its behalf. Here she is visiting a health centre in Burkina supported by the Fund.

ON HORSEBACK

A prizewinning jockey (right), Anne was a member of the British Olympic squad in 1976 and winner of the European Championships at Burghley, Lincolnshire, in 1971.

THE PRINCESS ROYAL

Born in 1950, and two years the junior of Prince Charles, Princess Anne has devoted herself in recent years to helping others. Some sectors of the popular press have described her as aloof, even arrogant, but she has more than acquitted herself with her tireless charitable work around the world.

EDWARD

Prince Edward, the youngest of the Queen's four children, followed in his eldest brother Charles's footsteps studying at Gordonstoun and graduating from Jesus College, Cambridge. He caused a minor controversy when he broke with the royal tradition of service in the armed forces and resigned his commission as a commando in the Royal Marines. Instead, he has pursued the family's love of amateur theatrics into the professional arena, taking a job at the offices of Andrew Lloyd-Webber's Really Useful company, where he answers the telephone as plain "Edward Windsor".

PRINCESS BEATRICE
Daughter of the Duke and Duchess of York, the young Princess Beatrice appears with her parents and grandmother, Queen Elizabeth (below). In March 1990 Beatrice acquired a sister, Eugenie Victoria.

ROYAL TEABOY
On his first day of work, Prince Edward passes a poster for Les Miserables (above), just one of the productions he worked on for Andrew Lloyd-Webber's Really Useful company.

PRINCESS MARGARET

Born in 1930, four years after her sister the Queen, Princess Margaret has had perhaps the unhappiest experience as a member of the Royal Family. Her intended marriage to Group Captain Peter Townsend was abandoned in 1955 when it was made known that Townsend had been divorced. Sharing her sister's devotion to duty, she put public life before private. In May 1960 she married the photographer Antony Armstrong-Jones, later Earl of Snowdon, giving birth to two children, Viscount Linley and Lady Sarah Armstrong-Jones. Princess Margaret and Snowdon separated in 1976 and were later divorced. Noted for her active involvement in the arts, Margaret takes a particular interest in dance and modern art.

ANDREW AND FERGIE

The marriage of Prince Andrew and Sarah Ferguson on 23 July 1986 was a spectacle second only to that of Charles and Diana five years earlier. Andrew had long been the subject of press speculation about his various female companions, gaining a reputation that merely fuelled press coverage of the royal romance. Daughter of Major Ronald Ferguson, then manager of Prince Charles's polo team, Sarah Ferguson was immediately nicknamed Fergie by the popular press, although her official name is the Duchess of York, as Prince Andrew and she were created Duke and Duchess of York on their wedding day.

PRINCESS MARGARET
Princess Margaret, a noted patron of the arts, attends a gala by the Royal Ballet School.

THE ROYAL WEDDING

THE MARRIAGE OF CHARLES AND DIANA

THE MARRIAGE OF PRINCE CHARLES and Lady Diana Spencer on Wednesday 29 July 1981 was unique in taking place in St Paul's Cathedral; traditionally, royal weddings are held in Westminster Abbey. The Prince of Wales had taken his time in deciding to settle down and marry; he had reached the age of 33 and had deliberated very hard on the responsibilities of his role and those of the woman who would one day be his queen. Lady Diana Frances Spencer, daughter of the Queen's equerry, the Earl Spencer, proved a hugely popular choice. Thirteen years her husband's junior, her shyness and beauty gave press and public much to talk about.

THE WEDDING

The day of the wedding was a national holiday, with all the pomp and pageantry befitting a fairytale romance. After the service, the wedding procession travelled through the centre of London, past thousands of well-wishers, some of whom had camped out for days to watch the event. More than 750 million television viewers worldwide watched the wedding.

ROYAL NEWLYWEDS
Charles and Diana, now married as the Prince and Princess of Wales, appear on the balcony of Buckingham Palace (above). Charles broke another royal tradition by publicly kissing his bride, to the delight of the crowds.

DRIVING HOME
The newly married couple return to Buckingham Palace in an open-top carriage (right). Charles wears his uniform as a naval commander, Diana the dress designed for her by David and Elizabeth Emmanuel.

THE FUTURE KING

THE TRAINING OF A KING

BORN IN 1948, it seems likely that Charles will have to wait many years before he accedes to the throne. Like his mother, he takes his responsibilities with the utmost seriousness, yet unlike his mother, who has been circumspect in all her dealings with government and state, Charles has actively courted publicity and attendant criticism in his pursuit of his beliefs, particularly on the issues of the environment and the supposed poverty of modern architecture. The most intellectual of the Windsors, a student of Gordonstoun and graduate of Trinity College, Cambridge, he has inherited his father's forthright attitude and applied it to many controversial issues.

HONORARY GRANDFATHER
Earl Mountbatten of Burma was a mentor to the young prince Charles, who termed him his "honorary grandfather" (left).

THE YOUNG FAMILY
The birth of Prince William (far right) in 1982 and Prince Harry (near right) in 1984 ensures the continuity of what has been referred to as the "Family Firm".

YOUNG LIFE
Prince Charles was the first member of the Royal Family to attend a normal day school, and later attended the rugged Gordonstoun Boys' School in Scotland and, briefly, Geelong Grammar School in Victoria, Australia. He was a student at Trinity College, Cambridge, where he studied archaeology and anthropology and pursued the familiar Windsor interest in amateur theatrics. Charles trained with the RAF on leaving college, and served with the Royal Navy from 1971 to 1976, finishing his career in the forces in charge of HMS *Bronington*.

"MONSTROUS CARBUNCLES"
Over the years Charles has been an outspoken critic of modern architecture, provoking some controversial debates. In 1989 he wrote A Vision of Britain and made a television documentary, both strongly critical of the way Britain's cities have been developed. In the photograph above Charles is shown deep in conversation on one of his favourite themes: community architecture.

VISION OF BRITAIN
Prince Charles and advisers spent a lot of time in London's East End researching material for his book and television documentary, A Vision of Britain.

PRINCESS DIANA
As a future Queen of England, Princess Diana has come under the most intense scrutiny from public and press alike. Suffering initially from shyness, she has gradually come to terms with her role and even revels in it. Her brief working career was spent teaching in a small, private kindergarten in West London. A glamorous socialite with a taste for clothes designed by top couturiers, Diana has also made a name for herself as a sponsor of charities, particularly those supporting children in need.

HIGH FASHION
Princess Diana's stylish dress sense (above) has been described by some as the best advertisement for British fashion so far.

ROYAL AWARENESS
Princess Diana has shown concern and interest in many controversial social issues. She hit the headlines when she opened the Landmark – a day centre for people with AIDS – in London (left).

Index

ACKNOWLEDGMENTS

Dorling Kindersley would like to thank Jane Thompson for drawing the royal coats of arms; Sandra Schneider for designing the family trees; John Gill for his help with the text; Peter Gamble for compiling the index; Joanne King, Kathy Lockley and Philippa Thomson for picture research; and Brian Rust and Steven Wooster for help with the design.

Picture Credits

Abbreviations: b = bottom; c = centre; l = left; r = right; t = top.

By gracious permission of Her Majesty the Queen: 50 bl © 1990, 63 br, 88-9, 94 bl, 96-7, 98-9 b, 99 tr, 103 l, 123 tl, 134 cl, 140 cl, 146-7, 148 cl, 168 c, 168-9 b, 169 c, 172 bl, 173 t, 176 bl, 184 cl, 188-9, 189 bl, 199 cr, 199 br, 203 l, 206 cl, 209.

Aerofilms: 30 cl. Ancient Art and Architecture Collection: 40 l, 43 l. Archives Nationales, Paris: 38 b Lauros-Giraudon. Ashmolean Museum: 12 tl Weidenfeld and Nicholson Archive; 12 cr.

Barnaby's Picture Library: 13 l, 14 tr, 43 br, 89 cr, 132 br, 139 tl, 139 bl, 139 cr, 164 bl, 184 br. Trustees of the Bedford Estate: 104 bl Bridgeman Art Library. Bible Society, London: 101 cl Bridgeman Art Library. Bibliothèque Nationale, Paris: 58 br Bridgeman Art Library; 60 cl, 64-5, 118-19 Weidenfeld and Nicholson Archive. Bibliothèque de Toulouse: 76 cr Bridgeman Art Library. Birmingham City Museums: 80 bl Bridgeman Art Library. Trustees of the Blair Collection: 125 tl Robert Harding Picture Library. Bodleian Library: 12 cr Weidenfeld and Nicholson Archive; 84 cr Bridgeman Art Library. Janet and Colin Bord: 52 bl. Bridgeman Art Library: 18 cl, 36 cb, 44 bl, 74-5, 138-9 c, 140 cr, 142 bl, 143 bl, 152 c, 162 bl, 162 cr, 167 cr, 171 t, 178 bl, 181 tr, 183 tr, 185 br, 186 br, 190 cr. Britain on View (BTA/ETB): 21 cl, 46 b. By courtesy of the Trustees of the British Museum: 9 c; 10 cl Bridgeman Art Library; 10 br, 11, 13 cr, 15 t; 15 br Weidenfeld and Nicholson Archive; 17 t, 22 ct, 22 cb, 23 c, 25 tl; 25 br, 27 b Weidenfeld and Nicholson Archive; 28-9, 28 br; 29 b Syndication International; 32-3, 33 br, 34 br, 35 c, 35 br, 36 ct, 37 c, 38 cl, 39 l, 42 cr; 44-5 Weidenfeld and Nicholson Archive; 48 bl Bridgeman Art Library; 48-9, 49 tr; 53 tr Weidenfeld and Nicholson Archive; 55 cr; 56 cr Pitkin Pictorials; 57 l Weidenfeld and Nicholson Archive; 58 cl; 60 b Bridgeman Art Library; 61 tr, 64 cl, 65 t, 68 bc, 68 cr, 70 cl, 70-71, 71 tr, 74 cl; 80 cr, 80-81, 83c Weidenfeld and Nicholson Archive; 84 cb Bridgeman Art Library; 89 tr Weidenfeld and Nicholson Archive; 93 cr Bridgeman Art Library; 95 cr Robert Harding Picture Library; 100 tr, 104 c; 109 b Bridgeman Art Library; 116-17 t Weidenfeld and Nicholson Archive; 120 b, 120-21 t, 158 c, 158cr. By kind permission of His Grace the Duke of Buccleuch and Queensbury: 88 cr Weidenfeld and Nicholson Archive; 116 cl, 119 cr Scottish Record Office.

Camera Press: 51 br, 66 cl, 201 tr, 204 cl, 215, 216 cl. J Allan Cash: 45 br, 56 bl, 88 bl, 96 c, 169 t. Celtic Picture Library: 54 bl, 54 cr, 55 ct. By permission of the Trustees of the Chatsworth Settlement: 133 br Robert Harding Picture Library. Christchurch Library: 60-61, 72 ct Bridgeman Art Library. Christie's Colour Library: 160 tr, 163 br, 165 tl. Corpus Christi College Library, Cambridge: 48 c. Création Cartier, Paris: 200 br.

Department of the Environment, Crown Copyright: 31 cr; 47 r Bridgeman Art Library; 132-3 c Syndication International; 161 b. By courtesy of the Dean and Chapter of Durham Cathedral: 114 tr.

Edinburgh Photographic Library: 117 ct, 117 c D Morrison. ET Archive: 105 cr, 157 c, 161 tl, 183 cl, 185 tc. Eton College Library: 52-3 Michael Holford; 79 c. Mary Evans Picture Library: 16-17 b, 78 cr, 97 cr 130 bl, 145 br, 158 cl, 159 br, 160 b, 165 cr, 167 tr, 168 tr, 169 cr, 170 tr, 174 c, 174 cr, 175 tr, 175 br, 178 cl, 178 cr, 179 br, 182-3 t, 186 cl, 187 ct, 192 tr, 198 tl, 198 bl, 203 br.

Giraudon: 170 b Bridgeman Art Library. Tim Graham: 210 b, 212 cl, 212 cr, 213 tl. Guildhall Library: 107 tr, 142-3 t, 165 b, 172-3 c, 186-7 ct Bridgeman Art Library.

Robert Harding Picture Library: 41 cb, 62 bl, 68 cl, 96 br, 103 c, 137 tl, 149 b, 161 tr, 163 cr, 176 c, 195 c. © Heinemann: 190 cl Weidenfeld and Nicholson Archive. By permission of the Controller of Her Majesty's Stationery Office, Crown Copyright: 4 ct, 119 c, 124 cr, 206 cr, 207 tl, 207 tr, 207 bc. Michael Holford: 11 cr, 14 bl, 16 cl, 20 cr, 20 bl, 21 t, 26 cr, 26 b, 32 br, 39 cr, 42 cl, 61 br, 69 l, 78 bl, 92 cl, 101 ct, 106 cr, 115 c, 121 bl, 155. House of Lords Record Office: 137 bl Bridgeman Art Library; 146 l, 152 cr. Hulton Deutsch Collection: 180 br, 182 bl, 183 bl, 188 cl, 188 b, 189 tr, 189 br, 193 tr, 197 tr, 198 tr, 202 b, 203 tr, 208 cr.

Illustrated London News: 156 cb, 192 bl, 194 ct, 197 l. Imperial War Museum: 205 tr Bridgeman Art Library.

Alan Jacobs Gallery, London: 140 b Bridgeman Art Library. Jarrold Colour Publications: 150.

Lambeth Palace Library: 76 bl, 86 cr. Library of Congress: 171 b. The Louvre: 99 cl Bridgeman Art Library.

Magdalene College Library, Cambridge: 44 c; 94 cl Robert Harding Picture Library. Mansell Collection: 75 tr, 106 cl, 130-31 t, 135 br, 141 br, 144 br, 153 cr, 166 c. Simon McBride: 86 bl. Archie Miles: 73 c. Musée Goya, Castres: 40-41 c Giraudon. Musée de Picardie, Amiens: 137 c Bridgeman Art Library. Museum of London: 135 cr Syndication International; 180 cl.

National Army Museum: 151 ET Archive.

National Galleries of Scotland: 111 c, 123 cr, 125 bl, 125 cr 164 tr. Trustees of the National Library of Scotland: 127 c. National Maritime Museum: 108 cl ET Archive. National Monuments Record for Wales: 75 br. National Museums of Scotland: 112 tr, 113 cr, 119 cb, 123 br, 129 br. Trustees of the National Portrait Gallery, London: 59 l, 72 cb, 77 l, 82 ct, 82 cb, 85 c, 90 ct, 90 cb, 93 c, 94 cr, 98 bl, 98 tr, 99 cr, 100 l, 101 br, 102 b, 104 cr, 105 l, 106 b, 107 l, 109 ct, 126 ct 126 cb, 128 cl, 128 bc, 129 l, 135 l, 143 cr, 144 cr, 145 l, 148-9 c, 149 t, 152 cl, 153 l, 154, 156 ct, 159 l, 163 l, 166 b, 166-7 c, 174 bl, 175 l, 179 l, 180 cr, 181 l, 191 l. National Trust Photographic Library: 102 br, 144 cl. Peter Newark's Western Americana: 170 cl. By kind permission of His Grace the Duke of Norfolk: 125 bl.

Popperfoto: 187 br, 191 br, 196 cl, 196 bc, 199 tl, 200 bl, 200 cr, 201 l, 201 br, 202 c, 204-205, 205 cr, 206 bc, 208 bl. Private Collection: 85 br, 128 cr, 133 ct, 134 br, 138 bl. Public Record Office, Crown Copyright: 24 br; 28 cl, 58 cr Syndication International; 131 cr, 131 bcr, 131 br.

By kind permission of the President and Fellows of Queen's College, Cambridge: 84 cl.

Retrograph Archive Collection: 190 bl. Rex Features: 193 bl, 208 br, 210 tl, 211 t, 211 c, 211 cr, 213 c, 213 b, 214, 216 b, 216-17, 217 ct. By kind permission of His Grace the Duke of Roxburghe: 115 tl National Library of Scotland. Board of Trustees of the Royal Armouries: 30-31 c, 81 t. Royal Holloway and Bedford New College: 87 cr Bridgeman Art Library.

St Edmundsbury Borough Council: 47 tl. St Faiths, Kings Lynn: 108-109 Bridgeman Art Library. Scottish Development Department: 112 bc, 113 tl, 114 c, 115 b, 116 br, 121 cr, 122 cr. Sealand Aerial Photography: 27 tl. Brian Shuel: 131 bl. Siena Duomo, Libreria Piccolomini: 122 bl Scala. Skyscan Balloon Photography: 8. Society of Antiquaries: 50 cr, 79 cr, 102 cl. Spectrum Colour Library: 10-11 t, 66 br, 173 br. Syndication International: 16 tr, 57 tr, 66-7 t, 109 cr, 136 bl, 196 cr, 208 cl, 211 b, 212 tr, 217 cr, 217 cb.

Trinity College Library, Cambridge: 38 cr.

Victoria and Albert Museum: 107 br Bridgeman Art Library; 158 b; 184-5 c Bridgeman Art Library.

Walker Art Gallery: 95 c; 141 l Robert Harding Picture Library. By courtesy of the Dean and Chapter of Westminster: 2; 24 cl Syndication International; 49 cr, 52 cr, 67; 77 cr Bridgeman Art Library; 92 bl, 206 t, 207 cr. Weston Park: 132 cl Bridgeman Art Library. Andy Williams ABIPP: 6, 7 c, 18-19, 50-51 t. Wilton House: 136 cr Bridgeman Art Library. Winchester Tourist Office: 91c.

Zefa: 32 bl, 41 tr, 55 b, 59 cr, 62-3 t, 110, 112-13, 118 cb, 143 br, 148 cr, 177, 183 br, 193 br, 194 c.